our best
THREAD CROCHET

LEISURE ARTS, INC.
Little Rock, Arkansas

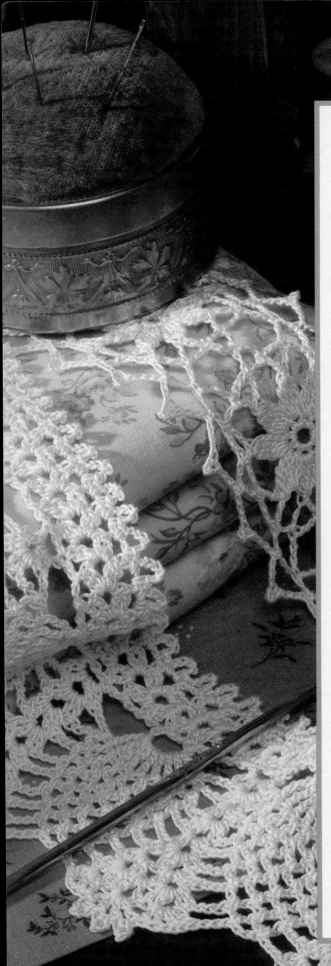

EDITORIAL STAFF

Vice President and Editor-in-Chief: Anne Van Wagner Childs
Executive Director: Sandra Graham Case
Editorial Director: Susan Frantz Wiles
Publications Director: Carla Bentley
Creative Art Director: Gloria Bearden
Senior Graphics Art Director: Melinda Stout

PRODUCTION

Managing Editor: Joan Gessner Beebe
Instructional Editors: Sue Galucki, Sarah J. Green,
   Valesha Marshell Kirksey, Tammy Kreimeyer, Frances Moore-Kyle,
   and Jackie Botnik Stanfill

EDITORIAL

Managing Editor: Linda L. Trimble
Senior Associate Editor: Tammi Williamson Bradley
Associate Editor: Robyn Sheffield-Edwards
Assistant Editors: Terri Leming Davidson and Darla Burdette Kelsay
Copy Editor: Laura Lee Weland

ART

Graphics Art Director: Rhonda Hodge Shelby
Senior Graphics Illustrator: Dianna K. Winters
Assistant Graphics Illustrators: Sonya McFatrich and Mary E. Wilhelm
Photography Stylists: Sondra Daniel, Karen Hall, Aurora Huston, and
   Christina Tiano Myers

BUSINESS STAFF

Publisher: Bruce Akin
Vice President, Finance: Tom Siebenmorgen
Vice President, Retail Sales: Thomas L. Carlisle
Retail Sales Director: Richard Tignor
Vice President, Retail Marketing: Pam Stebbins
Retail Marketing Director: Margaret Sweetin
Retail Customer Services Manager: Carolyn Pruss
General Merchandise Manager: Russ Barnett
Distribution Director: Ed M. Strackbein
Vice President, Marketing: Guy A. Crossley
Marketing Manager: Byron L. Taylor
Print Production Manager: Laura Lockhart

Library of Congress Catalog Number: 96-77624
International Standard Book Number 1-57486-055-0

*C*lassic looks have timeless appeal, and the proof is in this beautiful collection of thread crochet designs. In Our Best Thread Crochet, we've gathered a variety of our most popular projects into one exciting volume. As you browse through each section, you'll be treated to page after page of exquisite pieces created to let you make the most of your leisure time.

With our choice selections, you'll find it easy and enjoyable to bring charm into every room of your home. There are delicate doilies, lavish table toppers, and a potpourri of ornate edgings to embellish towels for the kitchen and bath. For those occasions when you want the gift to be as special as the recipient, turn to our collection of charming keepsakes. Welcoming a little one is a breeze when you follow our example of adding quick trims to purchased items. And the Christmas season will sparkle even more brightly with a lovely poinsettia doily, a glorious host of angels, and a flurry of delicate snowflakes.

Whether you're an experienced crocheter or a beginner, our easy-to-follow instructions, diagrams, and helpful hints make it simple to achieve beautiful, heirloom-quality results. So choose a pattern, grab your supplies, and enjoy Our Best Thread Crochet!

TABLE OF CONTENTS

THE CHARMING HOME

KEEPSAKE GIFTS

BABY BOUTIQUE

CHRISTMAS PRETTIES

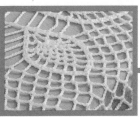

THE CHARMING HOME

The elegance of thread crochet makes it a wonderful decorating tool for bringing classic style to every room. And with the imaginative patterns in this collection, you can fill your home with beautiful accents! For the living room we have delightful doilies and a charming window dressing, and the dining room is brightened with airy table runners. You'll love the ornate edgings that dress up linens for the bedroom, bath, and kitchen. There's also a filet crochet mat to enhance a treasured photograph, a lacy lampshade cover, and more. With these lovely appointments, you'll find many ways to adorn your home with graceful crochet.

SHOWY TABLE TOPPER

You'll be showered with compliments when you drape a small table with this fanciful topper. As pretty as a peacock's showy feathers, the airy piece is worked in shells and clusters, then finished with picot shells.

Finished Size: 30"

MATERIALS
Bedspread Weight Cotton Thread (size 10):
670 yards
Steel crochet hook, size 3 (2.10 mm) **or** size needed for gauge

GAUGE: Rnds 1-4 = 4"

STITCH GUIDE

CLUSTER (uses next 4 dc)
★ YO, insert hook in **next** dc, YO and pull up a loop, YO and draw through 2 loops on hook; repeat from ★ 3 times **more**, YO and draw through all 5 loops on hook *(Figs. 12c & d, page 121)*.
BEGINNING CLUSTER (uses next 3 dc)
Ch 2, ★ YO, insert hook in **next** dc, YO and pull up a loop, YO and draw through 2 loops on hook; repeat from ★ 2 times **more**, YO and draw through all 4 loops on hook.
SHELL
(2 Dc, ch 2, 2 dc) in sp indicated.
PICOT SHELL
(2 Dc, ch 4, slip st in third ch from hook, ch 1, 2 dc) in sp indicated.

Ch 6; join with slip st to form a ring.

Rnd 1: Ch 1, sc in ring, (ch 6, sc in ring) 5 times, ch 3, dc in first sc to form last ch-6 loop: 6 ch-6 loops.

Rnd 2: Ch 12 (**counts as first dc plus ch 9, now and throughout**), (dc in next ch-6 sp, ch 9) around; join with slip st to first dc.

Rnd 3: Ch 3 (**counts as first dc, now and throughout**), 2 dc in same st, ch 9, (3 dc in next dc, ch 9) around; join with slip st to first dc: 18 dc.

Rnd 4: Ch 6, dc in next dc, ch 3, dc in next dc, ch 9, ★ dc in next dc, (ch 3, dc in next dc) twice, ch 9; repeat from ★ around; join with slip st to third ch of beginning ch-6.

Rnd 5: Ch 9, dc in next dc, ch 6, dc in next dc, ch 9, ★ dc in next dc, (ch 6, dc in next dc) twice, ch 9; repeat from ★ around; join with slip st to third ch of beginning ch-9.

Rnd 6: Ch 12, (dc in next dc, ch 9) around; join with slip st to first dc.

Rnd 7: Ch 12, (2 dc, ch 3, 2 dc) in next dc, ch 9, ★ (dc in next dc, ch 9) twice, (2 dc, ch 3, 2 dc) in next dc, ch 9; repeat from ★ around to last dc, dc in last dc, ch 9; join with slip st to first dc.

Rnd 8: Ch 12, dc in next 2 dc, ch 3, (dc, ch 3, dc) in next ch-3 sp, ch 3, dc in next 2 dc, ch 9, ★ (dc in next dc, ch 9) twice, dc in next 2 dc, ch 3, (dc, ch 3, dc) in next ch-3 sp, ch 3, dc in next 2 dc, ch 9; repeat from ★ around to last dc, dc in last dc, ch 9; join with slip st to first dc.

Rnd 9: Ch 12, dc in next 2 dc, ch 3, skip next ch-3 sp, dc in next ch-3 sp, (ch 1, dc in same sp) 6 times, ch 3, skip next dc, dc in next 2 dc, ch 9, ★ (dc in next dc, ch 9) twice, dc in next 2 dc, ch 3, skip next ch-3 sp, dc in next ch-3 sp, (ch 1, dc in same sp) 6 times, ch 3, skip next dc, dc in next 2 dc, ch 9; repeat from ★ around to last dc, dc in last dc, ch 9; join with slip st to first dc.

Rnd 10: Ch 12, dc in next 2 dc, ch 3, (sc in next ch-1 sp, ch 3) 6 times, skip next dc, dc in next 2 dc, ch 9, ★ (dc in next dc, ch 9) twice, dc in next 2 dc, ch 3, (sc in next ch-1 sp, ch 3) 6 times, skip next dc, dc in next 2 dc, ch 9; repeat from ★ around to last dc, dc in last dc, ch 9; join with slip st to first dc.

Rnd 11: Ch 12, dc in next 2 dc, ch 3, skip next ch-3 sp, (sc in next ch-3 sp, ch 3) 5 times, dc in next 2 dc, ch 9, ★ (dc in next dc, ch 9) twice, dc in next 2 dc, ch 3, skip next ch-3 sp, (sc in next ch-3 sp, ch 3) 5 times, dc in next 2 dc, ch 9; repeat from ★ around to last dc, dc in last dc, ch 9; join with slip st to first dc.

Rnd 12: Ch 12, dc in next 2 dc, ch 3, skip next ch-3 sp, (sc in next ch-3 sp, ch 3) 4 times, dc in next 2 dc, ch 9, ★ (dc in next dc, ch 9) twice, dc in next 2 dc, ch 3, skip next ch-3 sp, (sc in next ch-3 sp, ch 3) 4 times, dc in next 2 dc, ch 9; repeat from ★ around to last dc, dc in last dc, ch 9; join with slip st to first dc.

Rnd 13: Ch 3, (dc, ch 3, 2 dc) in same st, ch 9, ★ † dc in next 2 dc, ch 3, skip next ch-3 sp, (sc in next ch-3 sp, ch 3) 3 times, dc in next 2 dc, ch 9 †, [(2 dc, ch 3, 2 dc) in next dc, ch 9] twice; repeat from ★ 4 times **more**, then repeat from † to † once, (2 dc, ch 3, 2 dc) in last dc, ch 9; join with slip st to first dc.

Rnd 14: Ch 3, dc in next dc, ch 3, (dc, ch 3, dc) in next ch-3 sp, ch 3, dc in next 2 dc, ch 9, ★ † dc in next 2 dc, ch 3, skip next ch-3 sp, (sc in next ch-3 sp, ch 3) twice, dc in next 2 dc, ch 9 †, [dc in next 2 dc, ch 3, (dc, ch 3, dc) in next ch-3 sp, ch 3, dc in next 2 dc, ch 9] twice; repeat from ★ 4 times **more**, then repeat from † to † once, dc in next 2 dc, ch 3, (dc, ch 3, dc) in next ch-3 sp, ch 3, dc in last 2 dc, ch 9; join with slip st to first dc.

Rnd 15: Ch 3, dc in next dc, ch 3, skip next ch-3 sp, dc in next ch-3 sp, (ch 1, dc in same sp) 6 times, ch 3, skip next dc, dc in next 2 dc, ch 9, ★ † dc in next 2 dc, ch 3, skip next ch-3 sp, sc in next ch-3 sp, ch 3, dc in next 2 dc, ch 9 †, [dc in next 2 dc, ch 3, skip next ch-3 sp, dc in next ch-3 sp, (ch 1, dc in same sp) 6 times, ch 3, skip next dc, dc in next 2 dc, ch 9] twice; repeat from ★ 4 times **more**, then repeat from † to † once, dc in next 2 dc, ch 3, skip next ch-3 sp, dc in next ch-3 sp, (ch 1, dc in same sp) 6 times, ch 3, skip next dc, dc in last 2 dc, ch 9; join with slip st to first dc.

Rnd 16: Ch 3, dc in next dc, ch 3, (sc in next ch-1 sp, ch 3) 6 times, skip next dc, dc in next 2 dc, ch 9, work Cluster, ch 9, ★ [dc in next 2 dc, ch 3, (sc in next ch-1 sp, ch 3) 6 times, skip next dc, dc in next 2 dc, ch 9] twice, work Cluster, ch 9; repeat from ★ 4 times **more**, dc in next 2 dc, ch 3, (sc in next ch-1 sp, ch 3) 6 times, skip next dc, dc in last 2 dc, ch 9; join with slip st to first dc.

Rnd 17: Ch 3, dc in next dc, ★ † ch 3, skip next ch-3 sp, (sc in next ch-3 sp, ch 3) 5 times, dc in next 2 dc, ch 6, (sc in next loop, ch 6) twice, dc in next 2 dc, ch 3, skip next ch-3 sp, (sc in next ch-3 sp, ch 3) 5 times, dc in next 2 dc, ch 6, sc in next loop, ch 6 †, dc in next 2 dc; repeat from ★ 4 times **more**, then repeat from † to † once; join with slip st to first dc.

Rnd 18: Ch 3, dc in next dc, ★ † ch 3, skip next ch-3 sp, (sc in next ch-3 sp, ch 3) 4 times, dc in next 2 dc, ch 6, (sc in next loop, ch 6) 3 times, dc in next 2 dc, ch 3, skip next ch-3 sp, (sc in next ch-3 sp, ch 3) 4 times, dc in next 2 dc, ch 6, (sc in next loop, ch 6) twice †, dc in next 2 dc; repeat from ★ 4 times **more**, then repeat from † to † once; join with slip st to first dc.

Rnd 19: Ch 3, dc in next dc, ★ † ch 3, skip next ch-3 sp, (sc in next ch-3 sp, ch 3) 3 times, dc in next 2 dc, ch 6, (sc in next loop, ch 6) 4 times, dc in next 2 dc, ch 3, skip next ch-3 sp, (sc in next ch-3 sp, ch 3) 3 times, dc in next 2 dc, ch 6, (sc in next loop, ch 6) 3 times †, dc in next 2 dc; repeat from ★ 4 times **more**, then repeat from † to † once; join with slip st to first dc.

Rnd 20: Ch 3, dc in next dc, ★ † ch 3, skip next ch-3 sp, (sc in next ch-3 sp, ch 3) twice, dc in next 2 dc, ch 6, (sc in next loop, ch 6) 5 times, dc in next 2 dc, ch 3, skip next ch-3 sp, (sc in next ch-3 sp, ch 3) twice, dc in next 2 dc, ch 6, (sc in next loop, ch 6) 4 times †, dc in next 2 dc; repeat from ★ 4 times **more**, then repeat from † to † once; join with slip st to first dc.

Rnd 21: Ch 3, dc in next dc, ★ † ch 3, skip next ch-3 sp, sc in next ch-3 sp, ch 3, dc in next 2 dc, ch 6, (sc in next loop, ch 6) 6 times, dc in next 2 dc, ch 3, skip next ch-3 sp, sc in next ch-3 sp, ch 3, dc in next 2 dc, ch 6, (sc in next loop, ch 6) 5 times †, dc in next 2 dc; repeat from ★ 4 times **more**, then repeat from † to † once; join with slip st to first dc.

Rnd 22: Work beginning Cluster, ch 6, (sc in next loop, ch 6) 7 times, work Cluster, (ch 6, sc in next loop) 6 times, ★ ch 6, work Cluster, (ch 6, sc in next loop) 7 times, ch 6, work Cluster, (ch 6, sc in next loop) 6 times; repeat from ★ around, ch 3, dc in top of beginning Cluster to form last loop: 90 loops.

Rnds 23-25: Ch 1, sc in same loop, (ch 6, sc in next loop) around, ch 3, dc in first sc to form last loop.

Rnd 26: Ch 3, (dc, ch 3, 2 dc) in same loop, ch 6, (sc in next loop, ch 6) 4 times, ★ (2 dc, ch 3, 2 dc) in next loop, ch 6, (sc in next loop, ch 6) 4 times; repeat from ★ around; join with slip st to first dc.

Rnd 27: Ch 3, dc in next dc, ch 3, (dc, ch 3, dc) in next ch-3 sp, ch 3, dc in next 2 dc, ch 6, skip next loop, (sc in next loop, ch 6) 3 times, ★ dc in next 2 dc, ch 3, (dc, ch 3, dc) in next ch-3 sp, ch 3, dc in next 2 dc, ch 6, skip next loop, (sc in next loop, ch 6) 3 times; repeat from ★ around; join with slip st to first dc.

Rnd 28: Ch 3, dc in next dc, ch 3, skip next ch-3 sp, dc in next ch-3 sp, (ch 1, dc in same sp) 4 times, ch 3, skip next dc, dc in next 2 dc, ch 6, skip next loop, (sc in next loop, ch 6) twice, ★ dc in next 2 dc, ch 3, skip next ch-3 sp, dc in next ch-3 sp, (ch 1, dc in same sp) 4 times, ch 3, skip next dc, dc in next 2 dc, ch 6, skip next loop, (sc in next loop, ch 6) twice; repeat from ★ around; join with slip st to first dc.

Rnd 29: Ch 3, dc in next dc, ch 3, (sc in next ch-1 sp, ch 3) 4 times, skip next dc, dc in next 2 dc, ch 6, skip next loop, work Shell in next loop, ch 6, ★ dc in next 2 dc, ch 3, (sc in next ch-1 sp, ch 3) 4 times, skip next dc, dc in next 2 dc, ch 6, skip next loop, work Shell in next loop, ch 6; repeat from ★ around; join with slip st to first dc.

Rnd 30: Ch 3, dc in next dc, ch 3, skip next ch-3 sp, (sc in next ch-3 sp, ch 3) 3 times, dc in next 2 dc, ch 6, (2 dc, ch 2, work Shell) in next ch-2 sp, ch 6, ★ dc in next 2 dc, ch 3, skip next ch-3 sp, (sc in next ch-3 sp, ch 3) 3 times, dc in next 2 dc, ch 6, (2 dc, ch 2, work Shell) in next ch-2 sp, ch 6; repeat from ★ around; join with slip st to first dc.

Continued on page 10.

Rnd 31: Ch 3, dc in next dc, ch 3, skip next ch-3 sp, (sc in next ch-3 sp, ch 3) twice, dc in next 2 dc, ch 6, work Shell in each of next 2 ch-2 sps, ch 6, ★ dc in next 2 dc, ch 3, skip next ch-3 sp, (sc in next ch-3 sp, ch 3) twice, dc in next 2 dc, ch 6, work Shell in each of next 2 ch-2 sps, ch 6; repeat from ★ around; join with slip st to first dc.

Rnd 32: Ch 3, dc in next dc, ch 3, skip next ch-3 sp, sc in next ch-3 sp, ch 3, dc in next 2 dc, ch 6, (2 dc, ch 2, work Shell) in each of next 2 ch-2 sps, ch 6, ★ dc in next 2 dc, ch 3, skip next ch-3 sp, sc in next ch-3 sp, ch 3, dc in next 2 dc, ch 6, (2 dc, ch 2, work Shell) in each of next 2 ch-2 sps, ch 6; repeat from ★ around; join with slip st to first dc.

Rnd 33: Work beginning Cluster, ch 6, work Shell in each of next 4 ch-2 sps, ★ ch 6, work Cluster, ch 6, work Shell in each of next 4 ch-2 sps; repeat from ★ around, ch 3, dc in top of beginning Cluster to form last loop.

Rnd 34: Ch 1, sc in same loop, ch 3, sc in next loop, ch 3, (2 dc, ch 2, work Shell) in each of next 4 ch-2 sps, ch 3, ★ (sc in next loop, ch 3) twice, (2 dc, ch 2, work Shell) in each of next 4 ch-2 sps, ch 3; repeat from ★ around; join with slip st to first sc.

Rnd 35: Slip st in first 2 chs, ch 1, sc in same sp, ch 3, work Picot Shell in each of next 8 ch-2 sps, ch 3, ★ skip next ch-3 sp, sc in next ch-3 sp, ch 3, work Picot Shell in each of next 8 ch-2 sps, ch 3; repeat from ★ around; join with slip st to first sc, finish off.

See Washing and Blocking, page 124.

LOVELY LAMPSHADE COVER

An elegant accent for a traditional decor, our filet crochet lampshade cover features a repeated rose design. This lovely reflection of Victorian refinement is gathered at the top of the shade with satin ribbon.

MATERIALS

Bedspread Weight Cotton Thread (size 10):
  2 balls (282 yards per ball)
Steel crochet hook, size 6 (1.80 mm) **or** size needed for gauge
⅛"w ribbon - 2 yards

Note: Thread amounts given in Materials are for a Lampshade 6" across top x 10" across bottom x 8" high. To find approximate yardage for a different finished size, add or subtract 2 yards for each square inch. Lampshade must be a **minimum** of 6" high.

GAUGE: 14 ch-2 sps and 16 rows = 4"

BASIC CHART STITCHES

Beginning Space over Space: Ch 5, turn; dc in next dc.
Block over Space: 2 Dc in next ch-2 sp, dc in next dc.
Block over Block: Dc in next 3 dc.
Space over Block: Ch 2, skip next 2 dc, dc in next dc.
Space over Space: Ch 2, dc in next dc.

Note: Cover is worked in rows and then joined.

FOUNDATION

Row 1: Ch 7, dc in fourth ch from hook, ch 2, skip next 2 chs, dc in last ch.

Row 2: Ch 5 **(counts as first dc plus ch 2, now and throughout)**, turn; dc in last 2 sts.

Row 3: Ch 3 **(counts as first dc, now and throughout)**, turn; dc in next dc, ch 2, dc in last dc.

Repeat Rows 2 and 3 until piece measures same as height of shade plus 1", ending by working Row 3; do **not** finish off.

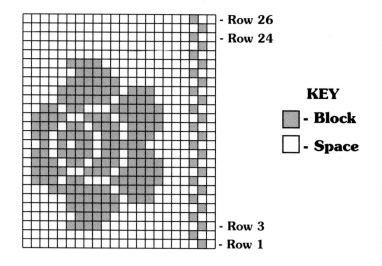

- Row 26
- Row 24

KEY
▨ - Block
☐ - Space

- Row 3
- Row 1

On right side rows, follow Chart from right to left; on wrong side rows, follow Chart from left to right.

BODY

Row 1: Do **not** turn; ch 5, working in end of rows, skip first row, dc in top of dc on next row, 2 dc in same row, dc in top of dc on next row, (ch 2, dc in top of dc on next row) 20 times, place marker around last dc made to mark beginning of Chart, ch 2, (dc in top of dc on next row, ch 2) across, dc in ch at base of last dc on Row 1 of Foundation.

Note: Move marker after each row is completed.

Row 2: Work Beginning Space over Space, work Space over Space across to marker, follow Chart from left to right across.

Row 3 (Right side): Follow Chart across to marker, work Space over Space across.

Note: Loop a short piece of thread around any stitch to mark Row 3 as **right** side.

Rows 4-26: Repeat Rows 2 and 3, 11 times; then repeat Row 2 once **more**.

Repeat Rows 3-26 until piece measures same as the distance around bottom of shade plus 1½", ending by working Row 24; do **not** finish off.

Continued on page 12.

Joining Row: With **right** side together and working in each st of last row **and** in end of rows on Foundation, slip st evenly across; do **not** finish off.

TOP EDGING

With **right** side facing, slip st across to first ch-2 sp on Foundation, ch 1, sc in same sp, ch 4; working in end of rows, sc in first row, ch 4, (sc in next row, ch 4) around; join with slip st to first sc, finish off.

BOTTOM EDGING

With **right** side facing, join thread with slip st in ch-2 on Foundation; ch 3, (dc, ch 4, 2 dc) in same sp; working in end of rows, ★ skip next row, (2 dc, ch 4, 2 dc) in next row; repeat from ★ around; join with slip st to first dc, finish off.

See Washing and Blocking, page 124.

Weave ribbon through the fourth line of spaces from Top Edging.

Pull ribbon to gather Cover around top of shade; tie ribbon ends into a bow to secure.

DELICATE DOILY

Grace a table or dresser with the old-fashioned loveliness of this delicate doily. A luxurious touch for your home, the project showcases an exquisite flower pattern surrounded by fans with picot trim.

Finished Size: 12" in diameter

MATERIALS

Cotton Crochet Thread (size 20):
   1 ball (300 yards per ball)
Steel crochet hook, size 7 (1.65 mm) **or** size needed for gauge

GAUGE: Rnds 1-5 = 2"

STITCH GUIDE

V-ST
(Dc, ch 3, dc) in second ch of next ch-3.
DECREASE (uses next 3 sts)
† YO, insert hook in **next** dc, YO and pull up a loop, YO and draw through 2 loops on hook †, skip next dc, repeat from † to † once, YO and draw through all 3 loops on hook **(counts as one dc)**.

Rnd 1 (Right side)**:** Ch 4, 17 dc in fourth ch from hook; join with slip st to top of beginning ch: 18 sts.

Rnd 2: Ch 3 **(counts as first dc, now and throughout)**, dc in same st and in next 2 dc, (2 dc in next dc, dc in next 2 dc) around; join with slip st to first dc: 24 dc.

Rnd 3: Ch 3, dc in same st and in next dc, (2 dc in next dc, dc in next dc) around; join with slip st to first dc: 36 dc.

Rnd 4: Ch 3, dc in next 5 dc, ch 3, (dc in next 6 dc, ch 3) around; join with slip st to first dc.

Rnd 5: Ch 3, ★ dc in next dc and in each dc across to next ch-3 sp, ch 1, work V-St, ch 1; repeat from ★ around; join with slip st to first dc.

Rnd 6: Ch 3, ★ dc in next dc and in each dc across to next ch-1 sp, ch 1, dc in next dc, ch 1, work V-St, ch 1, dc in next dc, ch 1; repeat from ★ around; join with slip st to first dc.

Rnd 7: Ch 3, ★ dc in next dc and in each dc across to next ch-1 sp, ch 1, (dc in next dc, ch 1) twice, work V-St, ch 1, (dc in next dc, ch 1) twice; repeat from ★ around; join with slip st to first dc.

Rnd 8: Ch 3, dc in next dc and in each dc across to next ch-1 sp, ch 1, (dc in next dc, ch 1) 3 times, work V-St, ch 1, (dc in next dc, ch 1) 3 times; repeat from ★ around; join with slip st to first dc.

Rnd 9: Ch 3, dc in next dc, ★ † 2 dc in next dc, ch 3, 2 dc in next dc, dc in next 2 dc, ch 1, (dc in next dc, ch 1) 4 times, dc in next ch-3 sp, ch 1, (dc in next dc, ch 1) 4 times †, dc in next 2 dc; repeat from ★ 4 times **more**, then repeat from † to † once; join with slip st to first dc.

Rnd 10: Ch 3, ★ dc in next dc and in each dc across to next ch-3 sp, ch 5, sc in next ch-3 sp, ch 5, dc in next 4 dc, ch 1, (dc in next dc, ch 1) 9 times; repeat from ★ around; join with slip st to first dc.

Rnd 11: Ch 3, ★ dc in next dc and in each dc across to next ch-5 sp, ch 5, (sc in next ch-5 sp, ch 5) twice, dc in next 4 dc, ch 1, (dc in next dc, ch 1) 9 times; repeat from ★ around; join with slip st to first dc.

Rnd 12: Ch 3, ★ dc in next dc and in each dc across to next ch-5 sp, ch 5, (sc in next ch-5 sp, ch 5) 3 times, dc in next 4 dc, ch 1, (dc in next dc, ch 1) 9 times; repeat from ★ around; join with slip st to first dc.

Rnd 13: Ch 3, ★ dc in next dc and in each dc across to next ch-5 sp, ch 5, (sc in next ch-5 sp, ch 5) 4 times, dc in next 4 dc, ch 1, (dc in next dc, ch 1) 3 times, decrease, ch 1, (dc in next dc, ch 1) 3 times; repeat from ★ around; join with slip st to first dc.

Rnd 14: Ch 3, ★ dc in next dc and in each dc across to next ch-5 sp, ch 5, (sc in next ch-5 sp, ch 5) 5 times, dc in next 4 dc, ch 1, (dc in next dc, ch 1) twice, decrease, ch 1, (dc in next dc, ch 1) twice; repeat from ★ around; join with slip st to first dc.

Rnd 15: Ch 3, ★ dc in next dc and in each dc across to next ch-5 sp, (ch 5, sc in next ch-5 sp) 3 times, ch 7, (sc in next ch-5 sp, ch 5) 3 times, dc in next 4 dc, ch 1, dc in next dc, ch 1, decrease, ch 1, dc in next dc, ch 1; repeat from ★ around; join with slip st to first dc.

Rnd 16: Ch 3, ★ dc in next dc and in each dc across to next ch-5 sp, (ch 5, sc in next ch-5 sp) 3 times, ch 1, 9 dc in next ch-7 sp, ch 1, (sc in next ch-5 sp, ch 5) 3 times, dc in next 4 dc, ch 1, decrease, ch 1; repeat from ★ around; join with slip st to first dc.

Rnd 17: Ch 3, ★ dc in next dc and in each dc across to next ch-5 sp, (ch 5, sc in next ch-5 sp) 3 times, ch 1, dc in next dc, † ch 3, YO, insert hook in same dc as last st made, YO and pull up a loop, YO and draw through 2 loops on hook, skip next dc, YO, insert hook in next dc, YO and pull up a loop, YO and draw through 2 loops on hook, YO and draw through all 3 loops on hook †, repeat from † to † 3 times **more**, ch 3, dc in same dc as last st made, ch 1, (sc in next ch-5 sp, ch 5) 3 times, dc in next 4 dc, skip next dc; repeat from ★ around; join with slip st to first dc.

Rnd 18: Ch 3, dc in next 3 dc, ★ † (ch 5, sc in next ch-5 sp) 3 times, ch 1, dc in next dc, (3 dc in next ch-3 sp, dc in next st) 5 times, ch 1, (sc in next ch-5 sp, ch 5) 3 times †, dc in next 8 dc; repeat from ★ 4 times **more**, then repeat from † to † once, dc in last 4 dc; join with slip st to first dc.

Continued on page 14.

Rnd 19: Ch 3, dc in next dc, ★ † (ch 5, sc in next ch-5 sp) 3 times, ch 1, dc in next dc, (ch 3, skip next dc, sc in next dc, ch 3, skip next dc, dc in next dc) 5 times, ch 1, (sc in next ch-5 sp, ch 5) 3 times, skip next 2 dc †, dc in next 4 dc; repeat from ★ 4 times **more**, then repeat from † to † once, dc in last 2 dc; join with slip st to first dc.

Rnd 20: Ch 8 **(counts as first dc plus ch 5)**, (sc in next ch-5 sp, ch 5) twice, sc in next ch-5 sp, ★ † ch 1, dc in next dc, (ch 7, dc in next dc) 5 times, ch 1, (sc in next ch-5 sp, ch 5) 3 times, skip next dc †, dc in next 2 dc, (ch 5, sc in next ch-5 sp) 3 times; repeat from ★ 4 times **more**, then repeat from † to † once, dc in last dc; join with slip st to first dc.

Rnd 21: Slip st in first 2 chs, ch 1, sc in same sp, (ch 5, sc in next ch-5 sp) twice, ★ † ch 1, dc in next dc, (7 dc in next ch-7 sp, dc in next dc) 5 times, ch 1, sc in next ch-5 sp †, (ch 5, sc in next ch-5 sp) 5 times; repeat from ★ 4 times **more**, then repeat from † to † once, (ch 5, sc in next ch-5 sp) twice, ch 2, dc in first sc to form last ch-5 sp.

Rnd 22: Ch 1, sc in same sp, (ch 5, sc in next ch-5 sp) twice, ★ † ch 1, dc in next dc, (ch 3, skip next dc, sc in next dc, ch 3, skip next dc, dc in next dc) 10 times, ch-1, sc in next ch-5 sp †, (ch 5, sc in next ch-5 sp) 4 times; repeat from ★ 4 times **more**, then repeat from † to † once, ch 5, sc in next ch-5 sp, ch 2, dc in first sc to form last ch-5 sp.

Rnd 23: Ch 1, sc in same sp, (ch 5, sc in next ch-5 sp) twice, ★ † ch 1, dc in next dc, (ch 5, dc in next dc) 10 times, ch 1, sc in next ch-5 sp †, (ch 5, sc in next ch-5 sp) 3 times; repeat from ★ 4 times **more**, then repeat from † to † once, ch 2, dc in first sc to form last ch-5 sp.

Rnd 24: Ch 1, sc in same sp, (ch 5, sc in next ch-5 sp) twice, ★ † ch 1, (dc in next dc, ch 3, sc in next ch-5 sp, ch 3, slip st in third ch from hook, ch 3) 10 times, dc in next dc, ch 1 †, sc in next ch-5 sp, (ch 5, sc in next ch-5 sp) twice; repeat from ★ 4 times **more**, then repeat from † to † once; join with slip st to first sc.

Rnd 25: Slip st in first 2 chs, ch 1, sc in same sp, ch 5, sc in next ch-5 sp, ★ † ch 1, tr in next dc, (ch 7, tr in next dc) 10 times, ch 1 †, sc in next ch-5 sp, ch 5, sc in next ch-5 sp; repeat from ★ 4 times **more**, then repeat from † to † once; join with slip st to first sc.

Rnd 26: Slip st in first 2 chs, ch 1, sc in same sp, ★ † ch 3, slip st in top of sc just made, ch 3, (2 dc, ch 4, slip st in fourth ch from hook, ch 1, 2 dc) in next tr, ch 3 †, sc in next sp; repeat from ★ around to last tr, then repeat from † to † once; join with slip st to first sc, finish off.

See Washing and Blocking, page 124.

DOILIES TO LOVE

Cotton doilies are a wonderful way to add traditional style to your home and protect your furniture, too. Crocheted in two different patterns, these lacy accents are simply delightful.

#1 CROWNS DOILY
Finished Size: 8" in diameter

MATERIALS
Bedspread Weight Cotton Thread (size 10): 60 yards
Steel crochet hook, size 8 (1.50 mm) **or** size needed for gauge

GAUGE: Rnds 1 and 2 = 2"

STITCH GUIDE

BEGINNING CLUSTER
Ch 3, ★ YO twice, insert hook in **same** sp, YO and pull up a loop, (YO and draw through 2 loops on hook) twice; repeat from ★ once **more**, YO and draw through all 3 loops on hook *(Figs. 12a & b, page 121)*.

CLUSTER
★ YO twice, insert hook in sp indicated, YO and pull up a loop, (YO and draw through 2 loops on hook) twice; repeat from ★ 2 times **more**, YO and draw through all 4 loops on hook.

DOUBLE TREBLE CROCHET *(abbreviated dtr)*
YO 3 times, insert hook in st or sp indicated, YO and pull up a loop, (YO and draw through 2 loops on hook) 4 times *(Figs. 10a & b, page 120)*.

Ch 8; join with slip st to form a ring.

Rnd 1 (Right side)**:** Ch 1, sc in ring, (ch 6, sc in ring) 5 times, ch 3, dc in first sc to form last sp: 6 ch-6 sps.

Rnd 2: Work beginning Cluster, ch 6, slip st in fourth ch from hook, ch 2, work Cluster in same sp, ch 6, slip st in fourth ch from hook, ch 2, work (Cluster, ch 6, slip st in fourth ch from hook, ch 2) twice in next ch-6 sp and in each ch-6 sp around; join with slip st to top of beginning Cluster: 12 Clusters.

Rnd 3: Ch 7, (dtr in same st, ch 2) 3 times, (dtr, ch 2) 4 times in next Cluster and in each Cluster around; join with slip st to fifth ch of beginning ch-7: 48 ch-2 sps.

Rnd 4: Slip st in next 2 chs and in next dtr, slip st in next ch-2 sp, work beginning Cluster, ch 6, slip st in fourth ch from hook, ch 2, work Cluster in same sp, ch 5, skip next ch-2 sp, sc in next ch-2 sp, ch 5, ★ skip next ch-2 sp, work Cluster in next ch-2 sp, ch 6, slip st in fourth ch from hook, ch 2, work Cluster in same sp, ch 5, skip next ch-2 sp, sc in next ch-2 sp, ch 5; repeat from ★ around; join with slip st to top of beginning Cluster: 24 Clusters.

Continued on page 16.

Rnd 5: Slip st in first ch-2 sp, ch 8, dtr in next ch-2 sp, ch 10, skip next 2 ch-5 sps, ★ dtr in next ch-2 sp, ch 3, dtr in next ch-2 sp, ch 10, skip next 2 ch-5 sps; repeat from ★ around; join with slip st to fifth ch of beginning ch-8.

Rnd 6: Slip st in first ch-3 sp, work beginning Cluster, ch 3, work Cluster in same sp, (ch 2, dtr) 6 times in next loop, ch 2, ★ work (Cluster, ch 3, Cluster) in next ch-3 sp, (ch 2, dtr) 6 times in next loop, ch 2; repeat from ★ around; join with slip st to top of beginning Cluster: 24 Clusters.

Rnd 7: Slip st in first ch-3 sp, ch 1, (sc, ch 4, sc) in same sp, ★ † ch 5, (dtr in next ch-2 sp, ch 2) 3 times, work Cluster in next ch-2 sp, ch 6, slip st in fourth ch from hook, ch 2, work Cluster in same sp, (ch 2, dtr in next ch-2 sp) 3 times, ch 5 †, (sc, ch 4, sc) in next ch-3 sp; repeat from ★ 10 times **more**, then repeat from † to † once; join with slip st to first sc, finish off.

See Washing and Blocking, page 124.

#2 SWEETHEART DOILY
Finished Size: 7$\frac{1}{2}$" in diameter

MATERIALS
Bedspread Weight Cotton Thread (size 10):
70 yards
Steel crochet hook, size 8 (1.50 mm) **or** size needed for gauge

GAUGE: Rnds 1 and 2 = 2$\frac{1}{4}$"

STITCH GUIDE

BEGINNING CLUSTER
Ch 3, ★ YO twice, insert hook in **same** st or sp, YO and pull up a loop, (YO and draw through 2 loops on hook) twice; repeat from ★ once **more**, YO and draw through all 3 loops on hook *(Figs. 12a & b, page 121)*.

CLUSTER
★ YO twice, insert hook in st or sp indicated, YO and pull up a loop, (YO and draw through 2 loops on hook) twice; repeat from ★ 2 times **more**, YO and draw through all 4 loops on hook.

SCALLOP
Ch 5, dc in fifth ch from hook.

DOUBLE TREBLE CROCHET
(abbreviated dtr)
YO 3 times, insert hook in st or sp indicated, YO and pull up a loop, (YO and draw through 2 loops on hook) 4 times *(Figs. 10a & b, page 120)*.

Ch 8; join with slip st to form a ring.

Rnd 1 (Right side): Slip st in ring, ch 8, dc in fifth ch from hook, (dc in ring, work Scallop) 5 times; join with slip st to third ch of beginning ch-8: 6 Scallops.

Rnd 2: Work (beginning Cluster, 2 Scallops, Cluster) in same st, ch 3, ★ work (Cluster, 2 Scallops, Cluster) in next dc, ch 3; repeat from ★ around; join with slip st to top of beginning Cluster: 12 Clusters.

Rnd 3: Ch 1, sc in same st, ★ † ch 9, sc in sp **between** Scallops, ch 9, sc in next Cluster and in next ch-3 sp †, sc in next Cluster; repeat from ★ 4 times **more**, then repeat from † to † once; join with slip st to first sc: 12 loops.

Rnd 4: Slip st in first 2 chs, ch 3 **(counts as first dc, now and throughout)**, 8 dc in same loop, sc in next sc, (9 dc in each of next 2 loops, sc in next sc) around to last loop, 9 dc in last loop; join with slip st to first dc: 12 9-dc groups.

Rnd 5: Ch 10, dc in fifth ch from hook, work Scallop, dtr in sp **before** first 9-dc group, ★ † ch 5, (dtr, work 2 Scallops, dtr) in next sc, ch 5 †, (dtr, work 2 Scallops, dtr) in sp **before** next 9-dc group; repeat from ★ 4 times **more**, then repeat from † to † once; join with slip st to fifth ch of beginning ch-10: 24 Scallops.

Rnd 6: Slip st in first Scallop (ch-4 sp), ch 10, dc in fifth ch from hook, work Scallop, dtr in same sp, (dtr, work 2 Scallops, dtr) in next Scallop and in each Scallop around; join with slip st to fifth ch of beginning ch-10: 48 Scallops.

Rnd 7: Slip st in first Scallop, ch 3, 3 dc in same sp, ch 1, 4 dc in next Scallop, work Scallop, ★ 4 dc in next Scallop, ch 1, 4 dc in next Scallop, work Scallop; repeat from ★ around; join with slip st to first dc: 48 4-dc groups.

Rnd 8: Slip st in next 3 dc and in next ch-1 sp, ch 10, dc in fifth ch from hook, work Scallop, dtr in same sp, (dtr, work 2 Scallops, dtr) in each Scallop and in each ch-1 sp around; join with slip st to fifth ch of beginning ch-10, finish off.

See Washing and Blocking, page 124.

CLASSIC COASTERS

*C*rafted in classic patterns and neutral colors, these handy coasters are ideal for entertaining. Both designs are crocheted using a combination of shells, treble crochet variations, and picot stitches.

COASTER #1
Finished Size: 5"

MATERIALS
Bedspread Weight Cotton Thread (size 10): 30 yards **each**
Steel crochet hook, size 6 (1.80 mm) **or** size needed for gauge

GAUGE: Rnds 1 and 2 (from Shell to Shell) = 1½"

STITCH GUIDE

BEGINNING SHELL
Ch 3 **(counts as first dc, now and throughout)**, (dc, ch 2, 2 dc) in sp indicated.
SHELL
(2 Dc, ch 2, 2 dc) in sp indicated.
PICOT
Ch 4, sc in fourth ch from hook.

Ch 6; join with slip st to form a ring.

Rnd 1 (Right side)**:** Work beginning Shell in ring, ch 7, (work Shell in ring, ch 7) 3 times; join with slip st to first dc: 4 ch-7 sps.

Note: Loop a short piece of thread around any stitch to mark Rnd 1 as **right** side.

Rnd 2: Slip st in next dc and in next ch-2 sp, work beginning Shell in same sp, ch 2, 7 tr in next ch-7 sp, ch 2, ★ work Shell in next Shell (ch-2 sp), ch 2, 7 tr in next ch-7 sp, ch 2; repeat from ★ around; join with slip st to first dc: 28 tr.

Rnd 3: Slip st in next dc and in next ch-2 sp, work beginning Shell in same sp, ch 2, dc in next tr, 2 dc in each of next 5 tr, dc in next tr, ch 2, skip next ch-2 sp, ★ work Shell in next Shell, ch 2, dc in next tr, 2 dc in each of next 5 tr, dc in next tr, ch 2, skip next ch-2 sp; repeat from ★ around; join with slip st to first dc: 64 dc.

Continued on page 18.

Rnds 4-6: Slip st in next dc and in next ch-2 sp, work beginning Shell in same sp, ch 2, skip next ch-2 sp, dc in next dc, (ch 1, dc in next dc) 11 times, ch 2, skip next ch-2 sp, ★ work Shell in next Shell, ch 2, skip next ch-2 sp, dc in next dc, (ch 1, dc in next dc) 11 times, ch 2, skip next ch-2 sp; repeat from ★ around; join with slip st to first dc.

Rnd 7: Slip st in next dc and in next ch-2 sp, ch 3, (dc, work Picot, 2 dc) in same sp, skip next ch-2 sp, dc in next dc, (work Picot, dc in next dc) 11 times, skip next ch-2 sp, ★ (2 dc, work Picot, 2 dc) in next Shell, skip next ch-2 sp, dc in next dc, (work Picot, dc in next dc) 11 times, skip next ch-2 sp; repeat from ★ around; join with slip st to first dc, finish off.

See Washing and Blocking, page 124.

COASTER #2
Finished Size: 4½"

MATERIALS
Bedspread Weight Cotton Thread (size 10):
  25 yards **each**
Steel crochet hook, size 6 (1.80 mm) **or** size needed for gauge

GAUGE: 18 dc = 2"

STITCH GUIDE

> **SHELL**
> (2 Dc, ch 2, 2 dc) in sp indicated.
> **DOUBLE TREBLE CROCHET**
> *(abbreviated dtr)*
> YO 3 times, insert hook in st or sp indicated, YO and pull up a loop, (YO and draw through 2 loops on hook) 4 times *(Figs. 10a & b, page 120).*
> **PICOT**
> Ch 4, sc in fourth ch from hook.

Ch 12; join with slip st to form a ring.

Row 1 (Right side)**:** Ch 5 **(counts as first dtr, now and throughout)**, work (Shell, ch 3, 15 tr, ch 3, Shell, dtr) in ring; do **not** join.

Note: Loop a short piece of yarn around any stitch to mark Row 1 as **right** side.

Row 2: Ch 5, turn; work Shell in next Shell (ch-2 sp), ch 3, dc in next tr, (ch 1, dc in next tr) 14 times, ch 3, work Shell in next Shell, dtr in last dtr: 18 sps.

Row 3: Ch 5, turn; work Shell in next Shell, ch 3, (sc in next ch-1 sp, ch 3) across to next Shell, work Shell in next Shell, dtr in last dtr: 17 sps.

Rows 4-14: Ch 5, turn; work Shell in next Shell, ch 3, skip next ch-3 sp, (sc in next ch-3 sp, ch 3) across to last ch-3 sp, skip last ch-3 sp, work Shell in next Shell, dtr in last dtr: 6 sps.

Row 15: Ch 5, turn; work Shell in next Shell, ch 3, skip next ch-3 sp, (sc in next ch-3 sp, ch 3) twice, work Shell in next Shell, dtr in last dtr: 5 sps.

Row 16: Ch 5, turn; work Shell in next Shell, skip next 3 ch-3 sps, work Shell in next Shell, dtr in last dtr: 2 Shells.

Row 17: Turn; slip st in first 2 dc and in next ch-2 sp, ch 1, sc in same sp, ch 5, sc in last Shell.

Edging: Do **not** turn; working in end of rows, slip st in next row, ch 1, (sc, work Picot, sc) in same row and in each row across to ring, (sc, work Picot, sc) in ring; (sc, work Picot, sc) in end of each of next 16 rows, (sc, work Picot, sc) in last ch-5 sp; join with slip st to first sc, finish off.

See Washing and Blocking, page 124.

FLORAL TABLE RUNNER

A garden of beautiful flowers blooms on this summer-fresh table runner! Instructions for the lacy accent are given in three sizes, but you can create any size runner you desire by adding or subtracting rows or the number of motifs in a row.

Finished Size: Small - 14" x 14"
  Medium - 14" x 33"
  Large - 14" x 52"

MATERIALS
Bedspread Weight Cotton Thread (size 10):
  Complete set - 2,350 yards
    Small - 330 yards
    Medium - 785 yards
    Large - 1,235 yards
Steel crochet hook, size 6 (1.80 mm) **or** size needed for gauge

GAUGE: Each Motif = 2³/₄"

STITCH GUIDE

BEGINNING CLUSTER (uses first 5 dc)
Ch 2, ★ YO, insert hook in **next** dc, YO and pull up a loop, YO and draw through 2 loops on hook; repeat from ★ 3 times **more**, YO and draw through all 5 loops on hook *(Figs. 12c & d, page 121)*.
CLUSTER (uses next 5 dc)
★ YO, insert hook in **next** dc, YO and pull up a loop, YO and draw through 2 loops on hook; repeat from ★ 4 times **more**, YO and draw through all 6 loops on hook.

FIRST MOTIF

Ch 6; join with slip st to form a ring.

Rnd 1 (Right side)**:** Ch 3 **(counts as first dc, now and throughout)**, 15 dc in ring; join with slip st to first dc: 16 dc.

Note: Loop a short piece of thread around any stitch to mark Rnd 1 as **right** side.

Rnd 2: Ch 7, skip next dc, (dc in next dc, ch 4, skip next dc) around; join with slip st to third ch of beginning ch-7: 8 ch-4 sps.

Rnd 3: Slip st in first ch-4 sp, ch 3, 4 dc in same sp, ch 1, (5 dc in next ch-4 sp, ch 1) around; join with slip st to first dc: 40 dc.

Rnd 4: Ch 3, dc in next 4 dc, ch 3, (dc in next 5 dc, ch 3) around; join with slip st to first dc.

Rnd 5: Work beginning Cluster, ch 12, (work Cluster, ch 12) around; join with slip st to top of beginning Cluster, finish off.

Continued on page 20.

ADDITIONAL MOTIFS

Work same as First Motif through Rnd 4.

Work One or Two Side Joining (**Fig. 22, page 123**), arranging Motifs as follows:

    Small - 5 rows of 5 Motifs **each**
    Medium - 5 rows of 12 Motifs **each**
    Large - 5 rows of 19 Motifs **each**

ONE SIDE JOINING

Work beginning Cluster, ch 6; holding Motifs with **wrong** sides together, slip st in corresponding loop on **previous Motif**, ch 6, work Cluster on **new Motif**, ch 6, slip st in corresponding loop on **previous Motif**, ch 6, (work Cluster on **new Motif**, ch 12) around; join with slip st to top of beginning Cluster, finish off.

TWO SIDE JOINING

Work beginning Cluster, ch 6; holding Motifs with **wrong** sides together, † slip st in corresponding loop on **previous Motif**, ch 6, work Cluster on **new Motif**, ch 6, slip st in corresponding loop on **previous Motif**, ch 6 †, work Cluster on **new Motif**, ch 6, repeat from † to † once, (work Cluster on **new Motif**, ch 12) around; join with slip st to top of beginning Cluster, finish off.

FILL-IN MOTIF

Ch 4; join with slip st to form a ring.

Rnd 1 (Right side): Ch 1, 8 sc in ring; join with slip st to first sc: 8 sc.

Rnd 2 (Joining rnd): ★ Ch 6, with **right** side of joined Motifs facing and working in space **between** Motifs, sc in corresponding ch-6 sp on Motif, hdc in second ch from hook and in next 4 chs, slip st in next sc on Fill-In Motif; repeat from ★ around working last slip st in first sc; finish off.

Repeat for each space between joined Motifs.

EDGING

With **right** side facing, join thread with slip st in last ch-6 sp before joining on any Motif; ch 1, 8 sc in same sp and in next ch-6 sp, 16 sc in each loop across to last ch-6 sp on same Motif, ★ 8 sc in each of next 2 ch-6 sps, 16 sc in each loop across to last loop on same Motif; repeat from ★ around; join with slip st to first sc, finish off.

See Washing and Blocking, page 124.

DREAMY BED LINENS

*S*weet dreams await when you adorn your bed linens with our feminine edgings. Attached to a purchased sheet, pillowcases, and shams, the oh-so-pretty trims are accented with satin ribbon.

MATERIALS

    Cotton Crochet Thread (size 10, 20, 30):
    Steel crochet hook,
        Size 10 thread - size 7 (1.65 mm)
        Size 20 thread - size 9 (1.40 mm)
        Size 30 thread - size 11 (1.10 mm)
        or size needed for gauge
    Sewing needle and thread
    Ribbon (for Edging #1 only)
    Bed Linens

EDGING #1

Thread Weight:	10	20	30
Width:	2¾"	2¼"	1¾"

STITCH GUIDE

PICOT
Ch 3, slip st in top of sc just made.

Ch 18.

Row 1 (Right side): Dc in ninth ch from hook, ch 3, skip next 2 chs, sc in next ch, ch 3, skip next 2 chs, dc in next ch, ch 2, skip next 2 chs, dc in last ch: 4 ch-sps.

Note: Loop a short piece of thread around any stitch to mark Row 1 as **right** side.

Row 2: Ch 5, turn; dc in next dc, ch 5, skip next 2 ch-3 sps, dc in next dc, ch 2, skip next 2 chs, dc in next ch: 3 ch-sps.

Row 3: Ch 5, turn; dc in **first** dc, ch 2, dc in next dc, ch 3, skip next 2 chs, sc in next ch, ch 3, dc in next dc, ch 2, skip next 2 chs, dc in next ch: 5 ch-sps.

Row 4: Ch 5, turn; dc in next dc, ch 5, skip next 2 ch-3 sps, dc in next dc, ch 2, dc in next dc, leave remaining ch-5 sp unworked: 3 ch-sps.

Row 5: Ch 5, turn; dc in next dc, ch 3, skip next 2 chs, sc in next ch, ch 3, dc in next dc, ch 2, skip next 2 chs, dc in next ch: 4 ch-sps.

Row 6: Ch 5, turn; dc in next dc, ch 5, skip next 2 ch-3 sps, dc in next dc, ch 2, skip next 2 chs, dc in next ch: 3 ch-sps.

Repeat Rows 3-6 for desired length, ending by working Row 5; do **not** finish off.

Picot Trim: Working in end of rows, slip st in first row, ch 3, dc in next row, ch 4, slip st in fourth ch from hook, ch 1, 2 dc in same row, ★ skip next row, 2 dc in next row, ch 4, slip st in fourth ch from hook, ch 1, 2 dc in same row; repeat from ★ across; finish off.

SCALLOP TRIM
Row 1: With **right** side facing and working in end of rows on opposite side of Edging, join thread with slip st in first row; ch 3, 4 dc in same row, ★ ch 2, skip next row, (dc, ch 2) twice in next row, skip next row, 5 dc in next row; repeat from ★ across.

Row 2: Turn; slip st in first 3 dc, ch 1, sc in same st, ★ ch 2, skip next 2 dc, dc in next dc, ch 2, (tr, ch 3, tr) in next ch-2 sp, ch 2, skip next dc, dc in next dc, ch 2, skip next 2 dc, sc in next dc; repeat from ★ across to last 2 sts, leave last 2 sts unworked.

Row 3: Ch 1, turn; 3 sc in first ch-2 sp, (sc, work Picot, sc) in next ch-2 sp, sc in next ch-3 sp, (work Picot, sc in same sp) 3 times, (sc, work Picot, sc) in next ch-2 sp, ★ 3 sc in each of next 2 ch-2 sps, (sc, work Picot, sc) in next ch-2 sp, sc in next ch-3 sp, (work Picot, sc in same sp) 3 times, (sc, work Picot, sc) in next ch-2 sp; repeat from ★ across to last ch-2 sp, 3 sc in last ch-2 sp; finish off.

See Washing and Blocking, page 124.
Referring to photo for placement, sew Edging to bed linen.

Continued on page 22.

EDGING #2

Thread Weight:	10	20	30
Width:	3"	2¼"	2"

Ch 27.

Row 1 (Right side): Dc in ninth ch from hook, ch 2, skip next 2 chs, dc in next ch, ch 2, skip next 2 chs, dc in next 4 chs, (ch 2, skip next 2 chs, dc in next ch) 3 times: 6 sps.

Note: Loop a short piece of thread around any stitch to mark Row 1 as **right** side.

Row 2: Ch 5 (**counts as first dc plus ch 2, now and throughout**), turn; dc in next dc, ch 2, dc in next dc, 2 dc in next ch-2 sp, dc in next dc, ch 2, skip next 2 dc, dc in next dc, 2 dc in next ch-2 sp, (dc in next dc, ch 2) twice, skip next 2 chs, dc in next ch: 12 dc and 5 ch-2 sps.

Row 3: Ch 5, turn; dc in next dc, 2 dc in next ch-2 sp, dc in next dc, ch 2, skip next 2 dc, dc in next dc, ch 2, dc in next dc, ch 2, skip next 2 dc, dc in next dc, 2 dc in next ch-2 sp, dc in next dc, ch 2, dc in last dc.

Row 4: Ch 5, turn; dc in next 4 dc, ch 2, dc in next dc, 2 dc in next ch-2 sp, dc in next dc, ch 2, dc in next 4 dc, ch 2, dc in last dc: 14 dc and 4 ch-2 sps.

Row 5: Ch 5, turn; dc in next 4 dc, (2 dc in next ch-2 sp, dc in next 4 dc) twice, ch 2, dc in last dc: 18 dc.

Row 6: Ch 5, turn; dc in next 4 dc, ch 2, (skip next 2 dc, dc in next 4 dc, ch 2) twice, dc in last dc: 14 dc.

Row 7: Ch 5, turn; dc in next 4 dc, ch 2, dc in next dc, ch 2, skip next 2 dc, dc in next dc, ch 2, dc in next 4 dc, ch 2, dc in last dc: 12 dc and 5 ch-2 sps.

Row 8: Ch 5, turn; dc in next dc, ch 2, skip next 2 dc, (dc in next dc, 2 dc in next ch-2 sp, dc in next dc, ch 2) twice, skip next 2 dc, dc in next dc, ch 2, dc in last dc.

Row 9: Ch 5, turn; (dc in next dc, ch 2) twice, skip next 2 dc, dc in next dc, 2 dc in next ch-2 sp, dc in next dc, ch 2, skip next 2 dc, dc in next dc, (ch 2, dc in next dc) twice: 10 dc.

Row 10: Ch 5, turn; dc in next dc, ch 2, dc in next dc, 2 dc in next ch-2 sp, dc in next dc, ch 2, skip next 2 dc, dc in next dc, 2 dc in next ch-2 sp, dc in next dc, (ch 2, dc in next dc) twice: 12 dc.

Repeat Rows 3-10 for desired length, ending by working a **wrong** side row; do **not** finish off.

SHELL TRIM

Row 1: Ch 7; working in end of rows, skip first 2 rows, sc in top of dc on next row, (ch 7, skip next row, sc in top of st on next row) across to last row, ch 4, skip next 2 chs on last row, dc in next ch to form last loop.

Row 2: Ch 3, turn; 2 dc in first ch, ch 3, slip st in top of dc just made, 2 dc in same ch, ★ ch 1, 3 dc in center ch of next loop, ch 3, slip st in top of dc just made, 2 dc in same ch; repeat from ★ across; finish off.

See Washing and Blocking, page 124.
Referring to photo for placement, sew Edging to bed linen.

EDGING #3

Thread Weight:	10	20	30
Width:	4¾"	4"	3½"

STITCH GUIDE

> **PICOT SHELL**
> 2 Dc in sp indicated, ch 4, slip st in top of dc just made, 2 dc in same sp.

Ch 31.

Row 1 (Right side): 3 Dc in fourth ch from hook, ch 3, skip next 2 chs, sc in next ch, ch 3, skip next 2 chs, (dc in next ch, ch 2, skip next 2 chs) 6 times, dc in last 4 chs: 8 sps.

Note: Loop a short piece of thread around any stitch to mark Row 1 as **right** side.

Row 2: Ch 11, turn; dc in ninth ch from hook and in next 2 chs, dc in next dc, ch 2, skip next 2 dc, dc in next dc, 2 dc in next ch-2 sp, dc in next dc, (ch 2, dc in next dc) 5 times, ch 5, skip next 2 ch-3 sps, dc in next dc, leave remaining sts unworked: 14 dc.

Row 3: Ch 3, turn; 3 dc in first dc, ch 3, skip next 2 chs, sc in next ch, ch 3, dc in next dc, (ch 2, dc in next dc) 4 times, 2 dc in next ch-2 sp, dc in next dc, ch 4, tr in next ch-2 sp, ch 4, skip next 3 dc, dc in next dc, 3 dc in last loop: 15 dc.

Row 4: Ch 11, turn; dc in ninth ch from hook and in next 2 chs, dc in next dc, ch 5, sc in next ch-4 sp, sc in next tr and in next ch-4 sp, ch 5, skip next 3 dc, dc in next dc, 2 dc in next ch-2 sp, dc in next dc, (ch 2, dc in next dc) 3 times, ch 5, skip next 2 ch-3 sps, dc in next dc, leave remaining sts unworked: 7 sps.

Row 5: Ch 3, turn; 3 dc in first dc, ch 3, skip next 2 chs, sc in next ch, ch 3, dc in next dc, (ch 2, dc in next dc) twice, 2 dc in next ch-2 sp, dc in next dc, ch 8, sc in next ch-5 sp, sc in next 3 sc and in next ch-5 sp, ch 8, skip next 3 dc, dc in next dc, 3 dc in last loop: 6 sps.

Row 6: Ch 11, turn; dc in ninth ch from hook and in next 2 chs, dc in next dc, ch 2, skip next 2 dc, dc in next dc, 3 dc in next ch-8 sp, ch 7, skip next sc, sc in next 3 sc, ch 7, 3 dc in next ch-8 sp, dc in next dc, ch 2, skip next 2 dc, dc in next dc, (ch 2, dc in next dc) twice, ch 5, skip next 2 ch-3 sps, dc in next dc, leave remaining sts unworked: 8 sps.

Row 7: Ch 3, turn; 3 dc in first dc, ch 3, skip next 2 chs, sc in next ch, ch 3, (dc in next dc, ch 2) 4 times, skip next 2 dc, dc in next dc, 3 dc in next ch-7 sp, ch 4, skip next sc, tr in next sc, ch 4, 3 dc in next ch-7 sp, dc in next dc, ch 4, tr in next ch-2 sp, ch 4, skip next 3 dc, dc in next dc, 3 dc in last loop: 10 sps.

Row 8: Ch 11, turn; dc in ninth ch from hook and in next 2 chs, dc in next dc, ch 5, sc in next ch-4 sp, sc in next tr and in next ch-4 sp, ch 5, skip next 3 dc, dc in next dc, 3 dc in next ch-4 sp, ch 2, 3 dc in next ch-4 sp, dc in next dc, ch 2, skip next 2 dc, dc in next dc, (ch 2, dc in next dc) 4 times, ch 5, skip next 2 ch-3 sps, dc in next dc, leave remaining sts unworked.

Row 9: Ch 3, turn; 3 dc in first dc, ch 3, skip next 2 chs, sc in next ch, ch 3, (dc in next dc, ch 2) 6 times, skip next 2 dc, dc in next dc, 2 dc in next ch-2 sp, dc in next dc, ch 8, sc in next ch-5 sp, sc in next 3 sc and in next ch-5 sp, ch 8, skip next 3 dc, dc in next dc, 3 dc in last loop (center of point): 10 sps.

Row 10: Ch 5, turn; skip first 3 dc, dc in next dc, 3 dc in first ch-8 sp, ch 7, skip next sc, sc in next 3 sc, ch 7, 3 dc in next ch-8 sp, dc in next dc, ch 2, skip next 2 dc, dc in next dc, 2 dc in next ch-2 sp, dc in next dc, (ch 2, dc in next dc) 5 times, ch 5, skip next 2 ch-3 sps, dc in next dc, leave remaining sts unworked.

Row 11: Ch 3, turn; 3 dc in first dc, ch 3, skip next 2 chs, sc in next ch, ch 3, dc in next dc, (ch 2, dc in next dc) 4 times, 2 dc in next ch-2 sp, dc in next dc, ch 4, tr in next ch-2 sp, ch 4, skip next 3 dc, dc in next dc, 3 dc in next ch-7 sp, ch 4, skip next sc, tr in next sc, ch 4, 3 dc in next ch-7 sp, dc in next dc, leave remaining sts unworked.

Row 12: Ch 5, turn; skip first 3 dc, dc in next dc, 3 dc in first ch-4 sp, ch 2, 3 dc in next ch-4 sp, dc in next dc, ch 5, sc in next ch-4 sp, sc in next tr and in next ch-4 sp, ch 5, skip next 3 dc, dc in next dc, 2 dc in next ch-2 sp, dc in next dc, (ch 2, dc in next dc) 3 times, ch 5, skip next 2 ch-3 sps, dc in next dc, leave remaining sts unworked: 8 sps.

Row 13: Ch 3, turn; 3 dc in first dc, ch 3, skip next 2 chs, sc in next ch, ch 3, dc in next dc, (ch 2, dc in next dc) twice, 2 dc in next ch-2 sp, dc in next dc, ch 8, sc in next ch-5 sp, sc in next 3 sc and in next ch-5 sp, ch 8, skip next 3 dc, dc in next dc, 2 dc in next ch-2 sp, dc in next dc, leave remaining sts unworked: 6 sps.

Repeat Rows 6-13 until 1" **less** than desired length, ending by working Row 13.

LAST 4 ROWS

Row 1: Ch 5, turn; skip first 3 dc, dc in next dc, 3 dc in next ch-8 sp, ch 7, skip next sc, sc in next 3 sc, ch 7, 3 dc in next ch-8 sp, dc in next dc, ch 2, skip next 2 dc, dc in next dc, (ch 2, dc in next dc) twice, ch 5, skip next 2 ch-3 sps, dc in next dc, leave remaining sts unworked: 7 sps.

Row 2: Ch 3, turn; 3 dc in first dc, ch 3, skip next 2 chs, sc in next ch, ch 3, (dc in next dc, ch 2) 4 times, skip next 2 dc, dc in next dc, 3 dc in next ch-7 sp, ch 4, skip next sc, tr in next sc, ch 4, 3 dc in next ch-7 sp, dc in next dc, leave remaining sts unworked: 8 sps.

Row 3: Ch 5, turn; skip first 3 dc, dc in next dc, 3 dc in first ch-4 sp, ch 2, 3 dc in next ch-4 sp, dc in next dc, ch 2, skip next 2 dc, dc in next dc, (ch 2, dc in next dc) 4 times, ch 5, skip next 2 ch-3 sps, dc in next dc, leave remaining sts unworked.

Row 4: Ch 3, turn; 3 dc in first dc, ch 3, skip next 2 chs, sc in next ch, ch 3, (dc in next dc, ch 2) 6 times, skip next 2 dc, dc in next dc, 2 dc in next ch-2 sp, dc in next dc; do **not** finish off.

PICOT SHELL TRIM

Ch 4; working in end of rows, skip first row, work Picot Shell in ch-5 sp of next row, ch 4, (sc in dc at base of dc on next row, ch 4, work Picot Shell in ch-5 sp of next row, ch 4) 3 times, sc in next row (center of point), ★ ch 4, work Picot Shell in ch-sp of next row, ch 4, sc in top of dc on next row, ch 4, work Picot Shell in ch-sp of next row, ch 4, sc in next row, ch 4, work Picot Shell in ch-5 sp of next row, ch 4, sc in dc at base of dc on next row, ch 4, work Picot Shell in ch-5 sp of next row, ch 4, sc in next row (center of point); repeat from ★ across to center of last point, (ch 4, work Picot Shell in ch-sp of next row, ch 4, sc in top of dc on next row) 4 times; finish off.

See Washing and Blocking, page 124.
Referring to photo for placement, sew Edging to bed linen.

MEMORY MAT

This filet crochet photo mat surrounds treasured family photographs with elegance. Dainty and delicate, it also makes a lovely gift for a bride to display her wedding portrait.

Finished Size: 6½" x 8¼"
(to fit an 8" x 10" frame)

MATERIALS
Bedspread Weight Cotton Thread (size 10):
  1 ball (282 yards per ball)
Steel crochet hook, size 12 (1.00 mm) **or** size
  needed for gauge
Photograph
8" x 10" Mat board
Spray mount
Fabric glue

GAUGE: 8 ch-2 sps and 10 rows = 2"

STITCH GUIDE

ADDING ON DOUBLE CROCHETS
YO, insert hook into base of last dc, YO and pull up a loop, YO and draw through one loop on hook, (YO and draw through 2 loops on hook) twice. Repeat as many times as instructed **(Fig. 21, page 123)**.

BOTTOM
Ch 81.

Row 1 (Right side)**:** Dc in fourth ch from hook and in each ch across: 79 sts.

Note: Loop a short piece of thread around any stitch to mark Row 1 as **right** side.

Row 2: Ch 3 **(counts as first dc, now and throughout)**, turn; dc in next 3 dc, [ch 2, skip next 2 dc, dc in next dc **(Space over Block made)]** across to last 3 sts, dc in last 3 sts **(Block over Block made)**.

Row 3: [Ch 3, turn; dc in next 3 dc **(beginning Block over Block made)]**, [ch 2, dc in next dc **(Space over Space made)]**, [2 dc in next ch-2 sp, dc in next dc **(Block over Space made)]**, work across following Chart.

Rows 4-7: Follow Chart.

LEFT SIDE
Row 8: Work Beginning Block, work 7 Spaces, work 3 Blocks, leave remaining sts unworked.

Row 9: Turn; slip st in first 7 dc, ch 3, work across following Chart.

Row 10: Follow Chart.

Row 11: [Turn; slip st in first 4 dc, ch 3 **(beginning decrease made)]**, work across following Chart.

Rows 12-25: Follow Chart.

Row 26: Work beginning Block, work 3 Spaces, work Block, add on 3 dc.

Rows 27-33: Follow Chart.

Row 34: Work beginning Block, work 7 Spaces, work Block, add on 6 dc; finish off.

KEY

▦	1 Block = 3 dc
☐	1 Space = ch 2, dc

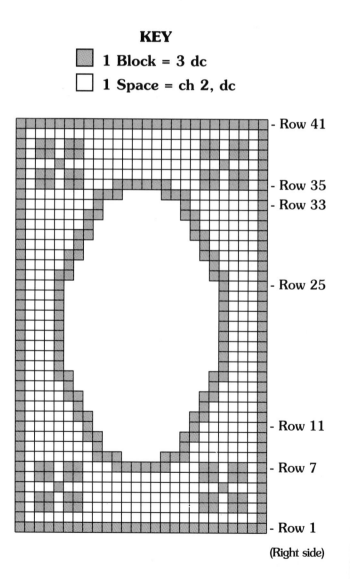

- Row 41

- Row 35

- Row 33

- Row 25

- Row 11

- Row 7

- Row 1

(Right side)

On right side rows follow Chart from right to left; on wrong side rows follow Chart from left to right.

RIGHT SIDE

Row 8: With **wrong** side facing, skip 11 dc from Left Side, join thread with slip st in next dc; ch 3, work across following Chart.

Row 9: Work beginning Block, work 7 Spaces, work Block, leave remaining 6 dc unworked.

Row 10: Follow Chart.

Row 11: Work beginning Block, work 6 Spaces, work Block, leave remaining 3 dc unworked **(ending decrease made)**.

Rows 12-25: Follow Chart.

Row 26: [Ch 5, turn; dc in fourth ch from hook, dc in next ch and in next dc **(beginning increase made)]**, work across following Chart.

Row 27-33: Follow Chart.

Row 34: Ch 8, turn; dc in fourth ch from hook, dc in next 4 chs and in next dc, work across following Chart.

TOP

Row 35: Work beginning Block, (work Space, work 2 Blocks) twice, work 3 Spaces, work Block, add on 11 dc, YO, insert hook into base of last dc worked **and** into top of first dc on Row 34 of Left Side, YO and pull up a loop, (YO, draw through 2 loops on hook) twice, dc in next 3 dc, work across following Chart.

Row 36-41: Follow Chart.

Finish off.

FINISHING

See Washing and Blocking, page 124.

Spray back of photograph with spray mount and place on center of mat board. Place crocheted piece on mat board and use fabric glue to secure.

ORNATE EDGINGS

These ornate edgings will lend added elegance to a set of linen guest towels. The five distinctive trims are simply whipstitched onto lengths of hemmed fabric.

MATERIALS
Cotton Crochet Thread (size 20):
    refer to individual projects for yardage
18" length 13½"w Bantry Cloth for each towel
Steel crochet hook, size 9 (1.40 mm) **or** size
    needed for gauge
Sewing thread to match towel
Sewing thread to match edging
Sewing machine
Straight pins
Hand sewing needle

FINISHING
See Washing and Blocking, page 124.

Press short edges of towel ¼" to wrong side; press to wrong side again. Using thread to match towel, machine stitch across each short edge of towel ³/₁₆" from outer pressed edge.

Matching **right** side of edging to **wrong** side of towel, refer to photo to pin edging to one short edge of towel, folding ends of edging to wrong side. Using thread to match edging, stitch edging in place.

EDGING #1
(Multiple of 12 chs plus 2)
Cotton Crochet Thread (size 20) - 35 yards

Finished Size: 14½" x 1¼"

GAUGE: 10 sc = 1"

STITCH GUIDE

> **PICOT**
> Ch 3, slip st in third ch from hook.

Ch 146.

Row 1 (Right side)**:** Sc in second ch from hook and in each ch across: 145 sc.

Note: Loop a short piece of thread around any stitch to mark Row 1 as **right** side.

Row 2: Ch 4 **(counts as first dc plus ch 1)**, turn; skip next sc, dc in next sc, ★ ch 1, skip next sc, dc in next sc; repeat from ★ across: 72 ch-1 sps.

Row 3: Ch 3 **(counts as first dc)**, turn; skip first ch-1 sp, dc in next ch-1 sp, working **around** dc just made, dc in skipped ch-1 sp, ★ dc in next ch-1 sp, working **around** dc just made, dc in previous ch-1 sp; repeat from ★ across to last dc, ch 1, dc in last dc: 145 sts.

Row 4: Ch 1, turn; sc in each dc and in each ch-1 sp across: 145 sc.

Row 5: Ch 1, turn; sc in first sc, ★ ch 5, skip next 3 sc, sc in next sc; repeat from ★ across: 36 ch-5 sps.

Row 6: Ch 1, turn; sc in first sc, ch 3, sc in next ch-5 sp, 8 dc in next ch-5 sp, sc in next ch-5 sp, ★ ch 5, sc in next ch-5 sp, 8 dc in next ch-5 sp, sc in next ch-5 sp; repeat from ★ across, ch 3, sc in last sc.

Row 7: Turn; skip first sc, slip st in next 2 chs, dc in next dc, (work Picot, dc in next dc) 7 times, ★ sc in next ch-5 sp, dc in next dc, (work Picot, dc in next dc) 7 times; repeat from ★ across to last 5 sts, skip next 2 sts, slip st in next 2 chs, leave remaining sc unworked; finish off.

Follow Finishing, first column, to hem towel and attach edging.

EDGING #2
(Multiple of 6 chs plus 2)
Cotton Crochet Thread (size 20) - 30 yards

Finished Size: 14½" x 1⅛"

GAUGE: 10 chs = 1"

STITCH GUIDE

> **CLUSTER** (uses next 2 tr)
> ★ YO twice, insert hook in next tr, YO and pull up a loop, (YO and draw through 2 loops on hook) twice; repeat from ★ once **more**, YO and draw through all 3 loops on hook.
> **PICOT**
> Ch 4, slip st in fourth ch from hook.

Ch 146.

Row 1 (Right side)**:** Sc in second ch from hook, ★ ch 3, skip next 2 chs, dc in next ch, ch 3, skip next 2 chs, sc in next ch; repeat from ★ across: 48 ch-3 sps.

Note: Loop a short piece of thread around any stitch to mark Row 1 as **right** side.

Row 2: Ch 1, turn; sc in first sc, 5 sc in each ch-3 sp across, sc in last sc: 242 sc.

Row 3: Ch 7 **(counts as first tr plus ch 3)**, turn; skip next 3 sc, tr in next 4 sc, ★ ch 5, skip next 6 sc, tr in next 4 sc; repeat from ★ across to last 4 sc, ch 3, skip next 3 sc, tr in last sc.

Row 4: Ch 1, turn; sc in first tr, work Picot twice, skip next tr, work Cluster, work Picot twice, ★ sc in next ch-5 sp, work Picot twice, skip next tr, work Cluster, work Picot twice; repeat from ★ across to last 2 tr, skip next tr, sc in last tr; finish off.

Follow Finishing, page 26, to hem towel and attach Edging.

EDGING #3
(Multiple of 6 chs plus 2)
Cotton Crochet Thread (size 20): 35 yards

Finished Size: 14½" x 1⅛"

GAUGE: 10 sc = 1"

Ch 146.

Row 1: Sc in second ch from hook and in each ch across: 145 sc.

Continued on page 28.

Row 2 (Right side)**:** Ch 5 **(counts as first dc plus ch 2)**, turn; skip next 2 sc, dc in next sc, ★ ch 2, skip next 2 sc, dc in next sc; repeat from ★ across: 48 ch-2 sps.

Note: Loop a short piece of thread around any stitch to mark Row 2 as **right** side.

Row 3: Ch 3 **(counts as first dc)**, turn; ★ 2 dc in next ch-2 sp, dc in next dc; repeat from ★ across: 145 dc.

Row 4: Ch 1, turn; sc in first dc ★ ch 2, skip next 2 dc, (tr, ch 4, slip st in fourth ch from hook) 4 times in next dc, ch 2, skip next 2 dc, sc in next dc; repeat from ★ across; finish off.

Follow Finishing, page 26, to hem towel and attach edging.

EDGING #4

(Multiple of 5 chs plus 2)
Cotton Crochet Thread (size 20): 55 yards

Finished Size: 14¹⁄₂" x 2"

GAUGE: 10 sc = 1"

STITCH GUIDE

> **PICOT**
> Ch 8, slip st in fourth ch from hook, ch 4.

Ch 147.

Row 1: Sc in second ch from hook and in each ch across: 146 sc.

Row 2 (Right side)**:** Ch 6 **(counts as first dc plus ch 3)**, turn; ★ skip next 4 sc, (dc, ch 3, dc) in next sc, ch 3; repeat from ★ across to last 5 sc, skip next 4 sc, dc in last sc: 57 ch-3 sps.

Note: Loop a short piece of thread around any stitch to mark Row 2 as **right** side.

Row 3: Ch 4 **(counts as first tr)**, turn; tr in next dc, (2 tr, ch 10, 2 tr) in next ch-3 sp, ★ tr in next dc, ch 1, tr in next dc, (2 tr, ch 10, 2 tr) in next ch-3 sp; repeat from ★ across to last 2 dc, tr in last 2 dc: 28 ch-10 sps.

Row 4: Ch 1, turn; sc in first tr, (7 dc, work Picot, 7 dc) in next ch-10 sp, ★ sc in next ch-1 sp, (7 dc, work Picot, 7 dc) in next ch-10 sp; repeat from ★ across to last 4 tr, skip next 3 tr, sc in last tr; finish off.

Follow Finishing, page 26, to hem towel and attach edging.

EDGING #5

(Multiple of 12 chs plus 3)
Cotton Crochet Thread (size 20): 30 yards

Finished Size: 14¹⁄₂" x 1¹⁄₂"

GAUGE: 10 dc = 1"

STITCH GUIDE

> **PICOT**
> Ch 6, slip st in fourth ch from hook, ch 2.

Ch 147.

Row 1 (Right side)**:** Dc in fourth ch from hook and in each ch across: 145 sts.

Note: Loop a short piece of thread around any stitch to mark Row 1 as **right** side.

Row 2: Ch 4 **(counts as first dc plus ch 1, now and throughout)**, turn; skip next dc, ★ dc in next dc, ch 1, skip next dc; repeat from ★ across to beginning ch, dc in top of beginning ch: 72 ch-1 sps.

Row 3: Ch 4, turn; sc in next ch-1 sp, (ch 1, sc in next ch-1 sp) twice, ★ ch 4, sc in next ch-1 sp, (ch 1, sc in next ch-1 sp) twice; repeat from ★ across, ch 1, dc in last dc: 23 ch-4 sps.

Row 4: Ch 6 **(counts as first tr plus ch 2)**, turn; tr in next ch-4 sp, (ch 1, tr in same sp) 5 times, ch 2, ★ sc in next ch-4 sp, ch 2, tr in next ch-4 sp, (ch 1, tr in same sp) 5 times, ch 2; repeat from ★ across to last dc, tr in last dc.

Row 5: Ch 4, turn; skip next ch-2 sp, (tr in next ch-1 sp and in next tr) twice, (tr, work Picot, tr) in next ch-1 sp, (tr in next tr and in next ch-1 sp) twice, ★ skip next 2 ch-2 sps, (tr in next ch-1 sp and in next tr) twice, (tr, work Picot, tr) in next ch-1 sp, (tr in next tr and in next ch-1 sp) twice; repeat from ★ across to last 2 tr, ch 1, skip next tr, dc in last tr; finish off.

Follow Finishing, page 26, to hem towel and attach edging.

LACY TOWEL SETS

*D*ecorative crocheted edgings turn ordinary towels into sophisticated accessories for the bath. Trimmed with two beautiful borders, our soft sets will make practical gifts with a personal touch.

MATERIALS

Bedspread Weight Cotton Thread (size 10):
2 balls (282 yards per ball) for **one** set
15¾"w hand towel
27½"w bath towel
12½" x 13 ½" washcloth
Steel crochet hook, size 8 (1.50 mm) **or** size needed for gauge
Straight pins
Sewing needle and thread

GAUGE: 10 dc = 1"

PEACH SET

Finished Size: Hand towel - 15¾" x 1¼"
Bath towel - 27½" x 1¼"
Washcloth - 52" x 1"

STITCH GUIDE

POPCORN

5 Dc in sp indicated, drop loop from hook, insert hook in first dc of 5-dc group, hook dropped loop and draw through *(Fig. 13, page 121)*.

Continued on page 30.

TOWELS
(Multiple of 3 chs)

Note: Instructions are written for hand towel with bath towel in parentheses.

Ch 159(276).

Row 1 (Right side): Dc in fourth ch from hook and in each ch across: 157(274) sts.

Note: Loop a short piece of thread around any stitch to mark Row 1 as **right** side.

Row 2: Ch 5 **(counts as first dc plus ch 2)**, turn; skip next 2 dc, dc in next dc, (ch 2, skip next 2 dc, dc in next st) across: 52(91) ch-2 sps.

Row 3: Ch 1, turn; sc in first dc, (2 sc in next ch-2 sp, sc in next dc) across: 157(274) sc.

Row 4: Ch 1, turn; sc in first sc, (ch 3, skip next 2 sc, sc in next sc) across: 52(91) ch-3 sps.

Row 5: Ch 4, turn; work Popcorn in first ch-3 sp, (ch 3, work Popcorn in next ch-3 sp) across to last sc, ch 1, dc in last sc: 52(91) Popcorns.

Row 6: Ch 1, turn; sc in first dc, ch 3, (sc in next ch-3 sp, ch 3) across to beginning ch-4, skip next ch, sc in next ch.

Row 7: Repeat Row 5.

Row 8: Ch 1, turn; sc in first dc, ch 5, slip st in fourth ch from hook, ch 2, ★ sc in next ch-3 sp, ch 5, slip st in fourth ch from hook, ch 2; repeat from ★ across to beginning ch-4, skip next ch, sc in next ch; finish off.

See Finishing, page 31.

WASHCLOTH
(Multiple of 3 chs)

Ch 525.

Row 1 (Right side): Dc in fourth ch from hook and in each ch across: 523 sts.

Note: Loop a short piece of thread around any stitch to mark Row 1 as **right** side.

Row 2: Ch 5, turn; skip next 2 dc, dc in next dc, (ch 2, skip next 2 dc, dc in next st) across: 174 ch-2 sps.

Row 3: Ch 1, turn; sc in first dc, (2 sc in next ch-2 sp, sc in next st) across: 523 sc.

Row 4: Ch 1, turn; sc in first sc, (ch 3, skip next 2 sc, sc in next sc) across: 174 ch-3 sps.

Row 5: Ch 4, turn; work Popcorn in first ch-3 sp, (ch 3, work Popcorn in next ch-3 sp) across, ch 1, dc in last sc: 174 Popcorns.

Row 6: Ch 1, turn; sc in first dc, ch 5, slip st in fourth ch from hook, ch 2, ★ sc in next ch-3 sp, ch 5, slip st in fourth ch from hook, ch 2; repeat from ★ across to beginning ch-4, skip next ch, sc in next ch; finish off leaving a long end for sewing.

See Finishing, page 31.

GREEN SET
Finished Size: Hand towel - 16¼" x 2"
Bath towel - 27½" x 2"
Washcloth - 52¼" x 1¼"

STITCH GUIDE

> **CLUSTER**
> ★ YO twice, insert hook in dc indicated, YO and pull up a loop, (YO and draw through 2 loops on hook) twice; repeat from ★ 2 times **more**, YO and draw through all 4 loops on hook *(Figs. 12a & b, page 121)*.

TOWELS
(Multiple of 8 chs plus 5)

Note: Instructions are written for hand towel with bath towel in parentheses.

Ch 165(277).

Row 1 (Right side): Dc in fourth ch from hook and in each ch across: 163(275) sts.

Note: Loop a short piece of thread around any stitch to mark Row 1 as **right** side.

Row 2: Ch 4 **(counts as first dc plus ch 1)**, turn; skip next dc, dc in next dc, (ch 1, skip next dc, dc in next st) across: 81(137) ch-1 sps.

Row 3: Ch 1, turn; sc in first dc and in next ch-1 sp, (sc in next dc and in next ch-1 sp) twice, ch 3, slip st in top of last sc made, ★ (sc in next dc and in next ch-1 sp) 4 times, ch 3, slip st in top of last sc made; repeat from ★ across to last 3 dc, sc in next dc, (sc in next ch-1 sp and in next dc) twice: 163(275) sc.

Row 4: Turn; slip st in first 2 sc, ch 3, 2 dc in same st, (ch 8, skip next 7 sc, 3 dc in next sc) across to last sc, leave last sc unworked.

Row 5: Ch 3, turn; dc in same st and in next dc, 2 dc in next dc, ★ ch 3, sc in next ch-8 sp, ch 3, 2 dc in next dc, dc in next dc, 2 dc in next dc; repeat from ★ across.

Row 6: Ch 4, turn; skip next dc, work Cluster in next dc, ★ ch 5, sc in next ch-3 sp, ch 3, sc in next ch-3 sp, ch 5, skip next 2 dc, work Cluster in next dc; repeat from ★ across to last 2 sts, skip next dc, tr in top of beginning ch-3: 21(35) Clusters.

Row 7: Turn; slip st in first tr, skip next Cluster, sc in next ch-5 sp, ch 3, 3 dc in next ch-3 sp, ch 3, ★ (sc in next ch-5 sp, ch 3) twice, 3 dc in next ch-3 sp, ch 3; repeat from ★ across to last ch-5 sp, sc in last ch-5 sp, skip next Cluster, slip st in last st.

Row 8: Ch 5, turn; 2 dc in next dc, dc in next dc, 2 dc in next dc, ★ ch 5, skip next ch-3 sp, sc in next ch-3 sp, ch 5, 2 dc in next dc, dc in next dc, 2 dc in next dc; repeat from ★ across to last ch-3 sp, ch 2, skip last ch-3 sp and next sc, dc in last slip st.

Row 9: Ch 1, turn; sc in first dc, ch 5, skip next 2 dc, work Cluster in next dc, ch 3, slip st in top of last Cluster made, ch 5, ★ sc in next ch-5 sp, ch 4, slip st in fourth ch from hook, ch 1, sc in next ch-5 sp, ch 5, skip next 2 dc, work Cluster in next dc, ch 3, slip st in top of last Cluster made, ch 5; repeat from ★ across to last ch-5 sp, skip next 2 chs, sc in next ch; finish off.

See Finishing, next column.

WASHCLOTH
(Multiple of 8 chs plus 3)

Ch 523.

Row 1 (Right side)**:** Dc in fourth ch from hook and in each ch across: 521 sts.

Note: Loop a short piece of thread around any stitch to mark Row 1 as **right** side.

Row 2: Ch 4, turn; skip next dc, dc in next dc, (ch 1, skip next dc, dc in next dc) across: 260 ch-1 sps.

Row 3: Ch 1, turn; sc in first dc and in next ch-1 sp, sc in next dc and in next ch-1 sp, ch 3, slip st in top of last sc made, ★ (sc in next dc and in next ch-1 sp) 4 times, ch 3, slip st in top of last sc made; repeat from ★ across to last 3 dc, sc in next dc, (sc in next ch-1 sp and in next dc) twice: 521 sc.

Row 4: Turn; slip st in first 2 sc, ch 3, 2 dc in same st, ch 8, (skip next 7 sc, 3 dc in next sc, ch 8) across to last 7 sc, skip next 6 sc, dc in last sc.

Row 5: Ch 6, turn; sc in first ch-8 sp, ch 3, 2 dc in next dc, dc in next dc, 2 dc in next dc, ★ ch 3, sc in next ch-8 sp, ch 3, 2 dc in next dc, dc in next dc, 2 dc in next dc; repeat from ★ across.

Row 6: Ch 4, turn; skip next dc, work Cluster in next dc, ch 3, slip st in top of last Cluster made, ch 5, sc in next ch-3 sp, ch 4, slip st in fourth ch from hook, ch 1, ★ sc in next ch-3 sp, ch 5, skip next 2 dc, work Cluster in next dc, ch 3, slip st in top of last Cluster made, ch 5, sc in next ch-3 sp, ch 4, slip st in fourth ch from hook, ch 1; repeat from ★ across to last ch-6 sp, sc in last ch-6 sp; finish off leaving a long end for sewing: 65 Clusters.

FINISHING
See Washing and Blocking, page 124.

Using photo as a guide for placement, pin **wrong** side of Edging to hemline on **right** side and baste in place. Hand or machine sew to secure. Remove basting thread.

Sew ends of washcloth Edging together.

BEAUTY BOX

Add a breath of beauty to the bath with this charming trinket box. Fill it with pretty soaps, bath beads, or other luxuries for a feminine pretty.

MATERIALS
Bedspread Weight Cotton Thread (size 10): 70 yards

Steel crochet hook, size 0 (3.25 mm) **or** size needed for gauge

Starching materials: Commercial fabric stiffener, resealable plastic bag, blocking board, plastic wrap, terry towel, paper towels, and stainless steel pins

Finishing materials - hot glue gun, glue sticks, ribbon, etc.

GAUGE: Rnds 1-3 = 1½"

BASE
BOTTOM
Rnd 1 (Right side)**:** Ch 2, 6 sc in second ch from hook; join with slip st to first sc.

Note: Loop a short piece of thread around any stitch to mark Rnd 1 as **right** side.

Rnd 2: Ch 6, dc in same st, ch 3, ★ (dc, ch 3, dc) in next sc, ch 3; repeat from ★ around; join with slip st to third ch of beginning ch-6: 12 ch-3 sps.

Rnd 3: Slip st in first ch-3 sp, ch 1, sc in same sp, ch 3, (sc in next ch-3 sp, ch 3) around; join with slip st to first sc: 12 sc.

Rnd 4: Ch 1, sc in same st, ch 5, (sc in next sc, ch 5) around; join with slip st to first sc.

Rnd 5: Ch 1, sc in same st, ch 7, (sc in next sc, ch 7) around; join with slip st to first sc.

Rnd 6: Ch 1, sc in same st, ch 9, (sc in next sc, ch 9) around; join with slip st to first sc.

Rnd 7: Ch 14, (dc in next sc, ch 11) around; join with slip st to third ch of beginning ch-14.

Rnd 8: Slip st in next 5 chs, ch 1, sc in same ch and in next 2 chs, ch 7, ★ skip next dc and next 4 chs, sc in next 3 chs, ch 7; repeat from ★ around to last dc, skip last dc; join with slip st to first sc: 36 sc.

Rnd 9: Ch 3, dc in each sc and in each ch around; join with slip st to top of beginning ch-3; do **not** finish off: 120 sts.

SIDES
Rnd 1: Ch 3, working in BLO *(Fig. 19, page 122),* dc in next dc and in each dc around; join with slip st to top of beginning ch-3.

Rnd 2: Ch 1, working in both loops, sc in same st, ch 3, skip next 3 dc, ★ sc in next dc, ch 3, skip next 3 dc; repeat from ★ around; join with slip st to first sc: 30 sc.

Rnd 3: Ch 1, sc in same st, ch 5, (sc in next sc, ch 5) around; join with slip st to first sc.

Rnd 4: Ch 1, sc in same st, ch 7, (sc in next sc, ch 7) around; join with slip st to first sc.

Rnd 5: Ch 1, sc in same st, ch 9, (sc in next sc, ch 9) around; join with slip st to first sc.

Rnd 6: Ch 12, (dc in next sc, ch 9) around; join with slip st to third ch of beginning ch-12.

Rnd 7: Slip st in next 4 chs, ch 1, sc in same ch and in next 2 chs, ch 1, ★ skip next dc and next 3 chs, sc in next 3 chs, ch 1; repeat from ★ around, skip last dc; join with slip st to first sc: 90 sc.

Rnd 8: Ch 3, dc in next sc and in each sc and each ch around; join with slip st to top of beginning ch-3, finish off.

TOP
Rnds 1-6: Work same as Base: 12 sc and 12 ch-9 sps.

Rnd 7: Ch 1, sc in same st, ch 11, (sc in next sc, ch 11) around; join with slip st to first sc.

Rnd 8: Ch 16, (dc in next sc, ch 13) around; join with slip st to third ch of beginning ch-16; do **not** finish off.

EDGING
Slip st in next ch, ch 1, sc in same ch and in next 2 chs, hdc in next ch, 2 dc in each of next 5 chs, hdc in next ch, sc in next 3 chs, ★ skip next dc, sc in next 3 chs, hdc in next ch, 2 dc in each of next 5 chs, hdc in next ch, sc in next 3 chs; repeat from ★ around; join with slip st to first sc, finish off.

FINISHING
See Starching and Blocking, page 124.

Using photo as a guide for placement, add finishing touches as desired.

WINDOW CHARM

Create a charming window dressing with this lacy crocheted valance. It features dainty house and tree motifs and is edged with a border of scallops.

Finished Size: 48" x 13"

MATERIALS
Bedspread Weight Cotton Thread (size 10):
   3 balls (282 yards per ball)
Steel crochet hook, size 7 (1.65 mm) **or** size
   needed for gauge

GAUGE: 18 dc and 8 rows = 2"

STITCH GUIDE

DOUBLE TREBLE CROCHET
(abbreviated dtr)
YO 3 times, insert hook in st indicated, YO and pull up a loop, (YO and draw through 2 loops on hook) 4 times *(Figs. 10a & b, page 120)*.
ROD LOOP
YO 3 times, insert hook in next dc, YO and pull up a loop, (YO and draw through 2 loops on hook) 3 times, YO 5 times, insert hook in free loop of dc in row **below** same dc, YO and pull up a loop, (YO and draw through 2 loops on hook) 5 times, YO and draw through all 3 loops on hook.

Ch 426.

Row 1 (Right side)**:** Dc in fourth ch from hook and in each ch across: 424 sts.

Note: Loop a short piece of thread around any stitch to mark Row 1 as **right** side.

Row 2: Ch 3 **(counts as first dc, now and throughout)**, turn; dc in next dc and in each dc across: 424 dc.

Row 3: [Ch 3, turn; dc in next 3 dc **(beginning Block over Block made)**], [ch 2, skip next 2 dc, dc in next dc **(Space over Block made)**], work Spaces across to last 3 dc, dc in last 3 dc **(Block over Block made)**.

Row 4: Work beginning Block, [ch 2, dc in next dc **(Space over Space made)**], [2 dc in next ch-2 sp, dc in next dc **(Block over Space made)**], work across following Chart.

Rows 5-44: Work across following Chart.

Row 45: Ch 3, turn; dc in next dc, dc in Front Loop Only of next dc *(Fig. 19, page 122)*, dc in **both** loops of next dc and in each dc across to last 3 dc, dc in Front Loop Only of next dc, dc in **both** loops of last 2 dc.

CHART

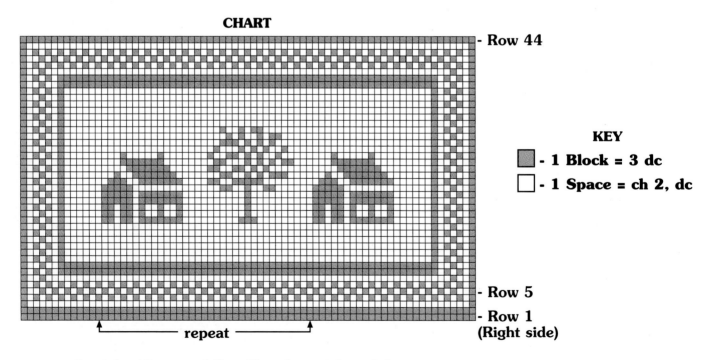

- Row 44

KEY

▨ - 1 Block = 3 dc

☐ - 1 Space = ch 2, dc

- Row 5

- Row 1
(Right side)

← repeat →

**On right side rows, follow Chart from right to left;
on wrong side rows, follow Chart from left to right.**

Row 46: Ch 5 **(counts as first dtr)**, turn; dtr in next dc, work Rod Loop, dtr in **both** loops of next 7 dc, ch 2, skip next 2 dc, dtr in next 16 dc, (ch 8, skip next 8 dc, dtr in next 16 dc) across to last 12 dc, ch 2, skip next 2 dc, dtr in next 7 dc, work Rod Loop, dtr in last 2 dc.

Row 47: Ch 3, turn; dc in next st and in each st and each ch across: 424 dc.

Row 48: Ch 3, turn; dc in next dc and in each dc across; do **not** finish off.

EDGING
Rnd 1: Ch 1, turn; 3 sc in first dc, sc in each dc across to last dc, 3 sc in last dc; work 98 sc evenly spaced across end of rows; working in free loops of beginning ch **(Fig. 20b, page 122)**, 3 sc in first ch, sc in each ch across to next corner ch, 3 sc in corner ch; work 98 sc evenly spaced across end of rows; join with slip st to first sc: 1052 sc.

Rnd 2: Do **not** turn; slip st in next 2 sc, ch 3, dc in next 3 sc, (ch 2, skip next 2 sc, dc in next 4 sc) across to next corner sc, ch 3, skip next sc, ★ dc in next 4 sc, (ch 2, skip next 2 sc, dc in next 4 sc) across to next corner sc, ch 3, skip next sc; repeat from ★ 2 times **more**; join with slip st to first dc.

Rnd 3: Slip st in next dc, ch 1, ★ sc in next dc, [(3 dc, ch 3, 3 dc) in next ch-2 sp, skip next 2 dc, sc in next dc] across to next corner ch-3 sp, (4 dc, ch 3, 4 dc) in corner sp, skip next 2 dc; repeat from ★ around; join with slip st to first sc, finish off.

See Washing and Blocking, page 124.

FRIENDLY WELCOME

As simple as it is beautiful, filet crochet is a longtime favorite for creating decorative home accessories. This heartwarming wall hanging is finished with easy-to-make tassels.

Finished Size: 11"w x 9"h

MATERIALS
Bedspread Weight Cotton Thread (size 10):
  95 yards
Steel crochet hook, size 10 (1.30 mm) **or** size
  needed for gauge
³⁄₈" wooden dowel - 12"
Wooden beads to fit dowel - 2

GAUGE: 21 dc and 8 rows = 2"

Ch 120.

Row 1 (Right side): Dc in fourth ch from hook and in each ch across: 118 sts.

Note: Loop a short piece of thread around any stitch to mark Row 1 as **right** side.

Row 2: Ch 3 **(counts as first dc, now and throughout)**, turn; dc in next 3 dc, **[**ch 2, skip next 2 dc, dc in next dc **(Space over Block made)]** across to last 3 sts, dc in last 3 sts **(Block over Block made)**: 37 Spaces.

Row 3: **[**Ch 3, turn; dc in next 3 dc **(beginning Block over Block made)]**, **[**ch 2, dc in next dc **(Space over Space made)]** across to last Block, work Block.

Row 4: Work beginning Block, work 3 Spaces, **[**2 dc in next ch-2 sp, dc in next dc **(Block over Space made)]**, work across following Chart.

Rows 5-34: Follow Chart.

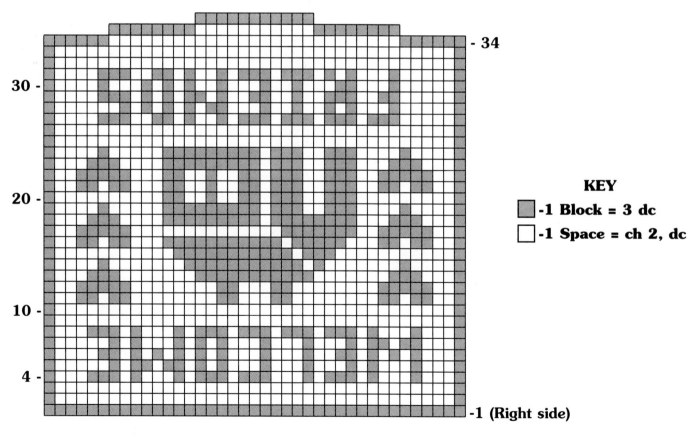

KEY
▨ -1 Block = 3 dc
☐ -1 Space = ch 2, dc

On right side rows follow Chart from right to left;
on wrong side rows follow Chart from left to right.

Row 35: Turn; slip st in first 19 dc, ch 3, work across following Chart, leave last 6 Blocks unworked.

Row 36: Turn; slip st in first 25 dc, ch 3, work across following Chart, leave last 8 Blocks unworked; finish off.

TOP LOOPS

With **right** side facing and working in free loops of beginning ch *(Fig. 20b, page 122)*, join thread with slip st in first ch; ch 1, sc in same st, (ch 16, skip next 8 chs, sc in next ch) across; finish off: 13 loops.

FINISHING

See Washing and Blocking, page 124.

Weave dowel through the Top Loops. Place a bead on each end of dowel, using a dot of glue to secure, if necessary.

Make 5 tassels *(Figs. 24a & b, page 123)*. Using photo as a guide for placement, attach tassels.

To hang in a window, use two small suction cup hooks and put the last loop of each end on the hook.

KITCHEN TOWEL TRIMS

Make everyday kitchen towels extraordinary with these fancy trimmings. They can be worked up quickly and attached to plain dish towels for unique housewarming gifts.

MATERIALS
Bedspread Weight Cotton Thread (size 10):
  Red - 1 ball (350 yards per ball)
Steel crochet hook, size 6 (1.80 mm) **or** size needed for gauge
Kitchen towels
Sewing needle and thread

FINISHING
See Washing and Blocking, page 124.

Using photo as a guide, place Trim along hemline on right side, folding ends to wrong side, and baste in place. Hand or machine sew to secure. Remove basting thread.

TRIM #1
(Multiple of 4 chs)

Finished Size: 20½" x 1"

Ch 184.

Row 1 (Right side)**:** Dc in sixth ch from hook, ★ ch 1, skip next ch, dc in next ch; repeat from ★ across: 90 sps.

Note: Loop a short piece of thread around any stitch to mark Row 1 as **right** side.

Row 2: Ch 3, turn; (dc in next ch-1 sp and in next dc) across to last ch-sp, dc around first ch and in next ch: 181 sts.

Row 3: Turn; slip st in first 3 dc, ch 3, 3 dc in same st, ch 3, **turn**; dc in top of beginning ch-3 to form loop, ch 3, **turn**; 4 dc in same loop, skip next 3 dc on Row 2, 4 dc in next dc, ★ ch 3, **turn**; dc in top of first dc of 4-dc group just made to form loop, ch 3, **turn**; 4 dc in same loop, skip next 3 dc on Row 2, 4 dc in next dc; repeat from ★ across to last 2 sts, leave last 2 sts unworked; finish off.

See Finishing, above.

TRIM #2
(Multiple of 9 chs plus 6)

Finished Size: 20½" x 1"

Ch 186.

Row 1 (Right side)**:** Dc in fourth ch from hook and in each ch across: 184 sts.

Note: Loop a short piece of thread around any stitch to mark Row 1 as **right** side.

Row 2: Ch 1, turn; sc in each st across.

Row 3: Ch 5 **(counts as first dc plus ch 2)**, turn; skip next 2 sc, dc in next sc, (ch 2, skip next 2 sc, dc in next sc) across: 61 ch-2 sps.

Row 4: Ch 3 **(counts as first dc)**, turn; 2 dc in first ch-2 sp, dc in next dc, ★ (ch 2, dc in next dc) twice, 2 dc in next ch-2 sp, dc in next dc; repeat from ★ across.

Row 5: Ch 1, turn; sc in first 4 dc, ★ (sc, ch 3, slip st in sc just made) twice in next ch-2 sp, sc in next ch-2 sp, ch 3, slip st in sc just made, sc in same sp and in next 4 dc; repeat from ★ across; finish off.

See Finishing, first column.

TRIM #3
(Multiple of 4 chs plus 3)

Finished Size: 20½" x 1½"

Ch 183.

Row 1 (Right side)**:** Dc in fourth ch from hook and in each ch across: 181 sts.

Note: Loop a short piece of thread around any stitch to mark Row 1 as **right** side.

Row 2: Ch 4 **(counts as first dc plus ch 1)**, turn; (skip next dc, dc in next dc, ch 1) across to last 2 sts, skip next dc, dc in last st: 90 ch-1 sps.

Row 3: Ch 3, turn; dc in each ch-1 sp and in each dc across: 181 sts.

Row 4: Ch 1, turn; sc in first dc, (ch 5, skip next 3 dc, sc in next st) across: 45 ch-5 sps.

Row 5: Ch 1, turn; (sc, ch 2, 4 dc) in first sp and in each ch-5 sp across.

Row 6: Turn; slip st in first 4 dc and in top of next ch-2, ch 1, sc in same st, (ch 5, skip next 5 sts, sc in top of next ch-2) across: 44 ch-5 sps.

Row 7: Ch 5, turn; slip st in fourth ch from hook, 4 dc in first sp, ★ sc in next sp, ch 5, slip st in fourth ch from hook, 4 dc in **same** sp; repeat from ★ across; finish off.

See Finishing, page 38.

DELIGHTFUL DISHCLOTHS

Scalloped edgings and cheerful colors give our handy all-cotton dishcloths their delightful appeal. These easy-to-make kitchen helpers are crocheted holding two strands of thread together.

Finished Size: 9" x 9"

MATERIALS
Bedspread Weight Cotton Thread (size 10):
Dishcloth #1
    Blue - 170 yards
    White - 70 yards
Dishcloth #2
    White - 175 yards
    Blue - 55 yards
Dishcloth #3
    Yellow - 220 yards
    Blue - 70 yards
Dishcloth #4
    Yellow - 260 yards
    White - 50 yards
Crochet hook, size D (3.25 mm) **or** size needed for gauge

GAUGE: With 2 strands of thread held together, 10 dc and 6 rows = 2"

Note: Dishcloths are worked holding 2 strands of thread together.

DISHCLOTH #1

STITCH GUIDE

CLUSTER (uses next 2 sts)
YO, insert hook in **same** st as last Cluster, YO and pull up a loop, YO and draw through 2 loops on hook, skip next ch, YO, insert hook in next st, YO and pull up a loop, YO and draw through 2 loops on hook, YO and draw through all 3 loops on hook *(Figs. 12c & d, page 121)*.

With 2 strands of Blue, ch 47.

Row 1 (Right side): YO, insert hook in third ch from hook, YO and pull up a loop, YO and draw through 2 loops on hook, skip next ch, YO, insert hook in next ch, YO and pull up a loop, YO and draw through 2 loops on hook, YO and draw through all 3 loops on hook **(beginning Cluster made)**, ch 1, (work Cluster, ch 1) across, dc in same ch as last Cluster: 22 Clusters.

Note: Loop a short piece of thread around any stitch to mark Row 1 as **right** side.

Row 2: Ch 1, turn; sc in first ch-1 sp, ch 1, (sc in next ch-1 sp, ch 1) across to beginning ch, sc around beginning ch: 23 sc.

Row 3: Ch 3, turn; YO, insert hook in first sc, YO and pull up a loop, YO and draw through 2 loops on hook, skip next ch, YO, insert hook in next sc, YO and pull up a loop, YO and draw through 2 loops on hook, YO and draw through all 3 loops on hook, ch 1, (work Cluster, ch 1) across, dc in same sc as last Cluster: 22 Clusters.

Repeat Rows 2 and 3 until piece measures 8", ending by working Row 3; finish off.

EDGING
Rnd 1: With **right** side facing, join 2 strands of White with slip st in any corner; ch 1, (3 sc in corner, work 41 sc evenly spaced across to next corner) around; join with slip st to first sc: 176 sc.

Rnd 2: Slip st in next sc, ch 3, (2 dc, ch 2, 3 dc) in same st, skip next 3 sc, ★ (3 dc, ch 2, 3 dc) in next sc, skip next 3 sc; repeat from ★ around; join with slip st to top of beginning ch-3, finish off.

DISHCLOTH #2
With 2 strands of White, ch 45.

Row 1 (Right side)**:** Dc in fourth ch from hook and in each ch across: 43 sts.

Note: Loop a short piece of thread around any stitch to mark Row 1 as **right** side.

Row 2: Ch 1, turn; (sc, 2 dc) in first dc, ★ skip next 2 dc, (sc, 2 dc) in next dc; repeat from ★ across to last 3 sts, skip next 2 dc, sc in last st: 14 groups.

Row 3: Ch 3, turn; dc in next dc and in each st across: 43 sts.

Repeat Rows 2 and 3 until piece measures 8", ending by working Row 3; finish off.

EDGING
Rnd 1: With **right** side facing, join 2 strands of Blue with slip st in any corner; ch 1, (3 sc in corner, work 42 sc evenly spaced across to next corner) around; join with slip st to first sc: 180 sc.

Rnd 2: Slip st in next sc, ch 1, (sc, 2 dc) in same st, skip next 2 sc, ★ (sc, 2 dc) in next sc, skip next 2 sc; repeat from ★ around; join with slip st to first sc, finish off.

DISHCLOTH #3

With 2 strands of Yellow, ch 51.

Row 1 (Right side)**:** Sc in fourth ch from hook, dc in next ch, (sc in next ch, dc in next ch) across: 49 sts.

Note: Loop a short piece of thread around any stitch to mark Row 1 as **right** side.

Row 2: Ch 3, turn; (sc in next sc, dc in next st) across.

Repeat Row 2 until piece measures 8"; finish off.

EDGING
Rnd 1: With **right** side facing, join 2 strands of Blue with slip st in any corner; ch 1, (3 sc in corner, work 43 sc evenly spaced across to next corner) around; join with slip st to first sc: 184 sc.

Continued on page 42.

Rnd 2: Slip st in next sc, ch 3, 4 dc in same st, ★ † skip next sc, sc in next sc, (skip next 2 sc, 5 dc in next sc, skip next 2 sc, sc in next sc) across to within one sc of next corner sc, skip next sc †, 5 dc in next sc; repeat from ★ 2 times **more**, then repeat from † to † once; join with slip st to top of beginning ch-3, finish off.

DISHCLOTH #4
With 2 strands of Yellow, ch 44.

Row 1 (Right side): (Sc, hdc, dc) in second ch from hook, ★ skip next 2 chs, (sc, hdc, dc) in next ch; repeat from ★ across to last 3 chs, skip next 2 chs, sc in last ch: 43 sts.

Note: Loop a short piece of thread around any stitch to mark Row 1 as **right** side.

Row 2: Ch 1, turn; (sc, hdc, dc) in first sc, ★ skip next 2 sts, (sc, hdc, dc) in next sc; repeat from ★ across to 3 last sts, skip next 2 sts, sc in last sc.

Repeat Row 2 until piece measures 8"; finish off.

EDGING
Rnd 1: With **right** side facing, join 2 strands of White with slip st in any corner; ch 1, (3 sc in corner, work 42 sc evenly spaced across to next corner) around; join with slip st to first sc: 180 sc.

Rnd 2: Slip st in next sc, ch 1, (sc, hdc, dc) in same st, skip next 2 sc, ★ (sc, hdc, dc) in next sc, skip next 2 sc; repeat from ★ around; join with slip st to first sc, finish off.

NOSTALGIC POT HOLDERS

*fun into your kitchen with these crocheted pot holders
undies. Whether you hang them simply for decoration
cook, these kitchen "drawers" are sure to bring a smile!*

Finished Size: 5 x 7

MATERIALS
Bedspread Weight Cotton Thread (size 10):
  Grandpa's Trunks: Red - 110 yards
  Gentleman's Trunks:
    Cream - 70 yards
    Red - 40 yards
  Lady's Bloomers:
    Cream - 140 yards
    Red - 10 yards
  Steel crochet hook, size 6 (1.80 mm) **or** size needed for gauge
  Grandpa's and Gentleman's Trunks: ¼" buttons - 2

GAUGE: 9 dc and 4 rnds = 1"

GRANDPA'S TRUNKS
BODY
With Red, ch 80; being careful not to twist chain, join with slip st to form a ring.

Rnd 1 (Right side): Ch 1, sc in each ch around; join with slip st to first sc: 80 sc.

Note: Loop a short piece of thread around any stitch to mark Rnd 1 as **right** side.

Hanging Loop: Ch 16, slip st in first ch to form a loop, turn; 24 sc in loop, slip st in first sc on Rnd 1.

Note: Work in Back Loops Only throughout *(Fig. 19, page 122).*

Rnd 2: Ch 3 **(counts as first dc, now and throughout)**, dc in next 19 sc, ch 1, dc in next 40 sc, ch 1, dc in last 20 sc; join with slip st to first dc: 80 dc.

Rnd 3: Ch 3, dc in next 19 dc, (dc, ch 1, dc) in next ch, dc in next 40 dc, (dc, ch 1, dc) in next ch, dc in last 20 dc; join with slip st to first dc: 84 dc.

Rnd 4 (Increase rnd): Ch 3, dc in next dc and in each dc across to first ch-1, (dc, ch 1, dc) in first ch, dc in each dc across to next ch, (dc, ch 1, dc) in next ch, dc in each dc around; join with slip st to first dc: 88 dc.

Rnds 5-13: Repeat Rnd 4, 9 times: 124 dc.

Do **not** finish off.

RIGHT LEG
Rnd 1: Ch 3, dc in next 30 dc, flattening piece so that ch-1 sps are together and skipping 62 dc in between, dc in ch of **both** front and back, dc in each dc around; join with slip st to first dc: 63 dc.

Rnds 2-5: Ch 3, dc in next dc and in each dc around; join with slip st to first dc.

Rnd 6: Ch 1, sc in each dc around; join with slip st to first sc, finish off.

LEFT LEG

Rnd 1: With **right** side facing, join thread with slip st in same center sp on Body as Right Leg; ch 3, dc in next dc and in each dc around; join with slip st to first dc: 63 dc.

Complete same as Right Leg.

Using photo as a guide for placement, add Buttons.

GENTLEMAN'S TRUNKS

Make same as Grandpa's Trunks, working in the following Stripe Sequence: 1 rnd Red, 2 rnds Cream; repeat these 3 rnds throughout.

LADY'S BLOOMERS

STITCH GUIDE

DECREASE (uses next 2 dc)
★ YO, insert hook in **next** dc, YO and pull up a loop, YO and draw through 2 loops on hook; repeat from ★ once **more**, YO and draw through all 3 loops on hook **(counts as one dc)**.

BODY

Work same as Grandpa's Trunks, working Rnd 1 and Hanging Loop with Red and remainder with Cream.

Continued on page 44.

RIGHT LEG

Rnd 1: Work same as Grandpa's Trunks, page 42: 63 dc.

Rnd 2 (Decrease rnd): Ch 3, decrease, dc in next dc and in each dc around; join with slip st to first dc: 62 dc.

Rnds 3-5: Repeat Rnd 2, 3 times: 59 dc.

Finish off.

Rnd 6: With **right** side facing, join Red with slip st in first st; ch 1, 2 sc in first dc, sc in each dc around; join with slip st to first sc, finish off: 60 sc.

EDGING

Rnd 1: With **right** side facing, join Cream with slip st in first st; ch 6, skip next 3 sc, (slip st in next sc, ch 6, skip next 3 sc) around; join with slip st to first slip st: 15 ch-6 sps.

Rnd 2: Ch 1, (sc, hdc, 2 dc, hdc, sc) in first sp, slip st in next slip st, ★ (sc, hdc, 2 dc, hdc, sc) in next ch-6 sp, slip st in next slip st; repeat from ★ around.

Rnd 3: Ch 6, ★ working **behind** sts on Rnd 2, slip st around post of next slip st *(Fig. 15, page 121)*, ch 6; repeat from ★ around; join with slip st to first slip st.

Rnds 4-6: Repeat Rnds 2 and 3 once, then repeat Rnd 2 once **more**.

Finish off.

LEFT LEG

Rnd 1: Work same as Grandpa's Trunks, page 43: 63 dc.

Rnd 2 (Decrease rnd): Ch 3, dc in next 30 dc, decrease, dc in next dc and in each dc around; join with slip st to first dc: 62 dc.

Complete same as Right Leg through Edging.

WAIST EDGING

With **right** side facing and working in free loops of beginning ch *(Fig. 20b, page 122)*, join Cream with slip st in any ch; ch 3, skip next ch, (slip st in next ch, ch 3, skip next ch) around; join with slip st to first slip st, finish off.

TEA JACKET BOUQUET

*W*hen you reach for that refreshing glass of iced tea this summer, make sure your glass is wearing one of our crocheted jackets. Accented with a sweet primrose, a sunny chrysanthemum, or a delicate dahlia, they make pretty alternatives to coasters.

Finished Size: 3¼" in diameter x 2¼"h

MATERIALS
Bedspread Weight Cotton Thread (size 10):
1 ball (225 yards) White will make 3
Primrose - Purple and Yellow
Chrysanthemum - Yellow
Little Dahlia - Red and Yellow
Leaves - Green
Steel crochet hook, size 7 (1.65 mm) **or** size needed for gauge
Tapestry needle

GAUGE: With 2 strands of thread held together, Bottom Rnds 1-5 = 3"

Note: Entire Jacket is worked holding 2 strands of thread together. Flowers and Leaves are worked with 1 strand of thread.

STITCH GUIDE

FRONT POST DOUBLE CROCHET (abbreviated FPdc)
YO, insert hook from **front** to **back** around post of st indicated, YO and pull up a loop *(Fig. 16, page 121)*, (YO and draw through 2 loops on hook) twice. Skip st behind FPdc.

BACK POST DOUBLE CROCHET (abbreviated BPdc)
YO, insert hook from **back** to **front** around post of st indicated, YO and pull up a loop *(Fig. 17, page 121)*, (YO and draw through 2 loops on hook) twice. Skip st in front of BPdc.

DOUBLE TREBLE CROCHET (abbreviated dtr)
YO 3 times, insert hook in st indicated, YO and pull up a loop, (YO and draw through 2 loops on hook) 4 times *(Figs. 10a & b, page 120)*.

Continued on page 46.

TEA JACKET

BOTTOM

Rnd 1 (Right side): With 2 strands of White, ch 4, 11 dc in fourth ch from hook; join with slip st to top of beginning ch: 12 sts.

Note: Loop a short piece of thread around any stitch to mark Rnd 1 as **right** side.

Rnd 2: Ch 3 (**counts as first dc, now and throughout**), dc in same st, 2 dc in next dc and in each dc around; join with slip st to first dc: 24 dc.

Rnd 3: Ch 3, dc in same st and in next dc, (2 dc in next dc, dc in next dc) around; join with slip st to first dc: 36 dc.

Rnd 4: Ch 3, dc in same st and in next 2 dc, (2 dc in next dc, dc in next 2 dc) around; join with slip st to first dc: 48 dc.

Rnd 5: Ch 1, sc in each dc around; join with slip st to first sc.

SIDES

Rnd 1: Ch 1, sc in Back Loop Only of each sc around *(Fig. 19, page 122)*; join with slip st to first sc.

Rnd 2: Ch 3, dc in Back Loop Only of next sc and in each sc around; join with slip st to both loops of first dc.

Rnds 3 and 4: Working from **front** to **back**, slip st around same st, ch 3, work FPdc around next 3 sts, work BPdc around next 4 sts, (work FPdc around next 4 sts, work BPdc around next 4 sts) around; join with slip st to first dc.

Rnds 5 and 6: Working from **back** to **front**, slip st around same st, ch 3, work BPdc around next 3 sts, work FPdc around next 4 sts, (work BPdc around next 4 sts, work FPdc around next 4 sts) around; join with slip st to first dc.

Rnds 7 and 8: Repeat Rnds 3 and 4.

Rnd 9: Ch 1, sc in each st around; join with slip st to first sc, finish off.

EDGING

With **right** side facing, top toward you, and working in free loops on Rnd 5 of Bottom *(Fig. 20a, page 122)*, join 2 strands of White with slip st in first sc; ch 1, sc in same st, 2 sc in next sc, (sc in next sc, 2 sc in next sc) around; join with slip st to first sc, finish off: 72 sc.

PRIMROSE

Rnd 1 (Right side): With 1 strand of Yellow, ch 2, 6 sc in second ch from hook; join with slip st to first sc, finish off.

Note: Loop a short piece of thread around any stitch to mark Rnd 1 as **right** side.

Rnd 2: With **right** side facing, join 1 strand of Purple with slip st in any sc; ch 1, 2 sc in each sc around; join with slip st to first sc: 12 sc.

Rnd 3: Ch 3, 2 dc in same st, (2 dc, ch 3, slip st) in next sc, ★ (slip st, ch 3, 2 dc) in next sc, (2 dc, ch 3, slip st) in next sc; repeat from ★ around; slip st in same sc as beginning ch-3; finish off: 6 Petals.

LEAF (Make 4)

With 1 strand of Green, ch 5, in fifth ch from hook work (2 tr, 2 dtr, ch 3, slip st in top of last dtr, 2 dtr, 2 tr, ch 4, slip st); finish off.

CHRYSANTHEMUM

With 1 strand of Yellow, ch 3; join with slip st to form a ring.

Rnd 1 (Right side): Ch 2, 13 hdc in ring; join with slip st to top of beginning ch: 14 sts.

Note: Loop a short piece of thread around any stitch to mark Rnd 1 as **right** side.

Rnd 2: Ch 1, sc in same st, skip next hdc, (sc in next hdc, skip next hdc) around; join with slip st to Front Loop Only of first sc *(Fig. 19, page 122)*: 7 sc.

Rnd 3: Ch 3, working in Front Loops Only, (tr, ch 3, slip st) in same st, (slip st, ch 3, tr, ch 3, slip st) in next sc and in each sc around (7 Petals); working in free loops of same rnd *(Fig. 20a, page 122)*, slip st in next sc, ch 2, hdc in same st, 2 hdc in next sc, hdc in next sc, 2 hdc in each of next 2 sc, hdc in next sc, 2 hdc in next sc; join with slip st to Front Loop Only of top of beginning ch-2: 12 sts.

Rnd 4: Ch 3, working in Front Loops Only, (tr, ch 3, slip st) in same st, (slip st, ch 3, tr, ch 3, slip st) in next hdc and in each hdc around (12 Petals); working in free loops of same rnd, slip st in next sc, ch 1, sc in same st and in next 4 hdc, 2 sc in next hdc, sc in next 5 hdc, 2 sc in last hdc; join with slip st to **both** loops of first sc: 14 sc.

Rnd 5: Ch 3, working in both loops, (2 tr, ch 3, slip st) in same st, (slip st, ch 3, 2 tr, ch 3, slip st) in next sc and in each sc around; finish off: 14 Petals.

LEAF (Make 2)
With 1 strand of Green, ch 5; (2 hdc, dc) in third ch from hook, ch 2, slip st in last dc made, (hdc, dc) in next ch, ch 2, slip st in last dc made, (2 hdc, 2 dc) in last ch, ch 2, slip st in last dc made, (dc, 2 hdc) in same ch; working in free loops of beginning ch *(Fig. 20b, page 122)*, dc in next ch, ch 2, slip st in last dc made, hdc in same ch, dc in next ch, ch 2, slip st in last dc made, (2 hdc, ch 2, slip st) in same ch; finish off leaving a long end for sewing.

LITTLE DAHLIA
CENTER
With 1 strand of Yellow, ch 3; join with slip st to form a ring.

Rnd 1 (Right side)**:** Ch 1, 8 sc in ring; join with slip st to Front Loop Only of first sc.

Note: Loop a short piece of thread around any stitch to mark Rnd 1 as **right** side.

Rnd 2: Working in Front Loops Only, (ch 3, slip st in next sc, ch 2, slip st in next sc) around; working in free loops of same rnd *(Fig. 20a, page 122)*, slip st in next sc, ch 1, sc in same st and in each sc around; join with slip st to first sc, finish off: 8 sc.

FIRST TOP PETAL
Row 1: With **right** side of Center facing, working behind chs and in Front Loops Only of sc, join 1 strand of Red with slip st in first sc; ch 3, 2 dc in same st and in next sc; leave remaining sc unworked: 5 dc.

Row 2: Ch 2, turn; ★ YO, insert hook in **next** dc, YO and pull up a loop, YO and draw through 2 loops on hook; repeat from ★ 2 times **more**, YO and draw through all 4 loops on hook, ch 2, slip st in last st; finish off.

REMAINING 3 TOP PETALS
Row 1: With **right** side of Center facing, working behind chs and in Front Loops Only of sc, join 1 strand of Red with slip st in next sc (to left of previous Petal); ch 3, 2 dc in same st and in next sc: 5 dc.

Row 2: Work same as First Top Petal.

FIRST BOTTOM PETAL
Row 1: With **right** side of Center facing and working in free loops behind Top Petals, join 1 strand of Red with slip st in second sc; ch 3, 2 dc in same st and in next sc; leave remaining sc unworked: 5 dc.

Row 2: Work same as First Top Petal.

REMAINING 3 BOTTOM PETALS
Row 1: With **right** side of Center facing and working in free loops behind Top Petals, join 1 strand of Red with slip st in next sc (to left of previous Petal); ch 3, 2 dc in same st and in next sc: 5 dc.

LEAF (Make 2)
Work same as Chrysanthemum Leaf.

FINISHING
Using photo as a guide for placement, attach Flower and Leaves to Tea Jacket.

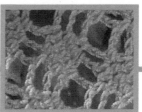

KEEPSAKE GIFTS

A handmade gift inspires warm thoughts of the giver long after it's been unwrapped. In this collection you'll discover a host of wonderful projects, from small "thinking-of-you" presents to ornate heirlooms, to please the special people in your life. For the bride, we've designed a Bible cover, sachet hangers, a ring bearer's pillow, and wedding bells. Girls of all ages will fall in love with our fashion doll bridal ensemble and doll-size afghan, or you can lift a friend's spirits with a beautiful bookmark or decorative birdcage. And let Grandmother know she's in your thoughts with our purse pretties and candy dish! Whatever you choose to offer, make it a gift from the heart as well as the hand, and it's sure to become a keepsake!

RING BEARER'S PILLOW

*F*eaturing a lacy latticework, this dreamy ring bearer's pillow is sure to become a cherished keepsake. A fanciful edging enhances the lovely wedding accessory, which is finished with tiny crocheted bells and an elegant bow.

Finished Size: 12" square

MATERIALS
- Bedspread Weight Cotton Thread (size 10): 620 yards
- Steel crochet hook, size 9 (1.40 mm) **or** size needed for gauge
- Finishing materials: 2 - 9" squares of fabric, polyester fiberfill, sewing machine, sewing thread, hand sewing needle, desired decorations (ribbons, pearls, etc.)
- Starching materials: Commercial fabric stiffener, resealable plastic bag, blocking board, plastic wrap, terry towel, paper towels, and stainless steel pins

GAUGE: (5 sc, ch 5) 3 times = $2\frac{3}{4}$"
and 12 rows = 2"

FORM
Matching **right** sides and raw edges, use a $\frac{1}{2}$" seam allowance to sew fabric squares together, leaving an opening at bottom edge. Clip seam allowances at corners. Turn form right side out, carefully pushing corners outward. Stuff form firmly and sew final closure by hand.

STITCH GUIDE

> **DOUBLE TREBLE CROCHET** *(abbreviated dtr)*
> YO 3 times, insert hook in st or sp indicated, YO and pull up a loop, (YO and draw through 2 loops on hook) 4 times *(Figs. 10a & b, page 120)*.
> **CLUSTER**
> ★ YO 3 times, insert hook in loop indicated, YO and pull up a loop, (YO and draw through 2 loops on hook) 3 times; repeat from ★ once **more**, YO and draw through all 3 loops on hook *(Figs. 12a & b, page 121)*.

BACK
Ch 68.

Row 1 (Right side)**:** Sc in second ch from hook and in each ch across: 67 sc.

Note: Loop a short piece of thread around any stitch to mark Row 1 as **right** side.

Row 2: Ch 1, turn; sc in first 4 sc, ch 5, ★ skip next 3 sc, sc in next 5 sc, ch 5; repeat from ★ 6 times **more**, skip next 3 sc, sc in last 4 sc: 8 ch-5 sps.

Row 3: Ch 1, turn; sc in first 3 sc, ★ ch 3, sc in next ch-5 sp, ch 3, skip next sc, sc in next 3 sc; repeat from ★ across: 16 ch-3 sps.

Row 4: Ch 1, turn; sc in first 2 sc, ch 3, sc in next ch-3 sp, sc in next sc and in next ch-3 sp, ch 3, ★ skip next sc, sc in next sc, ch 3, sc in next ch-3 sp, sc in next sc and in next ch-3 sp, ch 3; repeat from ★ across to last 3 sc, skip next sc, sc in last 2 sc.

Row 5: Ch 1, turn; sc in first sc, ch 3, sc in next ch-3 sp, sc in next 3 sc and in next ch-3 sp, ★ ch 5, sc in next ch-3 sp, sc in next 3 sc and in next ch-3 sp; repeat from ★ across to last 2 sc, ch 3, skip next sc, sc in last sc: 7 ch-5 sps and 2 ch-3 sps.

Row 6: Ch 1, turn; sc in first sc and in next ch-3 sp, ch 3, skip next sc, sc in next 3 sc, ch 3, ★ sc in next ch-5 sp, ch 3, skip next sc, sc in next 3 sc, ch 3; repeat from ★ 6 times **more**, sc in next ch-3 sp and in last sc: 16 ch-3 sps.

Row 7: Ch 1, turn; sc in first 2 sc and in next ch-3 sp, ch 3, skip next sc, sc in next sc, ch 3, ★ sc in next ch-3 sp, sc in next sc and in next ch-3 sp, ch 3, skip next sc, sc in next sc, ch 3; repeat from ★ 6 times **more**, sc in next ch-3 sp and in last 2 sc.

Row 8: Ch 1, turn; sc in first 3 sc and in next ch-3 sp, ch 5, sc in next ch-3 sp and in next 3 sc, ★ sc in next ch-3 sp, ch 5, sc in next ch-3 sp and in next 3 sc; repeat from ★ across: 8 ch-5 sps.

Rows 9-46: Repeat Rows 3-8, 6 times; then repeat Rows 3 and 4 once **more**.

Row 47: Ch 1, turn; sc in first sc, ch 3, ★ sc in next ch-3 sp, sc in next 3 sc and in next ch-3 sp, ch 3; repeat from ★ across to last 2 sc, skip next sc, sc in last sc; finish off: 9 ch-3 sps.

FRONT

Work same as Back; do **not** finish off.

JOINING

Place Front and Back with **wrong** sides together. With Front facing and working in **both** pieces, ch 1, 2 sc in same st; working in end of rows, sc in same row and in next 5 rows, 2 sc in next row, (sc in next row, 2 sc in next row) across to last 6 rows, sc in last 6 rows; working in free loops of beginning ch *(Fig. 20b, page 122)*, 3 sc in first ch, sc in next 65 chs, 3 sc in next ch; working in end of rows, sc in first 6 rows, 2 sc in next row, (sc in next row, 2 sc in next row) across to last 6 rows, sc in last 6 rows, insert form; working across last row, 3 sc in first sc, 2 sc in next ch-3 sp, sc in next 5 sc, (3 sc in next ch-3 sp, sc in next 5 sc) across to last ch-3 sp, 2 sc in last ch-3 sp, sc in same st as first sc, do **not** finish off: 272 sc.

EDGING

Rnd 1: Ch 3 (**counts as first dc**), do **not** turn; dc in same st and in each sc around working 3 dc in center sc of each corner 3-sc group, dc in same st as first dc; join with slip st to first dc: 280 dc.

Rnd 2: Ch 5 (**counts as first dc plus ch 2**), dc in same st, ch 2, ★ † skip next dc, dc in next dc, ch 2, (skip next 2 dc, dc in next dc, ch 2) across to next corner 3-dc group, skip next dc †, (dc, ch 2) 3 times in corner dc; repeat from ★ 2 times **more**, then repeat from † to † once, dc in same st as first dc, ch 2; join with slip st to first dc: 104 dc and 104 ch-2 sps.

Rnd 3: Ch 7 (**counts as first tr plus ch 3**), ★ † 2 dc in next dc, 3 dc in next ch-2 sp, 2 dc in next dc, ch 6, skip next dc, tr in next dc, ch 6, skip next dc, [dc in next dc, (2 dc in next ch-2 sp, dc in next dc) twice, ch 6, skip next dc, tr in next dc, ch 6, skip next dc] 3 times, 2 dc in next dc, 3 dc in next ch-2 sp, 2 dc in next dc, ch 3 †, tr in next dc, ch 3; repeat from ★ 2 times **more**, then repeat from † to † once; join with slip st to first tr: 140 dc and 20 tr.

Rnd 4: Ch 1, sc in same st, ★ † ch 4, skip next dc, dc in next 5 dc, (ch 7, sc in next tr, ch 7, skip next dc, dc in next 5 dc) 4 times, ch 4 †, sc in next tr; repeat from ★ 2 times **more**, then repeat from † to † once; join with slip st to first sc: 100 dc and 20 sc.

Rnd 5: Ch 1, (sc, ch 6, sc) in same st, ★ † ch 5, skip next dc, dc in next 3 dc, [ch 7, (sc, ch 6, sc) in next sc, ch 7, skip next dc, dc in next 3 dc] 4 times, ch 5 †, (sc, ch 6, sc) in next sc; repeat from ★ 2 times **more**, then repeat from † to † once; join with slip st to first sc: 60 ch-sps.

Rnd 6: Slip st in first ch-6 sp, ch 4, dtr in same sp, ch 4, (work Cluster in same sp, ch 4) 4 times, ★ † skip next dc, dc in next dc, [ch 3, skip next ch-sp, work Cluster in next ch-sp, (ch 4, work Cluster in same sp) 4 times, ch 3, skip next dc, dc in next dc] 4 times, ch 4, skip next ch-sp †, (work Cluster, ch 4) 5 times in next ch-sp; repeat from ★ 2 times **more**, then repeat from † to † once; join with slip st to first dtr, finish off.

BELL (Make 2)

Rnd 1 (Right side)**:** Ch 2, 10 sc in second ch from hook; do **not** join, place marker *(see Markers, page 123)*.

Note: Mark Rnd 1 as **right** side.

Rnd 2: 2 Sc in each sc around: 20 sc.

Rnds 3-9: Sc in each sc around.

Rnd 10: (Sc in next 4 sc, 2 sc in next sc) around: 24 sc.

Rnd 11: (Sc in next 3 sc, 2 sc in next sc) around: 30 sc.

Rnd 12: (Sc in next 2 sc, 2 sc in next sc) around; slip st in next sc, finish off.

FINISHING

See Starching and Blocking, page 124.

Decorate Pillow and Bells as desired.

DOLLY'S AFGHAN

A miniature variation of the popular granny square pattern, this darling afghan will please a favorite young miss or a friend who collects dolls. The dainty motifs work up quickly, so you can make one for yourself, too.

MATERIALS
Bedspread Weight Cotton Thread (size 10):
  Black - 70 yards
  White - 35 yards
  Variegated Pastels - 20 yards
Steel crochet hook, size 7 (1.65 mm)
Tapestry needle

Note: Gauge is not important. The afghan can be smaller or larger without changing the overall effect.

STITCH GUIDE

BEGINNING CLUSTER
Ch 2, ★ YO, insert hook in sp indicated, YO and pull up a loop, YO and draw through 2 loops on hook; repeat from ★ once **more**, YO and draw through all 3 loops on hook *(Figs. 12a & b, page 121)*.
CLUSTER
★ YO, insert hook in st or sp indicated, YO and pull up a loop, YO and draw through 2 loops on hook; repeat from ★ 2 times **more**, YO and draw through all 4 loops on hook.
PICOT
Ch 4, slip st in fourth ch from hook.

SQUARE (Make 12)
With Variegated Pastel, ch 5; join with slip st to form a ring.

Rnd 1 (Right side)**:** Work beginning Cluster in ring, ch 2, (work Cluster in ring, ch 2) 5 times; join with slip st to top of beginning Cluster, finish off: 6 Clusters.

Note: Loop a short piece of thread around any stitch to mark Rnd 1 as **right** side.

Rnd 2: With **right** side facing, join White with slip st in any ch-2 sp; work (beginning Cluster, ch 3, Cluster) in same sp, † ch 1, work Cluster in next ch-2 sp, ch 1, work (Cluster, ch 3, Cluster) in next ch-2 sp, ch 1, work Cluster in next Cluster, ch 1 †, work (Cluster, ch 3, Cluster) in next ch-2 sp, repeat from † to † once; join with slip st to top of beginning Cluster, finish off: 12 Clusters.

Rnd 3: With **right** side facing, join Black with slip st in any corner ch-3 sp; ch 3, (dc, ch 3, 2 dc) in same sp, ch 1, (2 dc in next ch-1 sp, ch 1) twice, ★ (2 dc, ch 3, 2 dc) in next corner ch-3 sp, ch 1, (2 dc in next ch-1 sp, ch 1) twice; repeat from ★ around; join with slip st to top of beginning ch-3, finish off.

ASSEMBLY
With **wrong** sides together, using Black, and working through **both** loops, whipstitch Squares together, forming 3 vertical strips of 4 squares each *(Fig. 23, page 123)*, beginning in center ch of first corner and ending in center ch of next corner; whipstitch strips together in same manner.

EDGING
Rnd 1: With **right** side facing, join Black with slip st in any corner ch-3 sp; ch 6, 2 dc in same sp, ch 1, (2 dc in next ch-sp, ch 1) across to next corner ch-3 sp, ★ (2 dc, ch 3, 2 dc) in corner sp, ch 1, (2 dc in next ch-sp, ch 1) across to next corner ch-3 sp; repeat from ★ around, dc in first corner sp; join with slip st to third ch of beginning ch-6: 70 ch-sps.

Rnd 2: Slip st in first corner ch-3 sp, work (beginning Cluster, Picot, Cluster, Picot) in same sp, ★ † (work Cluster in next ch-1 sp, work Picot) across to next corner ch-3 sp †, work (Cluster, Picot) twice in corner sp; repeat from ★ 2 times **more**, then repeat from † to † once; join with slip st to top of beginning Cluster, finish off.

FANCIFUL BOOKMARKS

Crocheted in three classic styles and accented with satin ribbons, these fanciful bookmarks will delight literature lovers. They're so quick to finish that you'll want to give them to all your friends.

MATERIALS

Bedspread Weight Cotton Thread (size 10):
  Pineapple (White) - 12 yards
  Long Strip (Green) - 15 yards
  Heart (Rose) - 9 yards
Steel crochet hook, size 5 (1.90 mm)
Ribbon

Note: Gauge is not important. The bookmarks can be smaller or larger without changing the overall effect.

STITCH GUIDE

> **SHELL**
> (2 Dc, ch 2, 2 dc) in st or sp indicated.
> **DOUBLE TREBLE CROCHET**
> *(abbreviated dtr)*
> YO 3 times, insert hook in sp indicated, YO and pull up a loop, (YO and draw through 2 loops on hook) 4 times *(Figs. 10a & b, page 120)*.

PINEAPPLE

Finished Size: 2½" wide x 3" long

Ch 10; join with slip st to form a ring.

Row 1 (Right side)**:** Ch 1, 11 sc in ring; do **not** join.

Note: Loop a short piece of thread around any stitch to mark Row 1 as **right** side.

Row 2: Ch 3, turn; (dc, ch 2, 2 dc) in same st, ch 3, skip next 4 sc, (dc, ch 5, dc) in next sc, ch 3, skip next 4 sc, work Shell in last sc.

Row 3: Ch 1, turn; skip first dc, slip st in next dc and in next ch-2 sp, ch 3, (dc, ch 2, 2 dc) in same sp, ch 3, skip next ch-3 sp, 9 tr in next ch-5 sp, ch 3, skip next ch-3 sp, work Shell in last ch-2 sp.

Row 4: Ch 1, turn; skip first dc, slip st in next dc and in next ch-2 sp, ch 3, (dc, ch 2, 2 dc) in same sp, ch 3, skip next ch-3 sp, dc in next tr, (ch 1, dc in next tr) 8 times, ch 3, skip next ch-3 sp, work Shell in last ch-2 sp.

Row 5: Ch 1, turn; skip first dc, slip st in next dc and in next ch-2 sp, ch 3, (dc, ch 2, 2 dc) in same sp, ch 3, skip next ch-3 sp, (sc in next ch-1 sp, ch 3) 8 times, skip next ch-3 sp, work Shell in last ch-2 sp.

Rows 6-11: Ch 1, turn; skip first dc, slip st in next dc and in next ch-2 sp, ch 3, (dc, ch 2, 2 dc) in same sp, ch 3, skip next ch-3 sp, (sc in next ch-3 sp, ch 3) across to last ch-3 sp, skip last ch-3 sp, work Shell in last ch-2 sp.

Row 12: Ch 1, turn; skip first dc, slip st in next dc and in next ch-2 sp, ch 3, (dc, ch 2, 2 dc) in same sp, ch 3, skip next ch-3 sp, sc in next ch-3 sp, ch 3, skip next ch-3 sp, work Shell in last ch-2 sp.

Row 13: Ch 1, turn; skip first dc, slip st in next dc and in next ch-2 sp, ch 3, (dc, ch 2, 2 dc) in same sp, skip next 2 ch-3 sps, work Shell in last ch-2 sp.

Row 14: Ch 1, turn; skip first dc, slip st in next dc and in next ch-2 sp, ch 3, dc in same sp, 2 dc in last ch-2 sp; finish off.

Fold an 18" length of ribbon in half. With **wrong** side facing, draw the folded end up through the beginning ring and pull the loose ends through the folded end; draw the knot up **tightly**.

LONG STRIP

Finished Size: 1½" wide x 2½" long

Ch 9.

Row 1: (Dc, ch 2, 2 dc) in fourth ch from hook, ch 5, skip next 4 chs, work Shell in last ch.

Row 2: Ch 1, turn; skip first dc, slip st in next dc and in next ch-2 sp, ch 3, (dc, ch 2, 2 dc) in same sp, ch 5, work Shell in last ch-2 sp.

Row 3: Ch 1, turn; skip first dc, slip st in next dc and in next ch-2 sp, ch 3, (dc, ch 2, 2 dc) in same sp, ch 2, working **around** next ch-5, sc in ch-5 sp in row **below**, ch 2, work Shell in last ch-2 sp.

Row 4: Ch 1, turn; skip first dc, slip st in next dc and in next ch-2 sp, ch 3, (dc, ch 2, 2 dc) in same sp, ch 4, skip next 2 ch-2 sps, work Shell in last ch-2 sp.

Rows 5 and 6: Ch 1, turn; skip first dc, slip st in next dc and in next ch-2 sp, ch 3, (dc, ch 2, 2 dc) in same sp, ch 5, work Shell in last ch-2 sp.

Rows 7-16: Repeat Rows 3-6 twice, then repeat Rows 3 and 4 once **more**.

Edging (Right side)**:** Ch 1, (sc, ch 3, sc) in end of each row across; ch 3, (sc, ch 3) 3 times in center ch-4 sp of beginning ch; (sc, ch 3, sc) in end of each row across; ch 3, (sc, ch 3) 3 times in ch-4 sp; join with slip st to first sc, finish off.

Using photo as a guide for placement, weave a 12" length of ribbon through center spaces.

HEART
Finished Size: 2¹/₂" x 2¹/₂"

Ch 6; join with slip st to form a ring.

Rnd 1: Ch 4 **(counts as first dc plus ch 1, now and throughout)**, (dc, ch 1) 7 times in ring; join with slip st to first dc: 8 dc.

Rnd 2: Ch 4, (dc, ch 1) twice in same st, dc in next dc, ch 1, (dc, ch 5, dc) in next dc, ch 1, dc in next dc, ch 1, ★ (dc, ch 1) 5 times in next dc, dc in next dc, ch 1; repeat from ★ once **more**, (dc, ch 1) twice in same dc as beginning ch-4; join with slip st to first dc: 21 dc.

Rnd 3: Ch 4, dc in same st, ch 3, skip next 2 dc, (sc, ch 3) twice in next dc and in next ch-5 sp, skip next dc, (sc, ch 3) twice in next dc, skip next 2 dc, dc in next dc, (ch 1, dc in same dc) twice, ch 3, skip next 2 dc, (sc, ch 3) twice in next dc, skip next 2 dc, (dc, ch 2, tr, ch 2, dc) in next dc, ch 3, skip next 2 dc, (sc, ch 3) twice in next dc, skip last 2 dc, dc in same dc as beginning ch-4, ch 1; join with slip st to first dc.

Top Of Heart: Skip first ch-3 sp, dtr in next ch-3 sp, (ch 2, dtr) 8 times in same sp, skip next ch-3 sp, slip st in next ch-3 sp, skip next ch-3 sp, dtr in next ch-3 sp, (ch 2, dtr) 8 times in same sp, skip next dc, slip st in next dc, leave remaining sts unworked.

Edging (Right side)**:** Ch 1, sc in same st, ch 3, sc in next dc, ch 3, (sc in next ch-3 sp, ch 3) 3 times, sc in next dc, ch 3, (sc, ch 3) twice in next tr, sc in next dc, ch 3, (sc in next ch-3 sp, ch 3) 3 times, (sc in next dc, ch 3) twice, (sc in next ch-2 sp, ch 3) 8 times, working **around** next slip st, sc in ch-3 sp in row **below**, ch 3, (sc in next ch-2 sp, ch 3) 8 times; join with slip st to first sc, finish off: 31 ch-3 sps.

Sew one end of a 12" length of ribbon to **wrong** side of Heart.

SENTIMENTAL BIBLE SET

A touching gift for the bride, this pretty Bible cover will add to the sentimental air of her special day. The cross-shaped bookmark, adorned with a ribbon rose, can be used to identify a special passage.

Finished Size: Fits a standard Bride's Bible 3¾" x 5¾"

MATERIALS

Bedspread Weight Cotton Thread (size 10):
  1 ball (282 yards per ball)
Steel crochet hook, size 6 (1.80 mm) **or** size needed for gauge
Straight pins
20" length of ⅜"w ribbon
One small ribbon rose
Sewing needle and matching thread

GAUGE: In pattern, 4 Shells and 6 rows = 2"

STITCH GUIDE

> **V-ST**
> (Tr, ch 1, tr) in st or sp indicated.
> **HALF TREBLE CROCHET** *(abbreviated htr)*
> YO twice, insert hook in sp indicated, YO and pull up a loop, YO and draw through 2 loops on hook, YO and draw through 3 loops on hook *(Figs. 8a & b, page 120)*.
> **SHELL**
> Htr in sp indicated, ch 1, (tr, ch 1) twice in same sp, htr in same sp.

BIBLE COVER
BODY
Ch 83.

Row 1: Work V-St in sixth ch from hook, ★ ch 3, skip next 4 chs, work V-St in next ch; repeat from ★ across to last 2 chs, skip next ch, tr in last ch: 16 V-Sts.

Row 2 (Right side): Ch 4 **(counts as first tr, now and throughout)**, turn; work Shell in first V-St (ch-1 sp) and in each V-St across, tr in top of beginning ch: 16 Shells.

Note: Loop a short piece of thread around any stitch to mark Row 2 as **right** side and bottom edge.

Row 3: Ch 4, turn; work V-St in first Shell (center ch-1 sp), ★ ch 3, work V-St in next Shell; repeat from ★ across, tr in last tr.

Rows 4-17: Repeat Rows 2 and 3, 7 times.

Edging: Ch 1, work 49 sc evenly spaced across end of rows to corner; working in free loops of beginning ch *(Fig. 20b, page 122)*, work 80 sc evenly spaced across to corner; work 49 sc evenly spaced across end of rows to corner; work 80 sc evenly spaced across to corner; join with slip st to first sc, finish off: 258 sc.

FACING (Make 2)
Ch 23.

Work same as Body to Edging: 4 V-Sts.

Edging: Ch 1, working in end of rows, work 49 sc evenly spaced across to corner; working in free loops of beginning ch, work 20 sc evenly spaced across to corner; work 49 sc evenly spaced across end of rows to corner, work 20 sc evenly spaced across to corner; join with slip st to first sc, finish off: 138 sc.

JOINING AND EDGING
With **wrong** sides and bottom edges together, pin Facings to Body, carefully matching stitches.

Rnd 1: With Body toward you, join thread with slip st in any sc of Body; ch 1, working through **both** loops of **both** pieces, sc in each sc around entire Body; join with slip st to first sc: 258 sc.

Rnd 2: Ch 4, skip next 2 sc, ★ hdc in next sc, ch 2, skip next 2 sc; repeat from ★ around; join with slip st to second ch of beginning ch-4: 86 ch-2 sps.

Rnd 3: Slip st in first ch-2 sp, ch 4, (dc, ch 1) 8 times in same sp, sc in next ch-2 sp, ch 1, ★ (dc, ch 1) 9 times in next ch-2 sp, sc in next ch-2 sp, ch 1; repeat from ★ around; join with slip st to third ch of beginning ch-4, finish off.

CROSS BOOKMARK
Finished Size: 2"w x 2⅝"h

STITCH GUIDE

> **ADDING ON DOUBLE CROCHETS**
> YO, insert hook into base of last dc *(Fig. 21, page 123)*, YO and pull up a loop, YO and draw through one loop on hook, (YO and draw through 2 loops on hook) twice **(one dc added on)**.

Ch 7.

Row 1 (Right side): Dc in fourth ch from hook and in each ch across: 5 sts.

Note: Loop a short piece of thread around any stitch to mark Row 1 as **right** side.

Rows 2-6: Ch 3 **(counts as first dc, now and throughout)**, turn; dc in next dc and in each st across: 5 dc.

Row 7: Ch 9, turn; dc in fourth ch from hook and in next 10 sts, add on 7 dc: 19 sts.

Row 8: Ch 3, turn; dc in next dc and in each dc across.

Row 9: Turn; slip st in next 7 dc, ch 3, dc in next 4 dc, leave remaining dc unworked: 5 dc.

Rows 10-12: Ch 3, turn; dc in next dc and in each dc across; do **not** finish off.

EDGING

Rnd 1: Ch 1, turn; sc evenly around Cross; join with slip st to first sc.

Rnd 2: Ch 1, sc in same st, ch 2, (sc in next sc, ch 2) around; join with slip st to first sc, finish off.

Sew small ribbon rose to center of Cross.

COUNTRY KITCHEN LACE

For a bit of down-home hospitality, surprise new friends with homemade goodies presented in country lace. The quaint crocheted jar lid cover and bread cloth trim will go nicely with your neighborly offerings.

MATERIALS
Bedspread Weight Cotton Thread (size 10):
   1 ball (282 yards per ball)
Steel crochet hook, size 7 (1.65 mm) **or** size
   needed for gauge
17" square of fabric
24" length of ¼"w ribbon

JAR LID COVER
Finished Size: To fit a 2½" diameter jar lid

GAUGE: Rnds 1-3 = 2"

STITCH GUIDE

> **V-ST**
> (Dc, ch 2, dc) in sp indicated.

Ch 10; join with slip st to form a ring.

Rnd 1 (Right side)**:** Ch 3 **(counts as first dc)**, 25 dc in ring; join with slip st to first dc. 26 dc.

Note: Loop a short piece of thread around any stitch to mark Rnd 1 as **right** side.

Rnd 2: Ch 4, (dc in next dc, ch 1) around; join with slip st to third ch of beginning ch-4: 26 ch-1 sps.

Rnd 3: Slip st in first ch-1 sp, ch 5 **(counts as first dc plus ch 2, now and throughout)**, dc in same sp, ch 2, ★ skip next ch-1 sp, work V-St in next ch-1 sp, ch 2; repeat from ★ around to last ch-1 sp, skip last ch-1 sp; join with slip st to first dc.

Rnd 4: Slip st in first ch-2 sp, ch 5, dc in same sp, ch 2, sc in next ch-2 sp, ch 2, ★ work V-St in next V-St (ch-2 sp), ch 2, sc in next ch-2 sp, ch 2; repeat from ★ around; join with slip st to first dc: 39 ch-2 sps.

Rnd 5: Slip st in first ch-2 sp, ch 5, dc in same sp, ch 2, sc in next sc, ch 2, ★ work V-St in next V-St, ch 2, sc in next sc, ch 2; repeat from ★ around; join with slip st to first dc.

Rnd 6: Slip st in first ch-2 sp, ch 5, dc in same sp, ch 3, sc in next sc, ch 3, ★ work V-St in next V-St, ch 3, sc in next sc, ch 3; repeat from ★ around; join with slip st to first dc: 26 ch-3 sps and 13 V-Sts.

Rnd 7: Slip st in first ch-2 sp, ch 5, dc in same sp, ch 4, sc in next sc, ch 4, ★ work V-St in next V-St, ch 4, sc in next sc, ch 4; repeat from ★ around; join with slip st to first dc.

Rnds 8 and 9: Slip st in first ch-2 sp, ch 5, dc in same sp, ch 5, sc in next sc, ch 5, ★ work V-St in next V-St, ch 5, sc in next sc, ch 5; repeat from ★ around; join with slip st to first dc.

Rnds 10 and 11: Slip st in first ch-2 sp, ch 5, dc in same sp, ch 6, sc in next sc, ch 6, ★ work V-St in next V-St, ch 6, sc in next sc, ch 6; repeat from ★ around; join with slip st to first dc.

Rnd 12: Slip st in first ch-2 sp, ch 5, dc in same sp, ch 7, sc in next sc, ch 7, ★ work V-St in next V-St, ch 7, sc in next sc, ch 7; repeat from ★ around; join with slip st to first dc.

Rnd 13: Slip st in first ch-2 sp, ch 8, slip st in fourth ch from hook, ch 1, dc in same sp, ch 7, sc in next sc, ch 7, ★ dc in next V-St, ch 5, slip st in fourth ch from hook, ch 1, dc in same sp, ch 7, sc in next sc, ch 7; repeat from ★ around; join with slip st to third ch of beginning ch-8, finish off.

FINISHING
Weave ribbon through Rnd 9, gather to fit lid, and tie ends in bow.

BREAD CLOTH
Finished Size: 20" x 20"

GAUGE: 20 sc = 2"

STITCH GUIDE

> **SHELL**
> (2 Dc, ch 2, 2 dc) in sp indicated.

Fold fabric over ¼" to the wrong side twice at each edge and sew in place. Press if desired.

Rnd 1 (Right side)**:** With **right** side of fabric facing and working over hemmed edges, join thread with slip st in any corner of fabric; ch 1, work 163 sc evenly spaced across each edge of fabric; join with slip st to first sc: 652 sc.

Rnd 2: Ch 5, skip next 2 sc, dc in next sc, (ch 2, skip next 2 sc, dc in next sc) 53 times, ★ ch 2, dc in next sc, (ch 2, skip next 2 sc, dc in next sc) 54 times; repeat from ★ 2 times **more**, ch 1, sc in third ch of beginning ch-5 to form last ch-2 sp: 220 ch-2 sps.

Rnd 3: Ch 3, (dc, ch 2, 2 dc) in same sp, ch 4, skip next ch-2 sp, work Shell in next ch-2 sp, (ch 4, skip next 2 ch-2 sps, work Shell in next ch-2 sp) 17 times, ★ (ch 4, skip next ch-2 sp, work Shell in next ch-2 sp) twice, (ch 4, skip next 2 ch-2 sps, work Shell in next ch-2 sp) 17 times; repeat from ★ 2 times **more**, ch 2, skip last ch-2 sp, hdc in top of beginning ch-3 to form last ch-4 sp: 76 Shells.

Rnd 4: Ch 1, sc in same sp, ch 2, work Shell in next Shell (ch-2 sp), ch 2, ★ sc in next ch-4 sp, ch 2, work Shell in next Shell, ch 2; repeat from ★ around; join with slip st to first sc.

Rnd 5: Ch 1, sc in same st, ch 2, work Shell in next Shell, ch 2, ★ sc in next sc, ch 2, work Shell in next Shell, ch 2; repeat from ★ around; join with slip st to first sc.

Rnd 6: Ch 1, sc in same st, ch 3, 2 dc in next Shell, ch 5, sc in fourth ch from hook, ch 1, 2 dc in same Shell, ch 3, ★ sc in next sc, ch 3, 2 dc in next Shell, ch 5, sc in fourth ch from hook, ch 1, 2 dc in same Shell, ch 3; repeat from ★ around; join with slip st to first sc, finish off.

"BERRY" CUTE COASTERS

Surprise a friend with these "berry" clever summertime treats! Arranged in a pretty basket, the fruity coasters look fresh-picked from the strawberry patch.

Finished Size: 4¼" x 4"

MATERIALS
Bedspread Weight Cotton Thread (size 10):
  Red - 1 ball (350 yards per ball)
  Green - 1 ball (350 yards per ball)
Steel crochet hook, size 6 (1.80 mm) **or** size
  needed for gauge

GAUGE: Rnds 1-4 = 2"

STITCH GUIDE

BEGINNING SHELL
Slip st in next dc and in first ch-2 sp, ch 3, (dc, ch 2, 2 dc) in same sp.
SHELL
(2 Dc, ch 2, 2 dc) in sp indicated.
FRONT POST DOUBLE CROCHET
(abbreviated FPdc)
YO, insert hook from **front** to **back** around post of next st, YO and pull up a loop even with last st made *(Fig. 16, page 121)*, (YO and draw through 2 loops on hook) twice.
DECREASE (uses next 2 FPdc)
★ YO, insert hook from **front** to **back** around post of next FPdc, YO and pull up a loop even with last st made, YO and draw through 2 loops on hook; repeat from ★ once **more**, YO and draw through all 3 loops on hook **(counts as one FPdc)**.

COASTER

With Green, ch 6; join with slip st to form a ring.

Rnd 1 (Right side)**:** Ch 3 **(counts as first dc, now and throughout)**, dc in ring, ch 2, (2 dc in ring, ch 2) 5 times; join with slip st to first dc: 6 ch-2 sps.

Note: Loop a short piece of thread around any stitch to mark Rnd 1 as **right** side.

Rnd 2: Work beginning Shell, † ch 2, work Shell in next ch-2 sp, ch 1, 11 dc in next ch-2 sp, ch 1 †, work Shell in next ch-2 sp, repeat from † to † once; join with slip st to first dc: 4 Shells.

Rnd 3: Work beginning Shell, † ch 2, skip next ch-2 sp, work Shell in next Shell (ch-2 sp), ch 1, 2 dc in each of next 4 dc, dc in next dc, 2 dc in next dc, dc in next dc, 2 dc in each of next 4 dc, ch 1 †, work Shell in next Shell, repeat from † to † once; join with slip st to first dc, finish off.

Rnd 4: With **right** side facing, join Red with slip st in ch-2 sp of beginning Shell; ch 3, (dc, ch 2, 2 dc) in same sp, † ch 2, work Shell in next Shell, ch 1, skip next ch-1 sp, work 2 FPdc around next dc, work FPdc around next 5 dc, work 2 FPdc around next dc, work FPdc around next 6 dc, work 2 FPdc around next dc, work FPdc around next 5 dc, work 2 FPdc around next dc, ch 1 †, work Shell in next Shell, repeat from † to † once; join with slip st to first dc: 48 FPdc.

Rnds 5-14: Work beginning Shell, † ch 2, work Shell in next Shell, ch 1, work FPdc around each of next 24 FPdc, ch 1 †, work Shell in next Shell, repeat from † to † once; join with slip st to first dc.

Rnd 15: Work beginning Shell, † ch 2, work Shell in next Shell, ch 1, decrease, work FPdc around each of next 3 FPdc, decrease, (work FPdc around each of next 4 FPdc, decrease) twice, FPdc around each of next 3 FPdc, decrease, ch 1 †, work Shell in next Shell, repeat from † to † once; join with slip st to first dc: 38 FPdc.

Rnd 16: Work beginning Shell, † ch 2, work Shell in next Shell, ch 1, work FPdc around each FPdc across to next ch-1 sp, ch 1 †, work Shell in next Shell, repeat from † to † once; join with slip st to first dc.

Rnd 17: Work beginning Shell, † ch 2, work Shell in next Shell, ch 1, decrease, work FPdc around next FPdc, decrease, (work FPdc around each of next 2 FPdc, decrease, work FPdc around next FPdc, decrease) twice, ch 1 †, work Shell in next Shell, repeat from † to † once; join with slip st to first dc: 26 FPdc.

Rnd 18: Repeat Rnd 16.

Rnd 19: Work beginning Shell, † ch 2, work Shell in next Shell, ch 1, decrease, work FPdc around next FPdc, decrease, work FPdc around each of next 3 FPdc, decrease, work FPdc around next FPdc, decrease, ch 1 †, work Shell in next Shell, repeat from † to † once; join with slip st to first dc: 18 FPdc.

Rnd 20: Work beginning Shell, † ch 2, work Shell in next Shell, ch 1, decrease twice, FPdc around next FPdc, decrease twice, ch 1 †, work Shell in next Shell, repeat from † to † once; join with slip st to first dc: 10 FPdc.

Rnd 21: Work beginning Shell, † ch 2, work Shell in next Shell, ch 1, decrease, FPdc around next FPdc, decrease, ch 1 †, work Shell in next Shell, repeat from † to † once; join with slip st to first dc: 6 FPdc.

Rnd 22: Slip st in next dc and in first ch-2 sp, ch 3, dc in same sp, 2 dc in next Shell, skip next ch-1 sp and next st, work FPdc around next FPdc, 2 dc in each of next 2 Shells, skip next ch-1 sp and next st, work FPdc around next FPdc; join with slip st to first dc, finish off.

BEAUTIFUL BELLS

Graceful adornments for wedding or anniversary gifts, our beautiful little bells are edged with delicate picots. Later, the package tie-ons can be hung on the Christmas tree for memorable ornaments.

MATERIALS
Bedspread Weight Cotton Thread (size 10):
   20 - 30 yards for **each** Bell
Steel crochet hook, size 5 (1.90 mm) **or** size
   needed for gauge
Starching materials: Stiffening solution, plastic
   wrap, rust-proof pins, 3" x 3" x 1" scrap of
   plastic foam, wide rubber band, firm bristle
   brush, and a 2½" plastic bell (available in the
   bridal section of your favorite craft store).

GAUGE: 19 sc and 20 rows = 2"

#1
STITCH GUIDE

PICOT
Ch 4, slip st in fourth ch from hook.

Rnd 1 (Hanger): Ch 12, join with slip st to form a ring; ch 1, 25 sc in ring; join with slip st to first sc.

Rnd 2 (Right side): Ch 7, tr in seventh ch from hook, ch 2, (tr in same st, ch 2) twice; join with slip st to fifth ch of beginning ch-7: 4 ch-2 sps.

Note: Loop a short piece of thread around any stitch to mark Rnd 2 as **right** side.

Rnd 3: Ch 1, sc in same st, 3 sc in first ch-2 sp, (sc in next tr, 3 sc in next ch-2 sp) around; join with slip st to first sc: 16 sc.

Rnd 4: ★ (Ch 7, slip st in fourth ch from hook) twice, ch 4, slip st in same st and in next 2 sc; repeat from ★ around; finish off: 8 loops.

Rnd 5: With **right** side facing, join thread with slip st in top of any loop; ch 1, sc in same loop, ch 4, (sc in next loop, ch 4) around; join with slip st to first sc: 8 ch-4 sps.

Rnd 6: Slip st in first ch-4 sp, ch 1, (2 sc, work Picot, 2 sc) in same sp and in each ch-4 sp around; join with slip st to first sc.

Rnd 7: Ch 1, sc in same st, ch 9, skip next Picot and next 2 sc, ★ sc in next sc, ch 9, skip next Picot and next 2 sc; repeat from ★ around; join with slip st to first sc.

Rnd 8: Ch 1, sc in same st, (sc, ch 3, sc, ch 4, sc, ch 3, sc) in first loop, ★ sc in next sc, (sc, ch 3, sc, ch 4, sc, ch 3, sc) in next loop; repeat from ★ around; join with slip st to first sc.

Rnd 9: Ch 2, sc in first ch-3 sp, 9 dc in next ch-4 sp, sc in next ch-3 sp, ch 2, skip next sc, slip st in next sc, ★ ch 2, sc in next ch-3 sp, 9 dc in next ch-4 sp, sc in next ch-3 sp, ch 2, skip next sc, slip st in next sc; repeat from ★ around; finish off.

Rnd 10: With **right** side facing, join thread with slip st in center dc of any 9-dc group; ch 1, sc in same st, ch 7, ★ sc in center dc of next 9-dc group, ch 7; repeat from ★ around; join with slip st to first sc: 8 ch-7 sps.

Rnd 11: Ch 1, sc in each ch and in each sc around; join with slip st to first sc: 64 sc.

Rnd 12: Ch 1, sc in each sc around; join with slip st to first sc.

Rnd 13: Ch 1, sc in same st and in next sc, ch 6, ★ skip next 4 sc, sc in next 4 sc, ch 6; repeat from ★ 6 times **more**, skip next 4 sc, sc in last 2 sc; join with slip st to first sc.

Rnd 14: Ch 1, sc in same st, (work Picot, 3 sc) twice in first loop, work Picot, ★ skip next sc, sc in next 2 sc, (work Picot, 3 sc) twice in next loop, work Picot; repeat from ★ around to last 2 sc, skip next sc, sc in last sc; join with slip st to first sc, finish off.

See Starching and Blocking, page 124.

#2
Rnd 1 (Hanger): Ch 12, join with slip st to form a ring; ch 1, 25 sc in ring; join with slip st to first sc.

Rnd 2 (Right side): Ch 7, tr in seventh ch from hook, ch 2, (tr in same st, ch 2) twice; join with slip st to fifth ch of beginning ch-7: 4 ch-2 sps.

Note: Loop a short piece of thread around any stitch to mark Rnd 2 as **right** side.

Rnd 3: Ch 1, sc in same st, 3 sc in first ch-2 sp, (sc in next tr, 3 sc in next ch-2 sp) around; join with slip st to first sc: 16 sc.

Rnd 4: Ch 1, sc in same st, (ch 3, sc in next sc) around, ch 1, hdc in first sc to form last ch-3 sp: 16 ch-3 sps.

Rnds 5-8: Ch 1, sc in same sp, (ch 3, sc in next ch-3 sp) around, ch 1, hdc in first sc to form last ch-3 sp.

Rnd 9: Ch 1, sc in same sp, 2 sc in next ch-3 sp and in each ch-3 sp around, sc in same sp as first sc; join with slip st to first sc: 32 sc.

Rnds 10 and 11: Ch 1, sc in each sc around; join with slip st to first sc.

Rnd 12: Ch 1, sc in first 3 sc, ch 15, ★ sc in next 4 sc, ch 15; repeat from ★ around to last sc, sc in last sc; join with slip st to first sc: 8 loops.

Rnd 13: Ch 1, sc in same st and in next sc, ch 2, 12 sc in first loop, ch 2, skip next sc, ★ sc in next 2 sc, ch 2, 12 sc in loop, ch 2, skip next sc; repeat from ★ around; join with slip st to first sc, finish off.

Rnd 14: With **right** side facing, join thread with slip st in sixth sc of any loop; ch 1, sc in same st and in next sc, ch 5, skip next 12 sc, (sc in next 2 sc, ch 5, skip next 12 sc) around; join with slip st to first sc: 16 sc.

Rnd 15: Ch 1, sc in same st and in next sc, sc in next 2 chs, 2 sc in next ch, sc in next 2 chs, ★ sc in next 2 sc and in next 2 chs, 2 sc in next ch, sc in next 2 chs; repeat from ★ around; join with slip st to first sc: 64 sc.

Rnd 16: Ch 1, sc in same st and in next 3 sc, (sc, ch 3, sc) in next sc, ★ sc in next 7 sc, (sc, ch 3, sc) in next sc; repeat from ★ 6 times **more**, sc in last 3 sc; join with slip st to first sc, finish off.

See Starching and Blocking, page 124.

VICTORIAN SACHETS

Our sweet Victorian sachets will fill the air with romance! Featuring picots or shells, the nostalgic fancies are finished with bridal net, metallic braid, satin bows, and ribbon roses.

MATERIALS (For One Sachet)
Bedspread Weight Cotton Thread (size 10):
 Picot (75 yards)
 Shell (45 yards)
Steel crochet hook, size 5 (1.90 mm) **or** size needed for gauge
Tapestry needle
Bridal net - 10" x 10"
Sewing needle and thread
Potpourri - approximately 1 ounce
¼" or ⅜"w ribbon
Optional: Ribbon roses, medium metallic braid, etc.

GAUGE: 18 dc = 2"

STITCH GUIDE

PICOT
Sc in sp indicated, ch 3, 2 dc in third ch from hook, slip st in sc just made.
BEGINNING SHELL
Ch 3, (2 dc, ch 3, 3 dc) in same sp.
SHELL
(3 Dc, ch 3, 3 dc) in sp indicated.

PICOT

Rnd 1 (Right side)**:** Ch 2, 8 sc in second ch from hook; join with slip st to first sc: 8 sc.

Note: Loop a short piece of thread around any stitch to mark Rnd 1 as **right** side.

Rnd 2: Ch 1, sc in same st, (ch 5, sc in next sc) around, ch 2, dc in first sc to form last ch-5 sp: 8 ch-5 sps.

Rnd 3: Ch 1, sc in same sp, (ch 5, sc in next ch-5 sp) around, ch 1, tr in first sc to form last ch-5 sp.

Rnd 4: Ch 1, (sc, ch 5, sc) in same sp, (ch 5, sc) twice in next ch-5 sp and in each ch-5 sp around, ch 2, dc in first sc to form last ch-5 sp: 16 ch-5 sps.

Rnds 5-17: Ch 1, work Picot in same sp, (ch 5, work Picot in next ch-5 sp) around, ch 2, dc in first sc to form last ch-5 sp: 16 Picots.

Rnds 18-21: Ch 1, sc in same sp, (ch 5, sc in next ch-5 sp) around, ch 2, dc in first sc to form last ch-5 sp.

Rnd 22: Ch 1, sc in same sp, ch 1, (tr, ch 1) 6 times in next ch-5 sp, ★ sc in next ch-5 sp, ch 1, (tr, ch 1) 6 times in next ch-5 sp; repeat from ★ around; join with slip st to first sc: 48 tr.

Rnd 23: Slip st in first ch-1 sp, (ch 3, slip st in next ch-1 sp) 6 times, skip next sc, ★ slip st in next ch-1 sp, (ch 3, slip st in next ch-1 sp) 6 times, skip next sc; repeat from ★ around; join with slip st to first slip st, finish off.

SHELL

Rnd 1 (Right side)**:** Ch 2, 8 sc in second ch from hook; join with slip st to first sc: 8 sc.

Note: Loop a short piece of thread around any stitch to mark Rnd 1 as **right** side.

Rnd 2: Ch 6, (dc in next sc, ch 3) around; join with slip st to third ch of beginning ch-6: 8 ch-3 sps.

Rnd 3: Slip st in first ch-3 sp, ch 3 **(counts as first dc, now and throughout)**, (dc, ch 3, 2 dc) in same sp, (2 dc, ch 3, 2 dc) in next ch-3 sp and in each ch-3 sp around; join with slip st to first dc: 32 dc.

Rnd 4: Slip st in next dc and in first ch-3 sp, work beginning Shell, skip next 4 dc, ★ work Shell in next ch-3 sp, skip next 4 dc; repeat from ★ around; join with slip st to first dc: 8 Shells.

Rnd 5: Slip st in next 2 dc and in first ch-3 sp, work beginning Shell, ch 3, ★ work Shell in next Shell (ch-3 sp), ch 3; repeat from ★ around; join with slip st to first dc.

Rnd 6: Slip st in next 2 dc and in first ch-3 sp, work beginning Shell, ch 2, sc in next ch-3 sp, ch 2, ★ work Shell in next Shell, ch 2, sc in next ch-3 sp, ch 2; repeat from ★ around; join with slip st to first dc.

Rnd 7: Slip st in next 2 dc and in first ch-3 sp, work beginning Shell, ch 5, skip next 2 ch-2 sps, ★ work Shell in next Shell, ch 5, skip next 2 ch-2 sps; repeat from ★ around; join with slip st to first dc.

Rnd 8: Slip st in next 2 dc and in first ch-3 sp, work beginning Shell, ch 2, sc in next ch-5 sp, ch 2, ★ work Shell in next Shell, ch 2, sc in next ch-5 sp, ch 2; repeat from ★ around; join with slip st to first dc.

Rnds 9-11: Repeat Rnds 7 and 8 once, then repeat Rnd 7 once **more**.

Rnd 12: Slip st in next 2 dc and in first ch-3 sp, ch 1, sc in same sp, ch 6, sc in next ch-5 sp, ★ ch 6, sc in next Shell, ch 6, sc in next ch-5 sp; repeat from ★ around, ch 3, dc in first sc to form last ch-6 sp: 16 ch-6 sps.

Rnds 13-17: Ch 1, sc in same sp, (ch 6, sc in next ch-6 sp) around, ch 3, dc in first sc to form last ch-6 sp.

Rnd 18: Ch 1, sc in same sp, ch 2, work Shell in next ch-6 sp, ch 2, ★ sc in next ch-6 sp, ch 2, work Shell in next ch-6 sp, ch 2; repeat from ★ around; join with slip st to first sc: 8 Shells.

Rnd 19: Slip st in first ch-2 sp, ch 3, (slip st, ch 3) twice in next Shell, ★ (slip st in next ch-2 sp, ch 3) twice, (slip st, ch 3) twice in next Shell; repeat from ★ around to last ch-2 sp, slip st in last ch-2 sp, ch 3; join with slip st to first slip st, finish off.

FINISHING

Make a Pouch as follows: Cut a 10" square from bridal net and fold in half, forming a 5" x 10" rectangle. Sew long ends ¹⁄₄" from edge. Fold short end together and sew a ¹⁄₄" seam, forming a tube; open seam and finger press. Fold bottom ¹⁄₄" to **wrong** side. Using a double strand of sewing thread, work small basting stitches ¹⁄₈" from edge. Repeat for top. Turn right side out. Gather bottom and knot securely. Whipstitch opening closed.

Fill with potpourri and close top in same manner.

Shape into a symmetrical ball.

Weave a length of ¹⁄₄" or ³⁄₈" ribbon through Rnd 19 of Picot Sachet or Rnd 15 of Shell Sachet, inserting pouch before closing; tie in a bow.

Add desired trims.

PRETTY LITTLE BIRDCAGES

Cheery springtime tokens, our crocheted birdcages are embellished with silk nosegays and little hummingbirds. The pretty tabletop accents will make thoughtful gifts for bird-watchers and nature lovers alike.

Finished Size: 4½" high x 4" in diameter

MATERIALS (For One Birdcage)
Bedspread Weight Cotton Thread (size 10):
   50 yards
Steel crochet hook, size 5 (1.90 mm) **or** size
   needed for gauge
Polyester fiberfill
Starching materials: Commercial fabric stiffener,
   resealable plastic bag, blocking board, plastic
   wrap, terry towel, paper towels, and stainless
   steel pins
Plastic foam
Glue gun
Flowers
Moss
Bird
8" length of ³/₈"w ribbon

GAUGE: Rnds 1 and 2 of Bottom = 1½"

STITCH GUIDE

> **DECREASE** (uses next 3 sc)
> ★ YO, insert hook in **next** sc, YO and pull up a loop, YO and draw through 2 loops on hook; repeat from ★ 2 times **more**, YO and draw through all 4 loops on hook.

BOTTOM

Ch 3; join with slip st to form a ring.

Rnd 1 (Right side): Ch 3 **(counts as first dc, now and throughout)**, 17 dc in ring; join with slip st to first dc: 18 dc.

Note: Loop a short piece of thread around any stitch to mark Rnd 1 as **right** side.

Rnd 2: Ch 5, (dc in next dc, ch 2) around; join with slip st to third ch of beginning ch-5: 18 ch-2 sps.

Rnd 3: Ch 6, (dc in next dc, ch 3) around; join with slip st to third ch of beginning ch-6: 18 ch-3 sps.

Rnd 4: Ch 3, 3 dc in first ch-3 sp, (dc in next dc, 3 dc in next ch-3 sp) around; join with slip st to first dc, do **not** finish off: 72 dc.

SIDES

Rnd 1: Ch 1, sc in Back Loop Only *(Fig. 19, page 122)* of each dc around; join with slip st to both loops of first sc.

Rnd 2: Ch 4, skip next sc, (dc in both loops of next sc, ch 1, skip next sc) around; join with slip st to third ch of beginning ch-4: 36 ch-1 sps.

Rnd 3: Ch 4, (dc in next dc, ch 1) around; join with slip st to third ch of beginning ch-4.

Rnd 4: Ch 7, skip next dc, (tr in next dc, ch 3, skip next dc) around; join with slip st to fourth ch of beginning ch-7: 18 ch-3 sps.

Rnds 5-7: Ch 7, (tr in next tr, ch 3) around; join with slip st to fourth ch of beginning ch-7.

Finish off.

TOP

Rnd 1 (Right side): Ch 4, 17 dc in fourth ch from hook; join with slip st to top of beginning ch: 18 sts.

Note: Mark Rnd 1 as **right** side.

Rnd 2: Ch 1, sc in each st around; join with slip st to first sc.

Rnd 3: Ch 2, ★ YO, insert hook in **next** sc, YO and pull up a loop, YO and draw through 2 loops on hook; repeat from ★ once **more**, YO and draw through all 3 loops on hook, decrease around; skip beginning ch-2 and join with slip st to next st: 6 sts.

Stuff firmly.

Rnd 4: Ch 4, dc in same st, ch 1, (dc, ch 1) twice in each decrease around; join with slip st to third ch of beginning ch-4: 12 ch-1 sps.

Rnd 5: Ch 4, (dc, ch 1) twice in next dc, ★ dc in next dc, ch 1, (dc, ch 1) twice in next dc; repeat from ★ around; join with slip st to third ch of beginning ch-4: 18 ch-1 sps.

Rnd 6: Ch 7, (tr in next dc, ch 3) around; join with slip st to fourth ch of beginning ch-7: 18 ch-3 sps.

Rnds 7 and 8: Ch 7, (tr in next tr, ch 3) around; join with slip st to fourth ch of beginning ch-7.

Rnd 9: Slip st in first ch-3 sp, ch 5, tr in same sp, (ch 1, tr) 5 times in same sp, sc in next ch-3 sp, ★ tr in next ch-3 sp, (ch 1, tr) 7 times in same sp, sc in next ch-3 sp; repeat from ★ around, tr in same sp as beginning ch-5, ch 1; join with slip st to fourth ch of beginning ch-5: 9 sc.

Rnd 10: Ch 1, sc in same st, (sc in next ch-1 sp and in next tr) 5 times, pull up a loop in next 2 ch-1 sps, YO and draw through all 3 loops on hook, ★ sc in next tr, (sc in next ch-1 sp and in next tr) 5 times, pull up a loop in next 2 ch-1 sps, YO and draw through all 3 loops on hook; repeat from ★ around; join with slip st to first sc, finish off.

Weave a 12" length of thread through top of Rnd 3; gather tightly and secure.

FINISHING

See Starching and Blocking, page 124.

Place a small piece of plastic foam in bottom of cage. Glue flowers and moss to plastic foam as desired. Glue Top to Sides. Tie ribbon in a bow and glue to Top. Glue bird in place.

BRIDE'S SACHET HANGER

Too exquisite to tuck away in the closet, this delicate hanger and sachet are just right for displaying something special. What a beautiful gift for a bride!

MATERIALS
Bedspread Weight Cotton Thread (size 10):
  1 ball (282 yards per ball)
Steel crochet hook, size 9 (1.40 mm) **or** size
  needed for gauge
Satin-covered padded hanger
¾ yard of ⅛"w ribbon
Potpourri
Tulle (fine bridal net)
Sewing needle

GAUGE: Rnds 1 and 2 = 1"

SACHET
FRONT
FIRST FLOWER
Ch 4; join with slip st to form a ring.

Rnd 1 (Right side)**:** Ch 3 **(counts as first dc, now and throughout)**, 13 dc in ring; join with slip st to first dc: 14 dc.

Note: Loop a short piece of thread around any stitch to mark Rnd 1 as **right** side.

Rnd 2: Ch 5, dc in same st, dc in next dc, ★ (dc, ch 2, dc) in next dc, dc in next dc; repeat from ★ around; join with slip st to third ch of beginning ch-5: 7 ch-2 sps.

Rnd 3: Slip st in first ch-2 sp, ch 3, (dc, ch 2, 2 dc) in same sp, skip next dc, dc in next dc, ★ (2 dc, ch 2, 2 dc) in next ch-2 sp, skip next dc, dc in next dc; repeat from ★ around; join with slip st to first dc.

Rnd 4: Slip st in next dc and in next ch-2 sp, ch 3, (2 dc, ch 2, 3 dc) in same sp, ch 4, ★ (3 dc, ch 2, 3 dc) in next ch-2 sp, ch 4; repeat from ★ around; join with slip st to first dc.

Rnd 5: Slip st in next 2 dc and in next ch-2 sp, ch 3, (2 dc, ch 2, 3 dc) in same sp, ch 3, working **around** next ch-4, sc in center dc on Rnd 3, ch 3, ★ (3 dc, ch 2, 3 dc) in next ch-2 sp, ch 3, working **around** next ch-4, sc in center dc on Rnd 3, ch 3; repeat from ★ around; join with slip st to first dc.

Rnd 6: Ch 1, sc in same st and in next 2 dc, 3 sc in next ch-2 sp, sc in next 3 dc, 2 sc in next ch-3 sp, slip st in next sc, 2 sc in next ch-3 sp, ★ sc in next 3 dc, 3 sc in next ch-2 sp, sc in next 3 dc, 2 sc in next ch-3 sp, slip st in next sc, 2 sc in next ch-3 sp; repeat from ★ around; join with slip st to first sc, finish off.

SECOND FLOWER
Rnd 1: With **right** side facing, working **behind** Rnd 5 and in center of ch-2 sps on Rnd 4, join thread with slip st in first ch-2 sp; ch 10, (slip st in next ch-2 sp, ch 10) around; join with slip st to first st: 7 loops.

Rnd 2: Slip st in first 3 chs, ch 3, (2 dc, ch 2, 3 dc, ch 2, sc, ch 1) in same sp, ★ sc in next loop, (ch 2, 3 dc in same loop) twice, ch 2, sc in same loop, ch 1; repeat from ★ around, sc in first loop, ch 2; join with slip st to first dc.

Rnd 3: Slip st in next 2 dc and in next ch-2 sp, ch 3, (2 dc, ch 2, 3 dc) in same sp, ch 9, skip next 3 sps, ★ (3 dc, ch 2, 3 dc) in next ch-2 sp, ch 9, skip next 3 sps; repeat from ★ around; join with slip st to first dc.

Rnd 4: Slip st in next 2 dc and in next ch-2 sp, ch 3, (2 dc, ch 2, 3 dc) in same sp, ch 5, working **around** next ch-9, sc in next ch-1 sp on Rnd 2, ch 5, ★ (3 dc, ch 2, 3 dc) in next ch-2 sp, ch 5, working **around** next ch-9, sc in next ch-1 sp on Rnd 2, ch 5; repeat from ★ around; join with slip st to first dc.

Rnd 5: Ch 1, sc in same st and in next 2 dc, 3 sc in next ch-2 sp, sc in next 3 dc, 4 sc in next ch-5 sp, slip st in next sc, 4 sc in next ch-5 sp, ★ sc in next 3 dc, 3 sc in next ch-2 sp, sc in next 3 dc, 4 sc in next ch-5 sp, slip st in next sc, 4 sc in next ch-5 sp; repeat from ★ around; join with slip st to first sc, finish off.

BORDER
Rnd 1: With **right** side facing, working **behind** Rnd 4 of Second Flower and in center of ch-2 sps on Rnd 3, join thread with slip st in first ch-2 sp; ch 14, (slip st in next ch-2 sp, ch 14) around; join with slip st to first st: 7 loops.

Rnd 2 (Eyelet rnd)**:** Slip st in first loop, ch 4, (dc, ch 1) 8 times in same loop, (dc, ch 1) 9 times in each loop around to last loop, dc in last loop (ch 1, dc in same loop) 8 times, sc in third ch of beginning ch-4 to form last sp: 63 sps.

Rnd 3: Ch 3, (2 dc, ch 2, 3 dc) in same sp, skip next 2 ch-1 sps, ★ (3 dc, ch 2, 3 dc) in next ch-1 sp, skip next 2 ch-1 sps; repeat from ★ around; join with slip st to first dc: 21 ch-2 sps.

Rnd 4: Slip st in next 2 dc and in next ch-2 sp, ch 3, (2 dc, ch 2, 3 dc) in same sp, ch 6, ★ (3 dc, ch 2, 3 dc) in next ch-2 sp, ch 6; repeat from ★ around; join with slip st to first dc.

Rnd 5: Slip st in next 2 dc and in next ch-2 sp, ch 3, (2 dc, ch 2, 3 dc) in same sp, ch 4, working **around** next ch-6, sc in sp **between** 3-dc groups on Rnd 3, ch 4, ★ (3 dc, ch 2, 3 dc) in next ch-2 sp, ch 4, working **around** next ch-6, sc in sp **between** 3-dc groups on Rnd 3, ch 4; repeat from ★ around; join with slip st to first dc.

Rnd 6: Ch 1, sc in same st and in next 2 dc, 3 sc in next ch-2 sp, sc in next 3 dc, 3 sc in next ch-4 sp, slip st in next sc, 3 sc in next ch-4 sp, ★ sc in next 3 dc, 3 sc in next ch-2 sp, sc in next 3 dc, 3 sc in next ch-4 sp, slip st in next sc, 3 sc in next ch-4 sp; repeat from ★ around; join with slip st to first sc, finish off.

BACK
Work same as Front through Border Rnd 2; finish off.

FINISHING
Using back as pattern, cut 2 pieces of tulle.

With **right** sides together, sew a ¼" seam, leaving an opening for turning. Turn right side out. Fill with potpourri; sew opening closed.

Holding **wrong** sides together, weave ribbon through ch-1 sps of Eyelet rnd, leaving a 1" loop at top for hanger and inserting potpourri pouch before closing; tie a bow.

HANGER COVER (Make 2)
Ch 4; join with slip st to form a ring.

Rnd 1 (Right side): Ch 3 **(counts as first dc, now and throughout)**, 9 dc in ring; join with slip st to first dc: 10 dc.

Note: Loop a short piece of thread around any stitch to mark Rnd 1 as **right** side.

Rnd 2: Ch 4, dc in same st, ch 1, dc in next dc, ch 1, ★ (dc, ch 1) twice in next dc, dc in next dc, ch 1; repeat from ★ around; join with slip st to third ch of beginning ch-4: 15 ch-1 sps.

Continued on page 70.

Rnd 3: Slip st in first ch-1 sp, ch 3, (2 dc, ch 2, 3 dc) in same sp, ch 1, skip next 2 ch-1 sps, ★ (3 dc, ch 2, 3 dc) in next ch-1 sp, ch 1, skip next 2 ch-1 sps; repeat from ★ around; join with slip st to first dc.

Rnd 4: Slip st in next 2 dc and in next ch-2 sp, ch 3, (2 dc, ch 2, 3 dc) in same sp, ch 4, skip next ch-1 sp, ★ (3 dc, ch 2, 3 dc) in next ch-2 sp, ch 4, skip next ch-1 sp; repeat from ★ around; join with slip st to first dc.

Rnd 5: Slip st in next 2 dc and in next ch-2 sp, ch 3, (2 dc, ch 2, 3 dc) in same sp, ch 3, working **around** next ch-4, sc in next ch-1 sp on Rnd 3, ch 3, ★ (3 dc, ch 2, 3 dc) in next ch-2 sp, ch 3, working **around** next ch-4, sc in next ch-1 sp on Rnd 3, ch 3; repeat from ★ around; join with slip st to first dc.

Rnd 6: Slip st in next 2 dc and in next ch-2 sp, ch 3, (2 dc, ch 2, 3 dc) in same sp, ch 3, skip next 2 ch-3 sps, ★ (3 dc, ch 2, 3 dc) in next ch-2 sp, ch 3, skip next 2 ch-3 sps; repeat from ★ around; join with slip st to first dc.

Rnd 7: Slip st in next 2 dc and in next ch-2 sp, ch 3, (2 dc, ch 2, 3 dc) in same sp, ch 4, skip next ch-3 sp, ★ (3 dc, ch 2, 3 dc) in next ch-2 sp, ch 4, skip next ch-3 sp; repeat from ★ around; join with slip st to first dc.

Rnd 8: Slip st in next 2 dc and in next ch-2 sp, ch 3, (2 dc, ch 2, 3 dc) in same sp, ch 3, working **around** next ch-4, sc in ch-3 sp in rnd **below**, ch 3, ★ (3 dc, ch 2, 3 dc) in next ch-2 sp, ch 3, working **around** next ch-4, sc in ch-3 sp in rnd **below**, ch 3; repeat from ★ around; join with slip st to first dc.

Rnds 9-32: Repeat Rnds 6-8, 8 times.

Rnd 33: Slip st in next 2 dc and in next ch-2 sp, ★ ch 8, skip next 2 ch-3 sps, slip st in next ch-2 sp; repeat from ★ around; finish off.

Slip covers onto hanger and join together by weaving ribbon through ch-8 sps on last Rnd; tie a bow.

DAINTY CANDY DISH

This dainty candy dish offers sweet surprises for family and guests. The stiffened bowl is a tasteful accent for any room.

Finished Size: 6" in diameter and 2¼" deep

MATERIALS
Bedspread Weight Cotton Thread (size 10):
80 yards
Steel crochet hook, size 7 (1.65 mm) **or** size needed for gauge
Starching materials: Commercial fabric stiffener, resealable plastic bag, blocking board, plastic wrap, terry towel, paper towels, and stainless steel pins

GAUGE: Rnds 1-5 = 2½"

Ch 5; join with slip st to form a ring.

Rnd 1 (Right side)**:** Ch 3 **(counts as first dc, now and throughout)**, 13 dc in ring; join with slip st to first dc: 14 dc.

Note: Loop a short piece of thread around any stitch to mark Rnd 1 as **right** side,

Rnd 2: Ch 4, ★ dc in next dc, ch 1; repeat from ★ around; join with slip st to third ch of beginning ch-4.

Rnd 3: Ch 3, 2 dc in next ch-1 sp, ★ dc in next dc, 2 dc in next ch-1 sp; repeat from ★ around; join with slip st to first dc: 42 dc.

Rnd 4: Ch 5 **(counts as first dc plus ch 2, now and throughout)**, skip next dc, ★ dc in next dc, ch 2, skip next dc; repeat from ★ around; join with slip st to first dc: 21 ch-2 sps.

Rnd 5: Ch 3, 3 dc in next ch-2 sp, ★ dc in next dc, 3 dc in next ch-2 sp; repeat from ★ around; join with slip st to first dc: 84 dc.

Rnd 6: Ch 5, skip next 2 dc, ★ dc in next dc, ch 2, skip next 2 dc; repeat from ★ around; join with slip st to first dc: 28 ch-2 sps.

Rnd 7: Ch 3, ★ 3 dc in next ch-2 sp, dc in next dc; repeat from ★ around to last ch-2 sp, 2 dc in last ch-2 sp; join with slip st to first dc: 111 dc.

Rnd 8: Ch 5, skip next 2 dc, ★ dc in next dc, ch 2, skip next 2 dc; repeat from ★ around; join with slip st to first dc: 37 ch-2 sps.

Rnd 9: Ch 3, ★ 2 dc in next ch-2 sp, dc in next dc; repeat from ★ around to last ch-2 sp, 3 dc in last ch-2 sp; join with slip st to first dc: 112 dc.

Rnd 10: Ch 1, sc in same st, ★ ch 5, skip next 3 dc, sc in next dc; repeat from ★ around to last 3 dc, ch 2, skip last 3 dc, dc in first sc to form last ch-5 sp: 28 ch-5 sps.

Rnd 11: Ch 1, sc in same sp, ch 5, sc in next ch-5 sp, 4 dc in next sc, ★ sc in next ch-5 sp, ch 5, sc in next ch-5 sp, 4 dc in next sc; repeat from ★ around; join with slip st to first sc: 14 ch-5 sps.

Rnd 12: Slip st in first 2 chs, ch 1, sc in same sp, ch 5, skip next 2 dc, sc in next dc, ★ ch 5, sc in next ch-5 sp, ch 5, skip next 2 dc, sc in next dc; repeat from ★ around, ch 2, dc in first sc to form last ch-5 sp: 28 ch-5 sps.

Rnds 13-17: Repeat Rnds 11 and 12 twice, then repeat Rnd 11 once **more**: 14 ch-5 sps.

Rnd 18: Slip st in first 2 chs, ch 1, sc in same sp, ch 5, skip next 2 dc, sc in next dc, ch 5, ★ sc in next ch-5 sp, ch 5, skip next 2 dc, sc in next dc, ch 5; repeat from ★ around; join with slip st to first sc: 28 ch-5 sps.

Rnd 19: Ch 3, 3 dc in next ch-5 sp, ★ dc in next sc, 3 dc in next ch-5 sp; repeat from ★ around; join with slip st to first dc: 112 dc.

Rnd 20: Ch 1, sc in same st, ch 1, skip next 3 dc, (tr, ch 1) 6 times in next dc, skip next 3 dc, ★ sc in next dc, ch 1, skip next 3 dc, (tr, ch 1) 6 times in next dc, skip next 3 dc; repeat from ★ around; join with slip st to first sc: 98 ch-1 sps.

Rnd 21: Ch 1, ★ sc in next ch-1 sp, (ch 3, sc in next ch-1 sp) 6 times; repeat from ★ around; join with slip st to first sc, finish off.

FINISHING

See Starching and Blocking, page 124.

PURSE PRETTIES

These lacy purse accessories will keep a lady's necessities neatly organized. Crocheted with a filigree shell pattern, the matching eyeglass case, tissue cover, and key ring are both pretty and practical. To add a fragrant touch to your gift, fill the key ring with potpourri.

MATERIALS
Bedspread Weight Cotton Thread (size 10):
    1 ball (325 yards) will make all 3 accessories
Steel crochet hook, size 1 (2.75 mm) **or** size
    needed for gauge
12" length of 1/8"w ribbon
1" Split ring
Satin - 7" x 10"
Tapestry needle
Sewing needle and thread
Potpourri - small amount

GAUGE: In pattern, 2 repeats = 2 1/2"

EYEGLASSES CASE
Ch 62.

Row 1: Sc in second ch from hook and in each ch across: 61 sc.

Row 2 (Right side)**:** Ch 1, turn; sc in first sc ★ ch 3, skip next 5 sc, dc in next sc, (ch 1, dc in same sc) 4 times, ch 3, skip next 5 sc, sc in next sc; repeat from ★ across.

Note: Loop a short piece of thread around any stitch to mark Row 2 as **right** side.

Row 3: Ch 3, turn; 2 dc in same st, ch 1, sc in next ch-1 sp, (ch 3, sc in next ch-1 sp) 3 times, ch 1, ★ (2 dc, ch 1, 2 dc) in next sc, ch 1, sc in next ch-1 sp, (ch 3, sc in next ch-1 sp) 3 times, ch 1; repeat from ★ 3 times **more**, 3 dc in last sc.

Row 4: Ch 3, turn; 2 dc in same st, ch 2, sc in next ch-3 sp, (ch 3, sc in next ch-3 sp) twice, ch 2, ★ skip next ch-1 sp, (2 dc, ch 1, 2 dc) in next ch-1 sp, ch 2, sc in next ch-3 sp, (ch 3, sc in next ch-3 sp) twice, ch 2; repeat from ★ 3 times **more**, 3 dc in last st.

Row 5: Ch 3, turn; 2 dc in same st, ch 3, skip next ch-2 sp, (sc in next ch-3 sp, ch 3) twice, ★ (2 dc, ch 1, 2 dc) in next ch-1 sp, ch 3, skip next ch-2 sp, (sc in next ch-3 sp, ch 3) twice; repeat from ★ 3 times **more**, 3 dc in last st.

Row 6: Ch 1, turn; sc in first dc, ch 3, skip next ch-3 sp, dc in next ch-3 sp, (ch 1, dc in same sp) 4 times, ch 3, skip next ch-3 sp, ★ sc in next ch-1 sp, ch 3, skip next ch-3 sp, dc in next ch-3 sp, (ch 1, dc in same sp) 4 times, ch 3, skip next ch-3 sp; repeat from ★ 3 times **more**, sc in last st.

Row 7-34: Repeat Rows 3-6, 7 times.

Do **not** finish off.

LINING
Using piece as a pattern and adding 1/2" along the top edge and 1/4" seam allowance along remaining edges, cut satin. Fold top edge over 1/4" to the **wrong** side twice and sew in place. With **right** sides together, sew a 1/4" seam along side and bottom. Turn right side out and press if desired.

EDGING
Row 1: Fold in half with **wrong** sides together, working in end of rows and through **both** thicknesses, ch 1, work 53 sc evenly spaced across to beginning ch; working in free loops of beginning ch *(Fig. 20b, page 122)*, 3 sc in first ch, work 29 sc evenly spaced across; finish off: 85 sc.

Row 2: Join thread with slip st in first sc on Row 1; ch 1, sc in same st, ★ skip next 2 sc, dc in next sc, (ch 1, dc in same st) twice, skip next 2 sc, sc in next sc; repeat from ★ across; finish off.

FINISHING
Insert Lining into piece and tack in place around top opening.

TISSUE COVER
FIRST SIDE
Ch 50.

Row 1 (Right side)**:** Sc in second ch from hook and in each ch across: 49 sc.

Note: Loop a short piece of thread around any stitch to mark Row 1 as **right** side.

Row 2: Ch 1, turn; sc in each sc across.

Row 3: Ch 1, turn; sc in first sc, ★ ch 3, skip next 5 sc, dc in next sc, (ch 1, dc in same st) 4 times, ch 3, skip next 5 sc, sc in next sc; repeat from ★ across.

Row 4: Ch 3, turn; 2 dc in same st, ch 1, sc in next ch-1 sp, (ch 3, sc in next ch-1 sp) 3 times, ch 1, ★ (2 dc, ch 1, 2 dc) in next sc, ch 1, sc in next ch-1 sp, (ch 3, sc in next ch-1 sp) 3 times, ch 1; repeat from ★ 2 times **more**, 3 dc in last sc.

Row 5: Ch 3, turn; 2 dc in same st, ch 2, sc in next ch-3 sp, (ch 3, sc in next ch-3 sp) twice, ch 2, ★ skip next ch-1 sp, (2 dc, ch 1, 2 dc) in next ch-1 sp, ch 2, sc in next ch-3 sp, (ch 3, sc in next ch-3 sp) twice, ch 2; repeat from ★ 2 times **more**, 3 dc in last st.

Row 6: Ch 3, turn; 2 dc in same st, ch 3, skip next ch-2 sp, (sc in next ch-3 sp, ch 3) twice, ★ (2 dc, ch 1, 2 dc) in next ch-1 sp, ch 3, skip next ch-2 sp, (sc in next ch-3 sp, ch 3) twice; repeat from ★ 2 times **more**, 3 dc in last st.

Row 7: Ch 1, turn; sc in first dc, ch 3, skip next ch-3 sp, dc in next ch-3 sp, (ch 1, dc in same sp) 4 times, ch 3, skip next ch-3 sp, ★ sc in next ch-1 sp, ch 3, skip next ch-3 sp, dc in next ch-3 sp, (ch 1, dc in same sp) 4 times, ch 3, skip next ch-3 sp; repeat from ★ 2 times **more**, sc in last st.

Rows 8-19: Repeat Rows 4-7, 3 times.

Finish off.

SECOND SIDE
Row 1: With **wrong** side facing and working in free loops of beginning ch *(Fig. 20b, page 122)*, join thread with slip st in first ch; ch 1, sc in each ch across: 49 sc.

Rows 2-18: Work same as Rows 3-19 of First Side.

Do **not** finish off.

With **right** side facing and working in end of rows, sc evenly across; finish off.

With **right** side facing, join thread with slip st in last st on Row 19 on First Side; ch 1, working in end of rows, sc evenly across; finish off.

Continued on page 74.

FINISHING

With **wrong** sides together, last row of each side centered over beginning ch **and** working in inside loops, whipstitch ends together **(Fig. 23, page 123)**. Turn **wrong** side out; with **right** sides together, fold corner with seam in center, sew across to each corner ¼" from end **(Fig. 1)**. Turn right side out.

Fig. 1

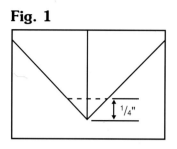

HEART SACHET KEY FOB
FIRST SIDE

Row 1 (Right side)**:** Ch 5, dc in fifth ch from hook **(4 skipped chs count as first dc plus ch 1)**, (ch 1, dc in same ch) 3 times: 4 ch-1 sps.

Note: Loop a short piece of thread around any stitch to mark Row 1 as **right** side.

Row 2: Ch 1, turn; sc in first ch-1 sp, (ch 3, sc in next ch-1 sp) 3 times.

Row 3: Ch 1, turn; sc in first ch-3 sp, (ch 3, sc in next ch-3 sp) twice.

Row 4: Ch 1, turn; sc in first ch-3 sp, ch 3, sc in next ch-3 sp, slip st in third ch of same ch-3 sp and in next sc.

Row 5: Ch 4 **(counts as first dc plus ch 1)**, turn; working **around** sts on Row 4, dc in first ch-3 sp on Row 3, (ch 1, dc in same sp) 3 times, ch 1, sc in ch-3 sp on Row 4, ch 1, skip next sc, dc in last ch-3 sp on Row 3, (ch 1, dc in same sp) 4 times.

Row 6: Ch 1, turn; sc in first ch-1 sp, (ch 3, sc in next ch-1 sp) 3 times, sc in next sc, skip next ch-1 sp, sc in next ch-1 sp, (ch 3, sc in next ch-1 sp) 3 times.

Row 7: Ch 1, turn; sc in first ch-3 sp, (ch 3, sc in next ch-3 sp) twice, slip st in same sp, skip next sc, sc in next sc, slip st in next ch-3 sp, sc in same sp, (ch 3, sc in next ch-3 sp) twice.

Row 8: Ch 1, turn; sc in first ch-3 sp, ch 3, sc in next ch-3 sp, slip st in same sp, skip next sc and next slip st, slip st in next sc, skip next slip st and next sc, slip st in next ch-3 sp, sc in same sp, ch 3, sc in next ch-3 sp; do **not** finish off.

EDGING

Rnd 1: Ch 1, turn; 5 sc in first ch-3 sp, slip st in next sc, slip st in next 3 slip sts and in next sc, 5 sc in next ch-3 sp, sc in next sc; working in end of rows, 2 sc in each of next 2 ch-sps, 4 sc in next dc row, 2 sc in next ch-sp, 4 sc in next dc row, 3 sc in beginning ch (tip), 4 sc in next dc row, 2 sc in next ch-sp, 4 sc in next dc row, 2 sc in each of next 2 ch-sps, sc in next sc; join with slip st to first sc: 43 sc.

Rnd 2: Ch 1, do **not** turn; sc in first 5 sc, slip st in next 5 slip sts, sc in next 20 sc, 2 sc in next sc, 3 sc in next sc (tip), 2 sc in next sc, sc in each sc around; join with slip st to first sc, finish off: 47 sc.

LINING

Using First Side as a pattern and adding ¼" seam allowance, cut 2 pieces of satin. With **right** sides together, sew a ¼" seam, leaving an opening for turning. Clip curves and corners; turn right side out. Fill with potpourri; sew opening closed.

SECOND SIDE

Work same as First Side, through Rnd 2 of Edging; do **not** finish off.

Rnd 3: With **wrong** sides together, matching sts and working through **both** pieces, ch 1, sc in first 5 sc, slip st in next 5 slip sts, sc in next sc, place marker around last sc made for Ruffle placement, sc in each sc around inserting lining before closing; join with slip st to first sc, finish off.

Ruffle: Join thread with slip st in marked sc, ★ dc in next sc, (ch 1, dc in same sc) twice, slip st in next sc; repeat from ★ around to last 5 slip sts, leave remaining slip sts unworked; finish off.

FINISHING

Join ribbon to split ring with a slip knot. Thread tapestry needle with ribbon and weave through center slip st at top of Heart. Tie in a bow.

FANTASY WEDDING ENSEMBLE

*F*ulfill a little girl's fantasy with our exquisitely detailed fashion doll wedding dress. The gown is complemented by a satin underskirt and a waist-length veil.

MATERIALS

Bedspread Weight Cotton Thread (size 10):
   2 balls (225 yards per ball)
Steel crochet hook, size 6 (1.80 mm) **or** size
   needed for gauge
Small snaps - 5
Sewing needle and thread
1" rubber band - 1

Bridal net - 15" x 17"
Satin fabric for Underskirt - 9" x 17"

GAUGE: 16 sc = 2"

Continued on page 76.

STITCH GUIDE

DECREASE (uses next 2 dc)
★ YO, insert hook in next dc and pull up a loop, YO and draw through 2 loops on hook; repeat from ★ once **more**, YO and draw through all 3 loops on hook.

WEDDING GOWN
SKIRT
Ch 64.

Row 1 (Right side): Sc in second ch from hook and in each ch across: 63 sc.

Note: Loop a short piece of thread around any stitch to mark Row 1 as **right** side.

Row 2: Ch 1, turn; sc in first 4 sc, ch 5, ★ skip next 3 sc, sc in next sc, ch 5; repeat from ★ across to last 7 sc, skip next 3 sc, sc in last 4 sc: 14 ch-5 sps.

Note: Begin working in rounds.

Rnd 1: Ch 3 **(counts as first dc, now and throughout)**, turn; dc in next 3 sc, ch 3, (sc, ch 3, sc) in center ch of first ch-5, ★ ch 5, (sc, ch 3, sc) in center ch of next ch-5; repeat from ★ around to last 4 sc, ch 3, dc in last 4 sc; join with slip st to first dc.

Rnd 2: Ch 3, turn; dc in next 4 dc, ch 5, skip first 2 ch-3 sps, ★ (sc, ch 3, sc) in center ch of next ch-5, ch 5; repeat from ★ around to last 2 ch-3 sps, skip last 2 ch-3 sps, dc in last 3 dc; join with slip st to first dc.

Rnd 3: Ch 3, turn; dc in next dc, 2 dc in each of next 2 dc, ch 5, (sc, ch 3, sc) in center ch of next ch-5, ★ ch 7, (sc, ch 3, sc) in center ch of next ch-5; repeat from ★ around to last 4 dc, ch 5, 2 dc in each of next 2 dc, dc in last 2 dc; join with slip st to first dc.

Note: Begin working in rows.

Row 1: Turn; slip st in next 6 dc, ch 10, skip first ch-5 sp, ★ (sc, ch 3, sc) in center ch of next ch-7, ch 7; repeat from ★ across to last ch-5 sp, skip last ch-5 sp, dc in next dc, leave remaining dc unworked.

Row 2: Ch 8, turn; (sc, ch 3, sc) in center ch of first ch-7, ch 7, ★ (sc, ch 3, sc) in center ch of next ch-7, ch 7; repeat from ★ across to last sp, skip next 3 chs, (sc, ch 3, sc) in next ch, ch 5, skip next 3 chs, dc in next ch.

Row 3: Ch 10, turn; skip first ch-5 sp, ★ (sc, ch 3, sc) in center ch of next ch-7, ch 7; repeat from ★ across to last sp, skip next 5 chs, dc in next ch.

Rows 4-15: Repeat Rows 2 and 3, 6 times.

Row 16: Ch 1, turn; sc in first dc, sc in each ch and in each sc across to last 2 chs, leave remaining chs unworked.

Row 17: Ch 1, turn; sc in each sc across.

Row 18: Ch 4, turn; 3 tr in first sc, 4 tr in each sc across; finish off.

BODICE
Row 1: With **right** side facing and working in free loops of beginning ch *(Fig. 20b, page 122)*, join thread with slip st in first ch; ch 1, sc in same st and in next ch, pull up a loop in next 2 chs, YO and draw through all 3 loops on hook, ★ pull up a loop in next 3 chs, YO and draw through all 4 loops on hook; repeat from ★ across to last 2 chs, sc in last 2 chs: 24 sts.

Row 2: Ch 1, turn; sc in each st across.

Row 3: Ch 1, turn; sc in first 4 sc, ★ 2 sc in next sc, sc in next 4 sc; repeat from ★ across: 28 sc.

Row 4: Ch 1, turn; sc in each sc across.

Row 5: Ch 1, turn; sc in first 4 sc, ★ 2 sc in next sc, sc in next 3 sc; repeat from ★ across: 34 sc.

Row 6: Ch 1, turn; sc in each sc across.

Row 7: Ch 1, turn; sc in first 4 sc, ★ 2 sc in next sc, sc in next 4 sc; repeat from ★ across: 40 sc.

Row 8: Ch 1, turn; sc in each sc across.

Row 9: Ch 1, turn; sc in first 5 sc, ★ 2 sc in next sc, sc in next 4 sc; repeat from ★ across: 47 sc.

Row 10: Ch 1, turn; sc in each sc across.

Row 11: Ch 1, turn; sc in first 5 sc, ★ 2 sc in next sc, sc in next 5 sc; repeat from ★ across: 54 sc.

Rows: 12-14: Ch 1, turn; sc in each sc across.

Row 15: Ch 1, turn; sc in first 8 sc, ch 8, skip next 6 sc (armhole), sc in next 12 sc, pull up a loop in next 2 sc, YO and draw through all 3 loops on hook, sc in next 12 sc, ch 8, skip next 6 sc (armhole), sc in last 8 sc: 41 sts and 2 ch-8 sps.

Row 16: Ch 1, turn; working in each sc and in each ch, sc in first 27 sts, pull up a loop in next 3 sc, YO and draw through all 4 loops on hook, sc in each st across: 55 sts.

Row 17: Ch 1, turn; sc in FLO of each sc across *(Fig. 19, page 122)*.

Row 18: Ch 3, turn; working in both loops, 2 dc in same st, 3 dc in each sc across; finish off.

EDGING
With **right** side facing and working in end of rows, join thread with slip st in Row 16; ch 1, sc evenly across to joining, slip st in joining, sc evenly across; finish off.

TRAIN

Row 1 (Ruffle): With **right** side facing and working in FLO of unworked sts on Skirt Rnd 3, join thread with slip st in first dc; ch 3, 2 dc in same st, 3 dc in each of next 9 dc: 30 dc.

Row 2: Turn; working in free loops of previous row, 2 dc in each of first 3 dc, dc in each dc across to last 3 dc, 2 dc in each of last 3 dc: 16 dc.

Row 3 (Ruffle): Turn; working in first dc on Ruffle **and** in FLO of first dc of previous row, slip st in first dc, ch 3, 2 dc in FLO of same st of previous row, 3 dc in FLO of each dc across: 48 dc.

Row 4: Turn; working in free loops of previous row, 2 dc in each of first 2 dc, dc in each dc across to last 2 dc, 2 dc in each of last 2 dc: 20 dc.

Rows 5-11: Repeat Rows 3 and 4, 3 times; then repeat Row 3 once **more**: 96 dc.

Rows 12-21: Repeat Rows 2 and 3, 5 times: 186 dc.

Row 22: Turn; working in free loops of previous row, 2 dc in first dc, dc in each dc across to last dc, 2 dc in last dc: 64 dc.

Row 23 (Ruffle): Turn; working in first dc on Ruffle **and** in FLO of first dc of previous row, slip st in first dc, ch 3, 2 dc in FLO of same st of previous row, 3 dc in FLO of each dc across: 192 dc.

Rows 24-33: Repeat Rows 22 and 23, 5 times: 222 dc.

Row 34: Turn; working in free loops of previous row, skip first dc, decrease, dc in each dc across to last 3 dc, decrease, leave remaining dc unworked: 70 dc.

Row 35 (Ruffle): Turn; working in first dc on Ruffle **and** in FLO of first dc of previous row, slip st in first dc, ch 3, 2 dc in FLO of same st of previous row, 3 dc in FLO of each dc across: 210 dc.

Rows 36-39: Repeat Rows 34 and 35 twice: 186 dc.

Row 40: Turn; working in free loops of previous row, skip first 3 dc, decrease, dc in each dc across to last 5 dc, decrease, leave remaining 3 dc unworked: 54 dc.

Row 41 (Ruffle): Turn; working in first dc on Ruffle **and** in FLO of first dc of previous row, slip st in first dc, ch 3, 2 dc in FLO of same st of previous row, 3 dc in FLO of each dc across: 162 dc.

Rows 42 and 43: Repeat Rows 40 and 41: 138 dc.

Finish off.

FINISHING

Sew Train to Skirt.

Add 3 snaps.

UNDERSKIRT

Trace pattern. Fold fabric in half widthwise. Place dotted edge of pattern along folded edge and pin in place. Cut out along solid lines.

Repeat using 9" x 17" piece of bridal net.

Holding net on **wrong** side of fabric, stitch 1/4" from top edge. Fold along stitching to **wrong** side, then fold over 1/4" again and press for waistband; sew in place.

With **right** sides together and sewing through all four layers, sew 1/4" seam from dot to bottom edge. Fold over 1/4" along opening to **wrong** side and press; sew in place.

Trim bridal net 1/4" along bottom edge.

Sew 1/4" hem in satin piece only.

Add snap.

HEADPIECE

Ch 38; join with slip st to form a ring, being careful not to twist ch.

Rnd 1 (Right side): Ch 1, holding chain and rubber band together and working over rubber band, sc in same ch and in each ch around; join with slip st to first sc: 38 sc.

Note: Mark Rnd 1 as **right** side.

Rnd 2: Ch 1, sc in same st, ch 3, (hdc in next sc, ch 3) 5 times, (dc in next sc, ch 3) 10 times, (hdc in next sc, ch 3) 5 times, (sc, slip st) in next sc, leave remaining 16 sc unworked; finish off.

Gather long edge of a 6" x 17" piece of bridal net; sew to wrong side of Headpiece behind ch-3 sps.

BABY BOUTIQUE

*F*inding the most adorable accessories for a little one is as easy as browsing through our baby boutique! These creative projects, which include a lacy layette and fancy footwear, offer fashion fun from head to toe. You'll especially enjoy our quick-to-finish shower gifts — the extra-soft blankets, thirsty bibs, and sweet sleeper are all made by embellishing plain fabric or garments! When you crochet these darling keepsakes, your loving stitches will be enjoyed for years to come.

STRAWBERRY LACE SET

For a special outing, dress your baby girl in this pretty layette, which includes a bonnet, a sacque, and booties fashioned in soft strawberry-pink thread. Instructions for the lacy ensemble are given for newborn to 3 months and 4 to 6 months.

Size: (Newborn to 3 months) and (4 to 6 months)

Size Note: Instructions are written for size Newborn to 3 months, with size 4 to 6 months in braces { }. Instructions will be easier to read if you circle all the numbers pertaining to your chosen size. If only one number is given, it applies to **both** sizes.

MATERIALS
Bedspread Weight Cotton Thread:
    4{5} balls (250 yards per ball)
Steel crochet hook, size 6 (1.80 mm) **or** size
    needed for gauge
4 yards of ⅛"w ribbon
Tapestry needle

GAUGE: 36 dc and 16 rows = 4"

STITCH GUIDE

V-ST
(Dc, ch 1, dc) in st or sp indicated.
SHELL
(2 Dc, ch 2, 2 dc) in sp or st indicated.
DECREASE
Pull up a loop in next 3 chs, YO and draw through all 4 loops on hook **(counts as one sc)**.

STRAWBERRY LACE PATTERN
Row 1 (Right side)**:** Ch 1, turn; sc in first dc, ch 1, skip next 2 dc, (dc, ch 1) 5 times in next dc, skip next 3 dc, sc in next dc, ★ ch 1, skip next 3 dc, (dc, ch 1) 5 times in next dc, skip next 3 dc, sc in next dc; repeat from ★ across.

Row 2: Ch 4 **(counts as first dc plus ch 1, now and throughout)**, turn; dc in same sc, ★ ch 1, skip next ch-1 sp, (sc in next ch-1 sp, ch 1) 4 times, work V-St in next sc; repeat from ★ across.

Row 3: Ch 4, turn; dc in first ch-1 sp, ★ ch 2, skip next ch-1 sp, (sc in next ch-1 sp, ch 2) 3 times, skip next ch-1 sp, work V-St in next ch-1 sp; repeat from ★ across.

Row 4: Ch 4, turn; dc in first ch-1 sp, ★ ch 2, skip next ch-2 sp, (sc in next ch-2 sp, ch 2) twice, skip next ch-2 sp, work V-St in next ch-1 sp; repeat from ★ across.

Row 5: Ch 1, turn; sc in first ch-1 sp, ★ ch 1, skip next ch-2 sp, (dc, ch 1) 5 times in next ch-2 sp, skip next ch-2 sp, sc in next ch-1 sp; repeat from ★ across.

Repeat Rows 2-5 for pattern.

SACQUE
YOKE
Ch 106{146}.

Row 1: Dc in fourth ch from hook **(3 skipped chs count as first dc)** and in next 14{20} chs, work Shell in next ch, dc in next 18{26} chs, work Shell in next ch, dc in next 32{44} chs, work Shell in next ch, dc in next 18{26} chs, work Shell in next ch, dc in last 16{22} chs: 116{156} dc.

Row 2 (Right side)**:** Ch 3 **(counts as first dc, now and throughout)**, turn; ★ dc in next dc and in each dc across to next ch-2 sp, work Shell in ch-2 sp; repeat from ★ 3 times **more**, dc in each dc across: 132{172} dc.

Note: Loop a short piece of thread around any stitch to mark Row 2 as **right** side.

Rows 3-12: Repeat Row 2, 10 times: 292{332} dc.

Row 13: Ch 3, turn; ★ dc in next dc and in each dc across to next ch-2 sp, 2 dc in ch-2 sp, skip next 66{74} dc (Sleeve), 2 dc in next ch-2 sp; repeat from ★ once **more**, dc in each dc across: 168{192} dc.

BODY
Work in Strawberry Lace Pattern until Body measures 6" from underarm, ending by working Pattern Row 5.

EDGING
Row 1: Ch 1, do **not** turn; sc in same corner, sc evenly along right front edge to next corner; working in free loops of beginning ch *(Fig. 20b, page 122)*, 2 sc in first ch, sc in next 14{20} chs, decrease, sc in next 16{24} chs, decrease, sc in next 30{42} chs, decrease, sc in next 16{24} chs, decrease, sc in next 15{21} chs.

Row 2: Ch 4, turn; skip next sc, dc in next sc, ★ ch 1, skip next sc, dc in next sc; repeat from ★ across neck edge, leave remaining sts unworked: 48{68} ch-1 sps.

Row 3: Turn; slip st in first ch-1 sp, ch 1, (sc, ch 3, sc) in same sp and in each ch-1 sp across; slip st in end of Edging Row 2, ch 1, sc evenly along left front edge; finish off.

SLEEVE

Row 1: With **wrong** side facing, join thread with slip st at underarm; ch 3, 2 dc in end of next row, dc in each dc around, 3 dc in end of next row: 72{80} dc.

Work in Strawberry Lace Pattern until Sleeve measures 5{6}" from underarm, ending by working Pattern Row 5.

EDGING

Row 1: Ch 1, turn; sc in first sc, sc in each ch-1 sp across: 55{61} sc.

Row 2: Ch 1, turn; sc in each sc across.

Row 3: Ch 4, turn; skip next sc, dc in next sc, ★ ch 1, skip next sc, dc in next sc; repeat from ★ across: 27{30} ch-1 sps.

Row 4: Turn; slip st in first ch-1 sp, ch 1, (sc, ch 3, sc) in same sp and in each ch-1 sp across; finish off leaving an 18" length for sewing.

Repeat for second Sleeve.

Sew Sleeve seams.

Weave a 36" length of ribbon through ch-1 sps at neck (Row 2) and an 18" length through ch-1 sps of each Sleeve (Row 3).

BOOTIES
SOLE
Ch 23{28}.

Rnd 1 (Right side)**:** 3 Sc in second ch from hook, sc in next 5{6} chs, hdc in next 5{6} chs, dc in next 10{13} chs, 7 dc in last ch; working in free loops of beginning ch **(Fig. 20b, page 122)**, dc in next 10{13} chs, hdc in next 5{6} chs, sc in next 5{6} chs; join with slip st to first sc: 50{60} sts.

Rnd 2: Ch 3 **(counts as first dc, now and throughout)**, turn; dc in same st and in next 20{25} sts, 2 dc in each of next 7 dc, dc in next 20{25} sts, 2 dc in each of last 2 sc; join with slip st to first dc: 60{70} dc.

Rnd 3: Ch 3, turn; 2 dc in next dc, dc in next dc, 2 dc in next dc, dc in next 21{26} dc, 2 dc in next dc, (dc in next dc, 2 dc in next dc) 6 times, dc in next 21{26} dc, 2 dc in last dc; join with slip st to first dc: 70{80} dc.

SIDES

Rnd 1: Ch 3, do **not** turn; working in Back Loops Only **(Fig. 19, page 122)**, dc in next dc and in each dc around; join with slip st to first dc.

Rnds 2-4: Ch 3, turn; working in both loops, dc in next dc and in each dc around; join with slip st to first dc.

Rnd 5: Ch 3, turn; dc in next 45{50} dc, place marker around last dc made for Instep joining, dc in next 24{29} dc; join with slip st to first dc, finish off.

INSTEP

Row 1: With **wrong** side facing, join thread with slip st in marked dc; ch 3, dc in next 15 dc, leave remaining sts unworked: 16 dc.

Rows 2-6: Ch 3, turn; dc in next dc and in each dc across.

Finish off leaving a 12" length for sewing.

With **right** side of Instep and Sides together and beginning 12{13} dc from Instep, sew Instep to Sides.

CUFF
Fold Bootie in half to find center back stitch.

Row 1: With **wrong** side facing, join thread with slip st in dc at center back; ch 1, sc in same st and in each dc across to Instep seam, 2 sc in seam, sc in next 14 dc across Instep, 2 sc in seam, sc in each dc across, sc in same st as first sc; do **not** join: 49{57} sc.

Row 2: Ch 4 **(counts as first dc plus ch 1)**, turn; skip next sc, dc in next sc, ★ ch 1, skip next sc, dc in next sc; repeat from ★ across: 24{28} ch-1 sps.

Row 3: Turn; slip st in first ch-1 sp, ch 3, dc in same sp, 2 dc in each ch-1 sp across: 48{56} dc.

Rows 4-8: Work Rows 1-5 of Strawberry Lace Pattern.

Finish off leaving a 12" length for sewing.

Sew back seam.

Repeat for second Bootie.

Weave an 18" length of ribbon through Row 2 of Cuff.

BONNET
BACK
Ch 26.

Row 1 (Right side)**:** Sc in second ch from hook, ★ ch 1, skip next 3 chs, (dc, ch 1) 5 times in next ch, skip next 3 chs, sc in next ch; repeat from ★ 2 times **more**.

Work Rows 2-5 of Strawberry Lace Pattern until Back measures 4{5}" from beginning ch, ending by working Pattern Row 4.

Finish off.

Continued on page 82.

CROWN

Row 1: With **wrong** side facing, join thread with slip st in first ch of beginning ch *(Fig. 20b, page 122)*; work 105{121} sc evenly spaced along sides and across top edge.

Row 2: Ch 1, turn; sc in first sc, ★ ch 1, skip next 3 sc, (dc, ch 1) 5 times in next sc, skip next 3 sc, sc in next sc; repeat from ★ across.

Work Rows 2-5 of Strawberry Lace Pattern until Crown measures 3½{4}", ending by working Pattern Row 5.

Edging: Ch 1, do **not** turn; sc evenly across bottom edge; finish off.

Sew on an 18" length of ribbon for each tie, using photo as a guide for placement.

BABY-SOFT BLANKETS

Beautiful crocheted edgings give these blankets a loving touch. Made from snuggly flannel, they're baby-soft and almost as sweet as the skin they were created to cover!

Finished Size: 37" square

MATERIALS
Bedspread Weight Cotton Thread (size 10):
  Edging #1 - Yellow, 2 balls (150 yards per ball)
  Edging #2 - Pink, 2 balls (150 yards per ball)
  Edging #3 - White, 1 ball (225 yards per ball)
Steel crochet hook, size 4 (2.00 mm) **or** size needed for gauge
1⅛ yards cotton flannel for **each** blanket
Scissors
6" diameter cardboard circle
Fabric marking pen
Sewing needle and thread

GAUGE: 25 sc = 4"

PREPARATION

Wash, dry, and press flannel. Trim flannel to a 36" square. To round corners, place cardboard circle on one corner of flannel with edge of circle even with edges of flannel. Use fabric marking pen to draw along edge of circle in corner; cut away excess flannel along drawn line. Repeat for remaining corners. Press all edges of blanket ¼" to wrong side and hand baste in place.

Note: Remove basting stitches after first round of Edging has been added.

When working stitches on first round of each Edging, insert hook through blanket ¼" from pressed edge.

EDGING #1

Rnd 1 (Right side): With **right** side of blanket facing, join thread with slip st at center of one rounded corner; ch 1, ★ work 216 sc evenly spaced across to center of next rounded corner; repeat from ★ 3 times **more**; join with slip st to first sc: 864 sc.

Rnd 2: Ch 5, dc in same st, skip next 2 sc, ★ (dc, ch 2, dc) in next sc, skip next 2 sc; repeat from ★ around; join with slip st to third ch of beginning ch-5: 288 ch-2 sps.

Rnd 3: Slip st in first ch-2 sp, ch 3, (dc, ch 3, 2 dc) in same sp, (2 dc, ch 3, 2 dc) in next ch-2 sp and in each ch-2 sp around; join with slip st to top of beginning ch-3, finish off.

EDGING #2

Rnd 1 (Right side): With **right** side of blanket facing, join thread with slip st at center of one rounded corner; ch 1, ★ work 216 sc evenly spaced across to center of next rounded corner; repeat from ★ 3 times **more**; join with slip st to first sc: 864 sc.

Rnd 2: Ch 3, dc in next sc and in each sc around; join with slip st to top of beginning ch-3.

Rnd 3: Ch 3, (2 dc, ch 2, 3 dc) in same st, skip next dc, sc in next dc, skip next dc, ★ (3 dc, ch 2, 3 dc) in next dc, skip next dc, sc in next dc, skip next dc; repeat from ★ around; join with slip st to top of beginning ch-3, finish off.

EDGING #3

Rnd 1 (Right side): With **right** side of blanket facing, join thread with slip st at center of one rounded corner; ch 1, ★ work 216 sc evenly spaced across to center of next rounded corner; repeat from ★ 3 times **more**; join with slip st to first sc: 864 sc.

Rnd 2: Ch 6, sc in same st, dc in next 2 sc, ★ (dc, ch 3, sc) in next sc, dc in next 2 sc; repeat from ★ around; join with slip st to third ch of beginning ch-6: 288 ch-3 sps.

Rnd 3: Slip st in first ch-3 sp, (sc, ch 3, 3 dc) in same sp and in each ch-3 sp around; join with slip st to first sc, finish off.

BABY'S BIBLE

This dainty cover for baby's first Bible makes a touching gift for a new arrival. Accented with ribbons and a dimensional rose, it's sure to become an heirloom.

Finished Size: 7⅝"w x 5¾"h
(Fits a 2⅞"w x 4½"h x ⅝"d Bible)

MATERIALS
Cotton Crochet Thread (size 30):
    White - 155 yards
    Yellow - 22 yards,
    Green - 6 yards
Steel crochet hook, size 13 (.85 mm) **or** size needed for gauge
Tapestry needle
2 - 12" lengths of ¹⁄₁₆"w ribbon for bow
1 - 12" length of ⅛"w ribbon for bow
⅔ yard of ¹⁄₁₆"w ribbon for weaving through Cover
Sewing needle and thread

GAUGE: [V-St, ch 3, (sc, ch 3) 4 times in next V-St, V-St] and 7 rows =1"

Gauge Swatch: 2⅝"w x 1"h
Ch 32.
Work same as Cover for 7 rows.
Finish off.

STITCH GUIDE

> **V-ST**
> (Dc, ch 2, dc) in st or sp indicated.

COVER
With White, ch 87.

Row 1 (Right side): Dc in fourth ch from hook, ★ ch 3, skip next 3 chs, (sc in next ch, ch 3) 4 times, skip next 3 chs, work V-St in next ch; repeat from ★ across to last 6 chs, ch 3, skip next 3 chs, sc in next ch, ch 3, sc in next ch, ch 1, hdc in last ch.

Note: Loop a short piece of thread around any stitch to mark Row 1 as **right** side.

Rows 2-32: Ch 4, turn; dc in first ch-1 sp, ch 3, ★ (sc, ch 3) 4 times in next V-St (ch-2 sp), skip next 2 ch-3 sps, work V-St in next ch-3 sp, ch 3; repeat from ★ across to last 2 ch-3 sps, skip last 2 ch-3 sps, (sc, ch 3, sc, ch 1, hdc) around turning ch; do **not** finish off.

EDGING
Rnd 1: Ch 1, turn; sc in same st, ch 3, skip next ch-3 sp, sc in next ch-3 sp, ch 3, [(sc, ch 3, sc) in next V-St, ch 3, sc in next ch-3 sp, ch 3, (skip next ch-3 sp, sc in next ch-3 sp, ch 3) twice] across; working in end of rows, (sc, ch 3, sc) in Row 32, place marker around last sc made for Inside Panel placement, ch 3, (sc in next row, ch 3) across to Row 1, (sc, ch 3, sc) in Row 1, ch 3; working over beginning ch, skip first sc, sc in sp **before** next sc, ch 3, sc in next sp, ch 3, [sc in same ch as next V-St **(Fig. 20b, page 122)**, ch 3, sc in next sp, ch 3, skip next sc, sc in sp **before** next sc, ch 3, skip next 2 sc, sc in sp **before** next sc, ch 3, sc in next sp, ch 3] across; working in end of rows, (sc, ch 3, sc) in Row 1, place marker around last sc made for Inside Panel placement, ch 3, (sc in next row, ch 3) across to Row 32, (sc, ch 3, sc) in Row 32, ch 3; join with slip st to first sc: 142 ch-3 sps.

Rnd 2: Slip st in next 2 chs, ch 1, sc in same sp, ch 3, sc in next ch-3 sp, ch 5, ★ sc in next ch-3 sp, ch 3, sc in next ch-3 sp, ch 5; repeat from ★ around; join with slip st to first sc: 142 sps.

Rnd 3: Slip st in next 2 chs, ch 1, sc in same sp, dc in next ch-5 sp, (ch 1, dc in same sp) 4 times, ★ sc in next ch-3 sp, dc in next ch-5 sp, (ch 1, dc in same sp) 4 times; repeat from ★ around; join with slip st to first sc.

Rnd 4: Ch 1, sc in same st and in next dc, sc in next ch-1 sp, sc in next dc and in next ch-1 sp, (sc, ch 3, sc) in next dc, sc in next ch-1 sp, sc in next dc and in next ch-1 sp, ★ sc in next 3 sts, sc in next ch-1 sp, sc in next dc and in next ch-1 sp, (sc, ch 3, sc) in next dc, sc in next ch-1 sp, sc in next dc and in next ch-1 sp; repeat from ★ around to last dc, sc in last dc; join with slip st to first sc; finish off.

FIRST INSIDE PANEL
Row 1: With **right** side of Cover facing, working **behind** Edging along one short edge **and** around posts of sc on Rnd 1 of Edging **(Fig. 15, page 121)**, and leaving an 8" length for sewing, join White with slip st around marked sc; ch 1, sc around same st, ch 3, sc around next sc, ch 3, ★ skip next sc, (sc around next sc, ch 3) 4 times; repeat from ★ 4 times **more**, skip next sc, sc around next sc, (ch 3, sc around next sc) 3 times: 25 ch-3 sps.

Row 2: Ch 5 **(counts as first dc plus ch 2, now and throughout)**, turn; dc in first ch-3 sp, (ch 2, dc in next ch-3 sp) across, ch 2, dc in last sc: 26 ch-2 sps.

Rows 3-8: Ch 5, turn; dc in next dc, (ch 2, dc in next dc) across.

Row 9: Ch 1, turn; (sc, ch 3, sc) in each ch-2 sp across; finish off leaving an 8" length for sewing.

SECOND INSIDE PANEL

Row 1: With **right** side of Cover facing, working **behind** Edging along remaining short edge **and** around posts of sc on Rnd 1 of Edging, and leaving an 8" length for sewing, join White with slip st around marked sc; ch 1, sc around same st, ch 3, sc around next sc, ch 3, ★ skip next sc, (sc around next sc, ch 3) 4 times; repeat from ★ 4 times **more**, skip next sc, sc around next sc, (ch 3, sc around next sc) 3 times: 25 ch-3 sps.

Rows 2-9: Work same as Rows 2-9 of First Inside Panel.

ROSE

With Yellow, ch 57.

Row 1 (Wrong side)**:** (Dc, ch 2, dc) in sixth ch from hook, ★ ch 2, skip next 2 chs, (dc, ch 2, dc) in next ch; repeat from ★ across: 36 sps.

Row 2: Ch 3, turn; 5 dc in next ch-2 sp, sc in next ch-2 sp, (6 dc in next ch-2 sp, sc in next ch-2 sp) 5 times, (9 dc in next ch-2 sp, sc in next ch-2 sp) 5 times, (12 dc in next ch-2 sp, sc in next sp) 7 times; finish off leaving a 10" length for sewing.

Thread tapestry needle with thread end. With **right** side facing and beginning with first petal made, refer to photo to roll Rose **tightly**; sew to secure.

Continued on page 86.

Rnd 2: Slip st in next sc, ch 1, 3 sc in same st, sc in each sc around, working 3 sc in each corner **and** increasing or decreasing as necessary to keep piece lying flat; join with slip st to first sc.

Rnd 3: Slip st in next sc, ch 1, sc in same st, (ch 6, skip next 3 sc, sc in next sc) around outside edge to center sc of next corner, ch 1, (slip st in next sc, ch 1) around; join with slip st to first sc.

Rnd 4: Ch 1, sc in same st, ★ ch 3, dc in third ch from hook, sc in next loop, ch 3, dc in third ch from hook, sc in next sc; repeat from ★ around outside edge to next corner, leave remaining sts unworked; finish off.

Add ribbon ties.

SWEET SLEEPER

Worked in a rainbow of pastel hues using simple stitches, this pretty yoke transforms a plain purchased gown into a precious nightie for baby. The sleeper closes with snaps and a ribbon tie.

MATERIALS
Infant gown with raglan sleeves and
   placket opening
Bedspread Weight Cotton Thread (size 10):
   Pink - 30 yards
   Blue, Yellow, and Green - 20 yards **each**
   White - 25 yards
Steel crochet hook, size 7 (1.65 mm) **or** size
   needed for gauge
Scissors
Fabric marking pen
8" diameter cardboard circle, cut in half
Sewing needle and thread
Embroidery floss - White
Embroidery needle
Snaps - 2
20" length of ⅛"w ribbon

GAUGE: 9 dc = 1"

PREPARATION
Wash, dry, and press gown. Mark center front and back of gown. Place cardboard half-circle on yoke with straight edges at shoulders and center of rounded edge centered with front of gown.
Mark gown along edge of circle with marking pen. Repeat for back of gown. Cut away excess yoke along drawn line. Hand baste raw edge of yoke ¼" to wrong side; press edge. Remove basting stitches after chain stitch foundation has been worked along edge.

CHAIN STITCH FOUNDATION
With **right** side of placket facing, using 6 strands of white embroidery floss and embroidery needle and beginning at left side edge of placket, work 191 chain stitches evenly spaced across edge of yoke to right side edge of placket as follows:

Chain Stitch is worked from right to left ⅛" from pressed edge. Make all stitches equal in length (there should be approximately 7 chains per inch). Come up at 1 and make a counterclockwise loop with the floss. Go down at 1 and come up at 2, keeping the floss below the point of the needle *(Fig. 1a)*. Make a loop with the floss and go down at 2; come up at 3, keeping floss below the point of the needle *(Fig. 1b)*. Secure last loop by bringing floss over loop and down.

Fig. 1a

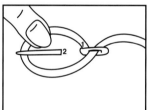

Fig. 1b

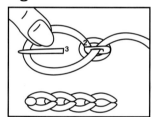

YOKE
STITCH GUIDE

> **FRONT POST DOUBLE CROCHET**
> *(abbreviated FPdc)*
> YO, insert hook from **front** to **back** around post of st indicated, YO and pull up a loop *(Fig. 16, page 121)*, (YO and draw through 2 loops on hook) twice.

Row 1: With **right** side facing and working in both loops of each chain st, join White with slip st in first chain st at left side of placket; ch 2 **(counts as first hdc, now and throughout)**, hdc in next st and in each st across; finish off: 191 hdc.

Row 2: With **right** side facing, join Pink with slip st in first hdc; ch 2, hdc in next hdc and in each hdc across.

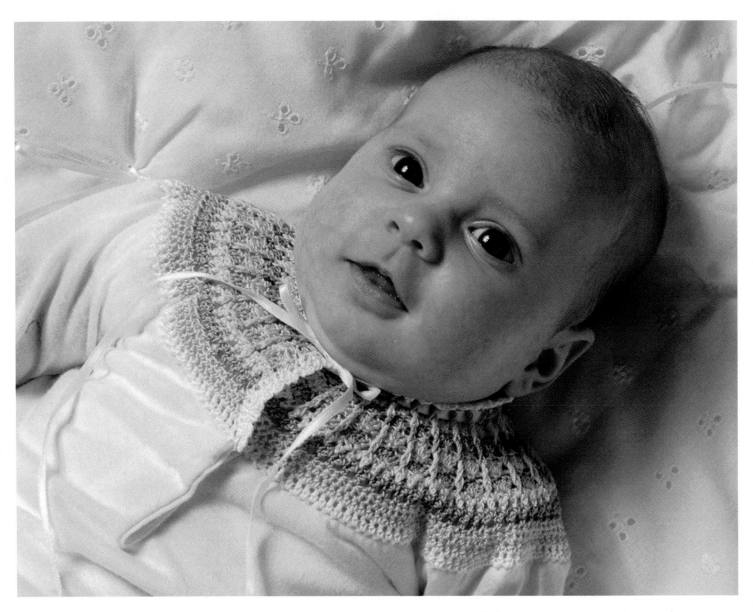

Row 3: Ch 2, turn; hdc in next hdc and in each hdc across; finish off.

Row 4: With **right** side facing, join Blue with slip st in first hdc; ch 1, sc in same st, ★ ch 3, skip next hdc, sc in next hdc; repeat from ★ across: 95 ch-3 sps.

Row 5: Ch 1, turn; sc in first sc, ch 1, (sc in next ch-3 sp, ch 1) across to last sc, sc in last sc; finish off: 97 sc.

Row 6: With **right** side facing, join Yellow with slip st in first sc; ch 1, sc in same st, (ch 3, sc in next sc) across: 96 ch-3 sps.

Row 7: Ch 1, turn; sc in first sc, ch 1, (sc in next ch-3 sp, ch 1) across to last sc, sc in last sc; finish off: 98 sc.

Row 8: With **right** side facing, join Green with slip st in first sc; ch 3 **(counts as first dc, now and throughout)**, skip next sc, 5 dc in next sc, ★ skip next sc, work FPdc around sc **below** next ch-1 sp,

skip next sc, 5 dc in next sc; repeat from ★ across to last 2 sc, skip next sc, dc in last sc; finish off: 32 5-dc groups.

Row 9: With **wrong** side facing, join Pink with slip st in first dc; ch 1, sc in same st, ch 3, (sc in center dc of next 5-dc group, ch 3) across to last dc, sc in last dc: 34 sc.

Row 10: Ch 3, turn; 4 dc in next sc, ★ work FPdc around FPdc **below** next ch-3, 4 dc in next sc; repeat from ★ across to last sc, dc in last sc; finish off: 32 4-dc groups.

Row 11: With **wrong** side facing, join Blue with slip st in first dc; ch 1, sc in same st, ch 3, (sc in second dc of next 4-dc group, ch 3) across to last dc, sc in last dc: 34 sc.

Row 12: Ch 3, turn; 3 dc in next sc, ★ work FPdc around FPdc **below** next ch-3, 3 dc in next sc; repeat from ★ across to last sc, dc in last sc; finish off: 32 3-dc groups.

Continued on page 90.

Row 13: With **wrong** side facing, join Yellow with slip st in first dc; ch 1, sc in same st, ch 2, (sc in center dc of next 3-dc group, ch 2) across to last dc, sc in last dc: 34 sc.

Row 14: Ch 3, turn; 3 dc in next sc, ★ work FPdc around FPdc **below** next ch-2, 3 dc in next sc; repeat from ★ across to last sc, dc in last sc; finish off: 32 3-dc groups.

Row 15: With **wrong** side facing, join Green with slip st in first dc; ch 1, sc in same st, ch 2, (sc in center dc of next 3-dc group, ch 2) across to last dc, sc in last dc: 34 sc.

Row 16: Ch 3, turn; 2 dc in next sc, ★ work FPdc around FPdc **below** next ch-2, 2 dc in next sc; repeat from ★ across to last sc, dc in last sc; finish off: 97 sts.

EDGING

Row 1: With **wrong** side facing, join White with slip st in end of first row on left neck edge; ch 1, work 24 sc evenly spaced along left neck edge; 2 sc in first dc on Row 16, ch 1, (skip next dc, sc in next dc, ch 1) across to last 2 dc, skip next dc, 2 sc in last dc; work 24 sc evenly spaced along right neck edge: 99 sc.

Row 2: Ch 1, turn; (sc, ch 3, sc) in first sc, skip next sc, ✝ (sc, ch 3, sc) in next sc, skip next sc ✝, repeat from ✝ to ✝ 11 times **more**, (sc, ch 3, sc) in each ch-1 sp across neck edge, ★ skip next sc, (sc, ch 3, sc) in next sc; repeat from ★ across; finish off.

Sew snaps to Yoke.

Weave ribbon behind post stitches on Row 16 and tie in a bow.

PRECIOUS ACCENTS

*P*erfect for shower gifts, our dainty baby buggy and bootie are charming little accents for the nursery. The stiffened designs are embellished with petite florals, ribbons, and lace.

MATERIALS
Bedspread Weight Cotton Thread (size 10):
  Buggy - 60 yards
  Bootie - 45 yards
Steel crochet hook, size 7 (1.65 mm) **or** size needed for gauge
Tracing paper
#2 pencil
Scissors
Starching materials: Commercial fabric stiffener, resealable plastic bag, blocking board, 3" diameter plastic foam cylinder, 1¾" square of ¼" thick cardboard, plastic wrap, terry towel, paper towels, and stainless steel pins
Finishing materials: clear-drying craft glue, assorted small flowers, ribbon

BABY BUGGY

GAUGE: Each Side = 3" diameter;
        Middle = 1½" x 7⅜";
        Each Wheel = 1⅝" diameter

SIDE A
Ch 4; join with slip st to form a ring.

Row 1 (Right side)**:** Ch 3 **(counts as first dc, now and throughout)**, 12 dc in ring: 13 dc.

Note: Loop a short piece of thread around any stitch to mark Row 1 as **right** side.

Row 2: Ch 3, turn; dc in same st, 2 dc in each of next 7 dc, (ch 1, dc in next dc) 5 times: 21 dc.

Row 3: Ch 5 **(counts as first dc plus ch 2)**, turn; (dc in next dc, ch 2) 4 times, (dc in next dc, 2 dc in next dc) 7 times, dc in last 2 dc: 28 dc.

Row 4: Ch 3, turn; (dc in next 2 dc, 2 dc in next dc) 7 times, dc in next dc, (ch 3, dc in next dc) 5 times: 35 dc.

Row 5: Ch 7 **(counts as first dc plus ch 4)**, turn; (dc in next dc, ch 4) 4 times, (dc in next 3 dc, 2 dc in next dc) 7 times, dc in last 2 dc: 42 dc.

Edging: Ch 1, do **not** turn; work 12 sc evenly spaced across end of rows to ring, sc in ring; work 12 sc evenly spaced across end of rows to next corner dc, 3 sc in corner dc, 4 sc in next ch-4 sp, (sc in next dc, 4 sc in next ch-4 sp) 4 times, sc in each dc across to last dc, 3 sc in last dc; join with slip st to first sc, finish off: 91 sc.

SIDE B
Ch 4; join with slip st to form a ring.

Row 1 (Right side)**:** Ch 3, 12 dc in ring: 13 dc.

Note: Mark Row 1 as **right** side.

Row 2: Ch 4 **(counts as first dc plus ch 1)**, turn; (dc in next dc, ch 1) 4 times, 2 dc in next dc and in each dc across: 21 dc.

Row 3: Ch 3, turn; dc in next dc, (2 dc in next dc, dc in next dc) 7 times, (ch 2, dc in next dc) 5 times: 28 dc.

Row 4: Ch 6 **(counts as first dc plus ch 3)**, turn; (dc in next dc, ch 3) 4 times, dc in next dc, 2 dc in next dc, (dc in next 2 dc, 2 dc in next dc) 6 times, dc in last 3 dc: 35 dc.

Row 5: Ch 3, turn; dc in next dc, (2 dc in next dc, dc in next 3 dc) 7 times, (ch 4, dc in next dc) 5 times: 42 dc.

Edging: Ch 1, do **not** turn; work 12 sc evenly spaced across end of rows to ring, sc in ring; work 12 sc evenly spaced across end of rows to next corner dc, 3 sc in corner dc; sc in each dc across to next ch-4 sp, 4 sc in ch-4 sp, (sc in next dc, 4 sc in next ch-4 sp) 4 times, 3 sc in last dc; join with slip st to first sc, finish off: 91 sc.

MIDDLE
Ch 16.

Row 1 (Right side)**:** Dc in fourth ch from hook and in each ch across **(3 skipped chs count as first dc)**: 14 dc.

Note: Mark Row 1 as **right** side.

Rows 2-27: Ch 3, turn; dc in next dc and in each dc across.

Finish off.

WHEEL (Make 4)
Ch 4; join with slip st to form a ring.

Rnd 1 (Right side)**:** Ch 3, 13 dc in ring; join with slip st to first dc: 14 dc.

Rnd 2: Ch 6 **(counts as first tr plus ch 2)**, (tr in next dc, ch 2) around; join with slip st to first tr: 14 ch-2 sps.

Rnd 3: Ch 1, sc in same st, 3 sc in next ch-2 sp, (sc in next tr, 3 sc in next ch-2 sp) around; join with slip st to first sc; finish off.

HANDLE
Ch 29, sc in second ch from hook and in each ch across; finish off: 28 sc.

Continued on page 92.

FINISHING
See Starching and Blocking, page 124.

Decorate as desired.

BABY BOOTIE
GAUGE: Rnds 1 and 2 = 1" x 2⅛"

STITCH GUIDE
DECREASE (uses next 2 dc)
★ YO, insert hook in **next** dc, YO and pull up a loop, YO and draw through 2 loops on hook; repeat from ★ once **more**, YO and draw through all 3 loops on hook **(counts as one dc)**.

SOLE AND SIDES
Ch 14.

Rnd 1 (Right side)**:** 4 Dc in fourth ch from hook **(3 skipped chs count as first dc, now and throughout)**, dc in next 9 chs, 5 dc in last ch; working in free loops of beginning ch **(Fig. 20b, page 122)**, dc in next 9 sts; join with slip st to first dc: 28 dc.

Note: Loop a short piece of thread around any stitch to mark Rnd 1 as **right** side.

Rnd 2: Ch 3 **(counts as first dc, now and throughout)**, dc in same st, 2 dc in each of next 4 dc, dc in next 9 dc, 2 dc in each of next 5 dc, dc in last 9 dc; join with slip st to first dc: 38 dc.

Rnd 3: Ch 3, dc in same st, 2 dc in each of next 9 dc, dc in next 9 dc, 2 dc in each of next 10 dc, dc in last 9 dc; join with slip st to first dc: 58 dc.

Rnd 4: Ch 3, dc in same st, (dc in next 2 dc, 2 dc in next dc) 6 times, dc in next 10 dc, 2 dc in next dc, (dc in next 2 dc, 2 dc in next dc) 6 times, dc in last 10 dc; join with slip st to Back Loop Only of first dc **(Fig. 19, page 122)**: 72 dc.

Rnd 5: Ch 3, working in Back Loops Only, dc in next dc and in each dc around; join with slip st to both loops of first dc.

Rnds 6 and 7: Ch 3, dc in both loops of next dc and in each dc around; join with slip st to first dc.

Rnd 8: Ch 3, dc in next 36 dc, decrease, (dc in next 2 dc, decrease) 6 times, dc in last 9 dc; join with slip st to first dc: 65 dc.

Rnd 9: Ch 3, dc in next 30 dc, place marker around last dc made for Row 1 joining, dc in next 6 dc, decrease 10 times, dc in last 8 dc; join with slip st to first dc, finish off: 55 dc.

CUFF
Row 1: Ch 5, with **wrong** side facing, join thread with slip st in marked dc; ch 1, sc in same st and in next 32 dc, leave remaining sts unworked: 33 sc.

Row 2: Ch 7, turn; dc in fourth ch from hook and in next 3 chs, dc in next sc and in each sc and in each ch across: 43 dc.

Row 3: Ch 3, turn; dc in next dc and in each dc across.

Row 4: Ch 1, turn; sc in first dc, (skip next 2 dc, 6 dc in next dc, skip next 2 dc, sc in next dc) across; finish off.

FINISHING
See Starching and Blocking, page 124.

Decorate as desired.

FOR TINY TOES
*B*abies will feel fancy right down to their toes when you slip their feet into these delicate booties. The boys' open-toe shoes have tasseled ties, and the girls' Mary Janes are trimmed with tiny appliqué flowers.

MATERIALS
Bedspread Weight Cotton Thread (size 10):
1 ball (225 yards per ball) will make both pairs
Steel crochet hook, size 4 (2.00 mm) **or** size needed for gauge
2 small buttons
Small appliqué flowers
Sewing needle and thread

GAUGE: 16 sc = 2"

Continued on page 94.

MARY JANE BOOTIES
SOLE
Ch 15.

Rnd 1 (Right side)**:** 5 Sc in second ch from hook, sc in each ch across to last ch, 5 sc in last ch; working in free loops of beginning ch **(Fig. 20b, page 122)**, sc in next 12 chs; join with slip st to first sc: 34 sc.

Note: Loop a short piece of thread around any stitch to mark Rnd 1 as **right** side.

Rnd 2: Ch 3 **(counts as first dc, now and throughout)**, dc in same st, 2 dc in each of next 4 sc, dc in next sc, hdc in next 6 sc, dc in next 5 sc, 2 dc in each of next 5 sc, dc in next 5 sc, hdc in next 6 sc, dc in last sc; join with slip st to first dc: 44 sts.

Rnd 3: Ch 1, sc in same st, 2 sc in next dc, (sc in next dc, 2 sc in next dc) 4 times, sc in next 13 sts, 2 sc in next dc, (sc in next dc, 2 sc in next dc) 4 times, sc in last 12 sts; join with slip st to first sc: 54 sc.

Rnd 4: Ch 3, (2 dc in next sc, dc in next 2 sc) 5 times, hdc in next sc, sc in next 4 sc, hdc in next sc, dc in next 6 sc, 2 dc in next sc, (dc in next 2 sc, 2 dc in next sc) 4 times, dc in next 6 sc, hdc in next sc, sc in next 4 sc, hdc in next sc, dc in last sc; join with slip st to first dc: 64 sts.

Rnd 5: Ch 1, sc in same st, 2 sc in next dc, (sc in next 3 dc, 2 sc in next dc) 4 times, sc in next 15 sts, 2 sc in next dc, (sc in next 3 dc, 2 sc in next dc) 4 times, sc in next 5 dc, place a marker around last sc made for joining placement, sc in last 9 sts; join with slip st to first sc, finish off: 74 sc.

INSTEP
Ch 3; join with slip st to form a ring.

Rnd 1 (Right side)**:** Ch 1, 12 sc in ring; join with slip st to first sc.

Note: Mark Rnd 1 as **right** side.

Rnd 2: Ch 3, dc in same st, 2 dc in each sc around; join with slip st to first dc: 24 dc.

Rnd 3: Ch 1, sc in same st and in next 2 dc, 2 sc in next dc, (sc in next 3 dc, 2 sc in next dc) around; join with slip st to first sc, do **not** finish off: 30 sc.

SIDES
Rnd 1: Ch 46; being careful not to twist ch and working in Back Loops Only **(Fig. 19, page 122)**, skip first 6 sc on Instep, sc in next 24 sc and in each ch around; join with slip st to both loops of first sc: 70 sc.

Rnds 2 and 3: Ch 3, working in both loops, dc in next st and in each st around; join with slip st to first dc.

Rnd 4: Ch 3, 2 dc in next dc, (dc in next 6 dc, 2 dc in next dc) 3 times, dc in last 47 dc; join with slip st to first dc, do **not** finish off: 74 dc.

Joining: Ch 1, with **wrong** side of Sole and Sides together and working in **both** pieces, sc in same st and in marked sc on Sole, sc in each st around; join with slip st to first sc, finish off.

Repeat for second Bootie.

LEFT BOOTIE
Strap: With **right** side facing and toe toward you, skip 5 sts from left side of Instep, join thread with slip st in next st; ch 16, sc in seventh ch from hook (buttonhole made), sc in each ch across.

Edging: Slip st in each st around opening, slip st in first 10 sts of Strap, 7 sc in buttonhole, slip st in each st across; finish off.

RIGHT BOOTIE
Strap: With **right** side facing and toe toward you, skip 6 sts from right side of Instep, join thread with slip st in next st; ch 16, sc in seventh ch from hook and in each ch across.

Edging: Work same as Left Bootie.

FINISHING
Using photo as a guide for placement, sew buttons to Sides and appliqués to toes.

OPEN-TOE BOOTIES
STITCH GUIDE

PUFF STITCH
(YO, insert hook in sp indicated, YO and pull up a loop even with loop on hook) 4 times, YO and draw through all 9 loops on hook **(Fig. 14, page 121)**, ch 1 to close.

SOLE
Work same as Mary Jane Booties through Rnd 4: 64 sts.

Rnd 5: Ch 1, sc in same st and in next 32 sts, (2 sc in next dc, sc in next 3 dc) 3 times, place a marker around last sc made for Top placement, 2 sc in next dc, sc in next 3 dc, 2 sc in next dc, sc in last 14 sts; join with slip st to first sc, finish off: 69 sts.

TOP

With **wrong** side of Sole facing, join thread with slip st in inside loop of marked st; ch 11, skip next 4 sc, slip st in inside loop of next sc.

Row 1 (Right side): Ch 1, turn; sc in first 5 chs, 3 sc in next ch, sc in next 5 chs, sc in inside loop of next 2 sc on Sole: 15 sc.

Row 2: Turn; skip first 2 sc, working in BLO **(Fig. 19, page 122)**, sc in each sc across, sc in inside loop of next 2 sc on Sole.

Row 3: Turn; skip first 2 sc, working in BLO, sc in next 6 sc, 3 sc in next sc, sc in next 6 sc, sc in inside loop of next 2 sc on Sole: 17 sc.

Row 4: Repeat Row 2.

Row 5: Turn; skip first 2 sc, working in BLO, sc in next 7 sc, 3 sc in next sc, sc in next 7 sc, sc in inside loop of next 2 sc on Sole: 19 sc.

Row 6: Repeat Row 2.

Row 7: Turn; skip first 2 sc, working in BLO, sc in next 8 sc, 3 sc in next sc, sc in next 8 sc, sc in inside loop of next 2 sc on Sole: 21 sc.

Row 8: Repeat Row 2.

Row 9: Turn; skip first 2 sc, working in BLO, sc in next 9 sc, 3 sc in next sc, sc in next 9 sc, sc in inside loop of next 2 sc on Sole: 23 sc.

Row 10: Repeat Row 2.

Row 11: Turn; skip first 2 sc, working in BLO, sc in next 10 sc, 3 sc in next sc, sc in next 10 sc, sc in inside loop of next 2 sc on Sole: 25 sc.

Row 12: Repeat Row 2.

Row 13: Turn; skip first 2 sc, working in BLO, sc in next 11 sc, 3 sc in next sc, sc in next 11 sc, sc in inside loop of next 2 sc on Sole: 27 sc.

Row 14: Turn; skip first 2 sc, working in BLO, sc in next 7 sc, place marker around last sc made to mark joining and Eyelet rnd, sc in next 5 sc, 3 sc in next sc, sc in next 12 sc, sc in inside loop of next 2 sc on Sole, do **not** finish off: 29 sc.

SIDES

Row 1: Turn; skip first 2 sc, working in BLO, sc in next 7 sc, leave remaining sc unworked: 7 sc.

Row 2: Ch 1, turn; working in BLO, sc in each sc across, sc in inside loop of next 2 sc on Sole: 9 sc.

Row 3: Turn; skip first 2 sc, working in BLO, sc in each sc across: 7 sc.

Repeat Rows 2 and 3 around to last sc on Sole, ending by working Row 3.

Next Row: Ch 1, turn; working in BLO, sc in each sc across, sc in inside loop of last sc on Sole: 8 sc.

Last Row: Turn; skip first sc, working in BLO, sc in each sc across; do **not** finish off: 7 sc.

Joining: Ch 1, turn; with **right** sides together, working through **both** loops of each sc on Sides **and** in BLO of Top, slip st in marked sc and in each st across; finish off.

Bottom Edging: With Top of Bootie facing, join thread with slip st in any free loop on Sole; ch 1, sc in same st and in each st around; join with slip st to first sc, finish off.

EDGING

Rnd 1 (Eyelet rnd): With **right** side facing, join thread with slip st in marked st on Top; ch 4, working in end of rows, skip next row, dc in next row, (ch 1, skip next row, dc in next row) around Sides; sc in each sc across Top; join with slip st to third ch of beginning ch-4.

Rnd 2: Ch 1, work Puff St in each ch-1 sp around, slip st in next sc on Top; finish off.

FINISHING

Make a 10" chain.
Make 2 Tassels **(Figs. 24a & b, page 123)**.
Weave chain through Eyelet rnd, then weave through center sc on Row 11 of Top.
Attach 1 Tassel to each end of chain.

Repeat for second Bootie.

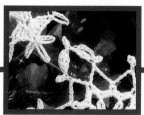

CHRISTMAS PRETTIES

The holiday season is especially joyous when you decorate your home with handmade touches! For this festive collection, we chose many of our favorite projects to help you deck the halls, stuff the stockings, and brighten the occasion in imaginative ways! You'll discover table toppers, a holiday wreath, and delicate snowflake ornaments to dress the tree. There's even a host of angels that will make heavenly gifts and cherished keepsakes. As you stitch these special designs, may you experience the merriment that comes with creating a handcrafted celebration.

4

3

LET IT SNOW!

Let it snow! Let it snow! Let it snow! And if it doesn't, you can create your own winter wonderland indoors with these dazzling snowflakes! The crystal-shaped designs are stiffened to make ornaments for the tree or pretty window decorations.

MATERIALS:

Bedspread Weight Cotton Thread (size 10):
10-20 yards for **each** Snowflake
Steel crochet hook, size 6 (1.80 mm)
Tapestry needle
Starching materials: Commercial fabric stiffener, resealable plastic bag, blocking board, plastic wrap, terry towel, paper towels, and stainless steel pins
Translucent nylon thread

Note: Gauge is not important. Snowflakes can be smaller or larger without changing the overall effect.

STITCH GUIDE

DOUBLE TREBLE CROCHET
(abbreviated dtr)
YO 3 times, insert hook in sp indicated, YO and pull up a loop, (YO and draw through 2 loops on hook) 4 times *(Figs. 10a & b, page 120)*.

2-DC CLUSTER
★ YO, insert hook in st indicated, YO and pull up a loop, YO and draw through 2 loops on hook; repeat from ★ once **more**, YO and draw through all 3 loops on hook *(Figs. 12a & b, page 121)*.

2-TR CLUSTER
★ YO twice, insert hook in st indicated, YO and pull up a loop, (YO and draw through 2 loops on hook) twice; repeat from ★ once **more**, YO and draw through all 3 loops on hook.

3-TR CLUSTER
★ YO twice, insert hook in st indicated, YO and pull up a loop, (YO and draw through 2 loops on hook) twice; repeat from ★ 2 times **more**, YO and draw through all 4 loops on hook.

TRIPLE TREBLE CROCHET
(abbreviated tr tr)
YO 4 times, insert hook in st indicated, YO and pull up a loop, (YO and draw through 2 loops on hook) 5 times *(Figs. 11a & b, page 120)*.

SNOWFLAKE #1

Ch 8; join with slip st to form a ring.

Rnd 1: Ch 5 **(counts as first dtr)**, (dtr, ch 5, slip st) in ring, ★ (ch 5, 3 dtr, ch 5, slip st) in ring; repeat from ★ 4 times **more**, ch 5, dtr in ring; join with slip st to first dtr: 6 3-dtr groups.

Rnd 2: ★ Ch 12, (work 2-dc Cluster, ch 2, slip st) in fourth ch from hook, slip st in next 5 chs, ch 9, slip st in second ch from hook and in next 5 chs, ch 8, (3-tr Cluster, ch 3, slip st) in fifth ch from hook, slip st in next 3 chs, ch 7, slip st in second ch from hook and in next 5 chs, slip st in free loop of adjacent ch and in next 2 chs, ch 9, (2-dc Cluster, ch 2, slip st) in fourth ch from hook, slip st in next 5 chs, slip st in free loop of adjacent ch and in next 3 chs, (ch 5, 2-tr Cluster in fifth ch from hook) twice, slip st in center dtr of next 3-dtr group; repeat from ★ around; finish off.

SNOWFLAKE #2

Ch 6; join with slip st to form a ring.

Rnd 1: Ch 12, slip st in fifth ch from hook, ★ † (ch 5, slip st in fifth ch from hook) twice, slip st in same ch as first slip st, ch 4, dc in ring, ch 10, slip st in second ch from hook and in next 3 chs, ch 9, slip st in second ch from hook and in next 4 chs, ch 5, slip st in third ch from hook and in next 2 chs, ch 6, slip st in second ch from hook and in next 4 chs, slip st in free loop of adjacent ch and in next 3 chs, ch 5, slip st in second ch from hook and in next 3 chs, slip st in free loop of adjacent ch and in next 5 chs, slip st in dc †, dc in ring, ch 9, slip st in fifth ch from hook; repeat from ★ 4 times **more**, then repeat from † to † once; join with slip st to third ch of beginning ch-12, finish off.

SNOWFLAKE #3

Ch 6; join with slip st to form a ring.

Rnd 1: Ch 1, 12 sc in ring; join with slip st to first sc.

Rnd 2: (Ch 11, slip st in next sc) around, ch 5, tr tr in same sc as previous joining to form last loop: 12 loops.

Rnd 3: Ch 1, sc in same loop, ch 5, (sc in next loop, ch 5) around; join with slip st to first sc.

Rnd 4: Slip st in first loop, ch 1, (3 sc, ch 3, 3 sc) in each loop around; join with slip st to first sc: 72 sc.

Rnd 5: Slip st across to first ch-3 sp, ch 1, sc in same sp, ★ † ch 5, tr in next ch-3 sp, ch 5, slip st in fifth ch from hook, (ch 5, 2-tr Cluster in fifth ch from hook, ch 5, slip st in fifth ch from hook) twice, tr in same ch-3 sp, ch 5 †, sc in next ch-3 sp; repeat from ★ 4 times **more**, then repeat from † to † once; join with slip st to first sc, finish off.

SNOWFLAKE #4

Ch 6; join with slip st to form a ring.

Rnd 1: Ch 1, 12 sc in ring; join with slip st to first sc.

Rnd 2: Ch 3 **(counts as first dc)**, dc in same st, ch 4, skip next sc, (2 dc in next sc, ch 4, skip next sc) around; join with slip st to first dc: 6 ch-4 sps.

Rnd 3: Ch 1, sc in same st and in next dc, ★ † 2 sc in next ch-4 sp, ch 15, slip st in 15th ch from hook to form a ring, ch 1, working around ring just made, 2 sc in ring, (ch 5, slip st in fifth ch from hook, 2 sc in ring) 3 times, ch 7, slip st in seventh ch from hook, 2 sc in ring, (ch 5, slip st in fifth ch from hook, 2 sc in ring) 3 times, 2 sc in same ch-4 sp †, sc in next 2 dc; repeat from ★ 4 times **more**, then repeat from † to † once; join with slip st to first sc, finish off.

SNOWFLAKE #5

Ch 8; join with slip st form a ring.

Rnd 1: Ch 1, 18 sc in ring; join with slip st to first sc.

Rnd 2: Ch 1, sc in same st and next 2 sc, ch 3, (sc in next 3 sc, ch 3) around; join with slip st to first sc: 6 ch-3 sps.

Rnd 3: Ch 1, sc in same st and in next 2 sc, (2 sc, ch 3, 2 sc) in next ch-3 sp, ★ sc in next 3 sc, (2 sc, ch 3, 2 sc) in next ch-3 sp; repeat from ★ around; join with slip st to first sc: 42 sc.

Rnd 4: Ch 1, sc in same st and in next 4 sc, (sc, ch 3, sc) in next ch-3 sp, ★ sc in next 7 sc, (sc, ch 3, sc) in next ch-3 sp; repeat from ★ around to last 2 sc, sc in last 2 sc; join with slip st to first sc: 54 sc.

Rnd 5: Slip st in next 5 sc, ch 4, tr in same st, 7 dc in next ch-3 sp, 2 tr in next sc, ★ skip next 7 sc, 2 tr in next sc, 7 dc in next ch-3 sp, 2 tr in next sc; repeat from ★ around; join with slip st to top of beginning ch-4.

Rnd 6: ★ Slip st in next 5 sts, (ch 7, slip st, ch 9, slip st, ch 7, slip st) in same st, slip st in next 6 sts, ch 7, slip st in same st; repeat from ★ around; join with slip st to first slip st, finish off.

FINISHING

See Starching and Blocking, page 124.

POTPOURRI BASKETS

Delight a friend on your Christmas list with these lacy crocheted baskets filled with potpourri. Trimmed with satin ribbon, they'll add a romantic touch to a room.

MATERIALS

Bedspread Weight Cotton Thread (size 10):
  Large Basket - 80 yards
  Small Basket - 50 yards
Steel crochet hook, size 6 (1.80 mm) **or** size needed for gauge
1½ yards of ¼"w ribbon for Large Basket
¾ yard of ¼"w ribbon for Small Basket
Starching materials: Commercial fabric stiffener, marking pen, resealable plastic bag, plastic wrap, 6¼" diameter can for Large Basket, 4" diameter can for Small Basket, terry towel, and paper towels

GAUGE: Rnds 1-4 = 3"

LARGE BASKET
Finished Size: 6¼" in diameter

BOTTOM
Ch 6; join with slip st to form a ring.

Rnd 1 (Right side)**: Ch 3 (counts as first dc, now and throughout)**, 23 dc in ring; join with slip st to first dc: 24 dc.

Note: Loop a short piece of thread around any stitch to mark Rnd 1 as **right** side.

Rnd 2: Ch 4 **(counts as first dc plus ch 1, now and throughout)**, (dc in next dc, ch 1) around; join with slip st to first dc: 24 ch-1 sps.

Rnd 3: Ch 5 **(counts as first dc plus ch 2, now and throughout)**, (dc in next dc, ch 2) around; join with slip st to first dc.

Rnd 4: Ch 4, dc in first ch-2 sp, ch 1, ★ dc in next dc, ch 1, dc in next ch-2 sp, ch 1; repeat from ★ around; join with slip st to first dc: 48 dc.

Rnd 5: Ch 4, (dc in next dc, ch 1) around; join with slip st to first dc.

Rnds 6-8: Ch 5, (dc in next dc, ch 2) around; join with slip st to first dc.

Rnd 9: Ch 3, 2 dc in first ch-2 sp, ★ dc in next dc, 2 dc in next ch-2 sp; repeat from ★ around; join with slip st to first dc: 144 dc.

SIDES
Rnd 1: Ch 3, dc in Back Loop Only of next dc and in each dc around *(Fig. 19, page 122)*; join with slip st to first dc.

Rnd 2: Ch 5, working in both loops, skip next 2 dc, (dc in next dc, ch 2, skip next 2 dc) around; join with slip st to first dc: 48 ch-2 sps.

Rnds 3-5: Ch 5, (dc in next dc, ch 2) around; join with slip st to first dc.

Rnd 6: Ch 1, work (sc, ch 3, sc, ch 5, sc, ch 3, sc) in same st, ★ ch 3, skip next dc, work (sc, ch 3, sc, ch 5, sc, ch 3, sc) in next dc; repeat from ★ around to last dc, ch 1, skip last dc, hdc in first sc to form last ch-3 sp.

Rnd 7: Ch 8, skip next 3 sps, ★ slip st in center ch of next ch-3, ch 8, skip next 3 sps; repeat from ★ around; join with slip st to base of beginning ch.

Rnd 8: Slip st in first ch-8 sp, ch 1, 10 sc in same sp and in each ch-8 sp around; join with slip st to first sc, finish off.

SMALL BASKET
Finished Size: 4" in diameter

BOTTOM
Work same as Large Basket through Rnd 5.

Rnd 6: Slip st in first ch-1 sp, ch 3, dc in same sp, 2 dc in each ch-1 sp around; join with slip st to first dc: 96 dc.

SIDES
Work same as Large Basket.

FINISHING
See Starching and Blocking, page 124.

Decorate as follows:
Large Basket: Weave a 21" length of ribbon through Rnd 2 of Sides; tack in place.

Repeat for Rnd 5 of Sides.

Small Basket: Weave a 15" length of ribbon through Rnd 5 of Sides; tack in place.

Both Baskets: Make a bow for each with a 12" length of ribbon and tack to top ribbon.

SO-PRETTY SNOWFLAKES

Enjoy a white Christmas no matter where you live by crocheting a flurry of these three-dimensional snowflakes. Not only will they make lovely ornaments for your tree, but they can also be used as fancy winter accents for your home.

MATERIALS
Bedspread Weight Cotton Thread (size 10):
   1 ball (225 yards) will make all three Snowflakes
Steel crochet hook, size 6 (1.80 mm)
Tapestry needle
Starching materials: 8" x 12" heavy cardboard, commercial fabric stiffener, resealable plastic bag, blocking board, plastic wrap, terry towel, paper towels, stainless steel pins, transparent tape, tracing paper, and waterproof marking pen
Finishing materials: Glue gun, glue sticks, and translucent nylon thread

Note: Gauge is not important. Snowflakes can be smaller or larger without changing the overall effect.

STITCH GUIDE

PICOT
Slip st in third ch from hook.
CLUSTER
YO twice, insert hook in fourth ch from hook, YO and pull up a loop, (YO and draw through 2 loops on hook) twice, ★ YO twice, insert hook in **same** ch, YO and pull up a loop, (YO and draw through 2 loops on hook) twice; repeat from ★ once **more**, YO and draw through all 4 loops on hook *(Figs. 12a & b, page 121)*.
DOUBLE TREBLE CROCHET
(abbreviated dtr)
YO 3 times, insert hook in st indicated, YO and pull up a loop, (YO and draw through 2 loops on hook) 4 times *(Figs. 10a & b, page 120)*.
PICOT GROUP
Slip st in third ch from hook, (ch 3, slip st in same ch as last slip st) twice.

SNOWFLAKE #1 (Make 3)
Ch 7; join with slip st to form a ring.

Rnd 1 (Right side)**:** Ch 4 **(counts as first tr)**, 2 tr in ring, ch 3, (3 tr in ring, ch 3) 5 times; join with slip st to first tr: 18 tr and 6 ch-3 sps.

*Note: Loop a short piece of thread around any stitch to mark Rnd 1 as **right** side.*

Rnd 2: Slip st in next tr, ★ † ch 5, work Picot, ch 6, work Picot, ch 3, slip st in same tr and in next tr, (slip st, ch 3, slip st) in next ch-3 sp †, slip st in next 2 tr; repeat from ★ 4 times **more**; then repeat from † to † once; join with slip st first slip st, finish off: 12 Picots.

Rnd 3: With **right** side facing, join thread with slip st in center ch of ch-3 **between** first 2 Picots; ★ ch 6, work Picot, ch 15, slip st in 14th ch from hook and in same ch as last slip st, ch 8, slip st in sixth ch from hook, ch 10, slip st in same ch as last slip st, ch 6, slip st in sixth ch from hook and in same ch as last slip st, slip st in next 2 chs and in same ch as first slip st, ch 15, slip st in 14th ch from hook and in same st as last slip st, ch 3, slip st in same st as last slip st, slip st in next 3 chs and in same ch of ch-3 as previous slip st, ch 3, sc in next Picot, ch 5, slip st in fourth ch from hook, ch 2, sc in next Picot, ch 3, slip st in center ch of next ch-3 sp; repeat from ★ around; finish off.

SNOWFLAKE #2 (Make 3)
Ch 5; join with slip st to form a ring.

Rnd 1: Ch 8, work Cluster, ★ tr in ring, ch 4, work Cluster; repeat from ★ 4 times **more**; join with slip st to fourth ch of beginning ch-8: 6 Clusters.

Rnd 2: Ch 1, sc in same st, (ch 9, sc in next tr) 5 times, ch 4, dtr in first sc to form last loop: 6 loops.

Rnd 3: Ch 1, sc in same st, ch 7, work Picot group, ch 5, ★ sc in center ch of next loop, ch 7, work Picot group, ch 5; repeat from ★ around; join with slip st to first sc.

Rnd 4: ★ Ch 13, slip st in seventh ch from hook, ch 8, slip st in sixth ch from hook, ch 10, slip st in same ch as last slip st, ch 5, slip st in fifth ch from hook and in same ch as last slip st, slip st in next 2 chs and in same ch as first slip st, ch 7, slip st in same ch as last slip st, slip st in next 6 chs and at base of beginning ch-13, ch 9, tr in center Picot of next Picot group, (ch 10, slip st in tr just made) twice, ch 9, slip st in next sc; repeat from ★ around; finish off.

SNOWFLAKE #3 (Make 3)

Rnd 1: Ch 2, 12 sc in second ch from hook; join with slip st to first sc.

Rnd 2: Ch 1, sc in same st, ch 3, skip next sc, (sc in next sc, ch 3, skip next sc) around; join with slip st to first sc: 6 ch-3 sps.

Rnd 3: Slip st in first ch-3 sp, ch 3 **(counts as first dc)**, 2 dc in same sp, ch 1, (3 dc in next ch-3 sp, ch 1) around; join with slip st to first dc: 18 dc and 6 ch-1 sps.

Rnd 4: Slip st in next 2 dc and in next ch-1 sp, ch 4 **(counts as first tr)**, (tr, ch 6, 2 tr) in same sp, ch 1, ★ (2 tr, ch 6, 2 tr) in next ch-1 sp, ch 1; repeat from ★ around; join with slip st to first tr: 24 tr and 6 ch-6 sps.

Rnd 5: Ch 1, sc in same st and in next tr, (3 sc, ch 13, 3 sc) in next ch-6 sp, sc in next 2 tr, (sc, ch 3, sc) in next ch-1 sp, ★ sc in next 2 tr, (3 sc, ch 13, 3 sc) in next ch-6 sp, sc in next 2 tr, (sc, ch 3, sc) in next ch-1 sp; repeat from ★ around; join with slip st to first sc: 6 loops.

Rnd 6: Slip st in next 2 sc, ch 1, sc in same sc and in next 2 sc, sc in next loop, (ch 3, sc in same loop) 13 times, sc in next 3 sc, ch 2, (sc, ch 4, sc) in next ch-3 sp, ch 2, skip next 3 sc, ★ sc in next 3 sc and in next loop, (ch 3, sc in same loop) 13 times, sc in next 3 sc, ch 2, (sc, ch 4, sc) in next ch-3 sp, ch 2, skip next 3 sc; repeat from ★ around; join with slip st to first sc, finish off.

FINISHING

See Starching and Blocking, page 124.

HEIRLOOM ANGEL

*E*mbellished with pearl beads, this graceful angel makes a lovely showpiece for the table or treetop. The heavenly project is destined to become a cherished family heirloom.

Finished Size: 11¼"h

MATERIALS
Bedspread Weight Cotton Thread (size 10):
  120 yards
Steel crochet hook, size 7 (1.65 mm) **or** size needed
  for gauge
343 - 3 mm pearl beads
#24 tapestry needle
Polyester fiberfill
Starching materials: Commercial fabric stiffener,
  resealable plastic bag, blocking board, plastic foam
  cone, plastic wrap, terry towel, paper towels, and
  stainless steel pins
Clear-drying craft glue

GAUGE: 10 sc and 8 rnds = 1"

WORKING WITH PEARLS
Pearls must be strung onto thread before you begin to crochet. As you crochet, push pearls down out of the way and do **not** use unless instructed. When instructed to add pearl, slide pearl next to last st made. Pearls will be on the **right** side of work.

STITCH GUIDE

> **DECREASE**
> Pull up a loop in next 2 sts, YO and draw through
> all 3 loops on hook **(counts as one sc)**.

HEAD AND BODY
String 237 pearls onto thread.

Rnd 1 (Right side)**:** Ch 2, 6 sc in second ch from hook; do **not** join, place marker **(see Markers, page 122)**: 6 sc.

Note: Loop a short piece of thread around any stitch to mark Rnd 1 as **right** side.

Rnd 2: 2 Sc in each sc around: 12 sc.

Rnd 3: (Sc in next sc, 2 sc in next sc) around: 18 sc.

Rnd 4: (Sc in next 2 sc, 2 sc in next sc) around: 24 sc.

Rnd 5: (Sc in next 3 sc, 2 sc in next sc) around: 30 sc.

Rnd 6: (Sc in next 4 sc, 2 sc in next sc) around: 36 sc.

Rnd 7: (Sc in next 5 sc, 2 sc in next sc) around: 42 sc.

Rnd 8: (Sc in next 6 sc, 2 sc in next sc) around: 48 sc.

Rnds 9-12: Sc in each sc around.

Rnd 13: (Sc in next 6 sc, decrease) around: 42 sc.

Rnd 14: (Sc in next 5 sc, decrease) around: 36 sc.

Rnd 15: (Sc in next 4 sc, decrease) around: 30 sc.

Rnd 16: (Sc in next 3 sc, decrease) around: 24 sc.

Rnd 17: (Sc in next 2 sc, decrease) around: 18 sc.

Rnd 18: (Sc in next sc, decrease) around: 12 sc.

Stuff head firmly with polyester fiberfill.

Rnd 19: Decrease around: 6 sc.

Rnd 20: (Wrong side)**:** Slip st in next sc, ch 3 **(counts as first dc, now and throughout)**, **turn**; 2 dc in same st, 3 dc in each sc around; join with slip st to first dc: 18 dc.

Rnd 21: Ch 3, dc in same st and in next dc, (2 dc in next dc, dc in next dc) around; join with slip st to first dc: 27 dc.

Rnd 22: Ch 3, dc in same st, 2 dc in each of next 2 dc, add pearl, (2 dc in each of next 3 dc, add pearl) around; join with slip st to first dc: 54 dc.

Rnd 23: Ch 3, dc in same st, 2 dc in next dc and in each dc around; join with slip st to first dc: 108 dc.

Rnd 24: Ch 3, dc in next 2 dc, add pearl, (dc in next 3 dc, add pearl) around; join with slip st to first dc.

Rnd 25: Ch 3, dc in next dc and in each dc around; join with slip st to first dc.

Rnd 26: Ch 3, dc in same st, 2 dc in each of next 4 dc, skip next 42 dc, 2 dc in each of next 12 dc, skip next 42 dc, 2 dc in each of next 7 dc; join with slip st to first dc: 48 dc.

Rnd 27: Ch 4 **(counts as first dc plus ch 1, now and throughout)**, (dc in next dc, ch 1) around; join with slip st to first dc.

Rnd 28: Ch 8 **(counts as first dc plus ch 5, now and throughout)**, skip next dc, (dc in next dc, ch 5, skip next dc) around; join with slip st to first dc: 24 dc.

Rnd 29: Ch 5 **(counts as first dc plus ch 2, now and throughout)**, sc in third ch of next ch-5, add pearl, ch 2, ★ dc in next dc, ch 2, sc in third ch of next ch-5, add pearl, ch 2; repeat from ★ around; join with slip st to first dc.

Rnd 30: Ch 8, (dc in next dc, ch 5) around; join with slip st to first dc.

Rnds 31-42: Repeat Rnds 29 and 30, 6 times.

Rnd 43: Slip st in next ch-5 sp, ch 1, (sc, 4 dc, add pearl, 3 dc, sc) in same sp and in each ch-5 sp around; join with slip st to first dc; finish off.

WING EDGING

String 8 pearls onto thread.

With **wrong** side facing, join thread with slip st in first skipped dc on Rnd 25; ch 1, sc in same st, skip next 2 dc, (4 dc, add pearl, 3 dc) in next dc, skip next 2 dc, sc in next dc, ★ skip next dc, (4 dc, add pearl, 3 dc) in next dc, skip next 2 dc, sc in next dc; repeat from ★ 6 times **more**; join with slip st to first sc; finish off.

Repeat for remaining wing.

HALO

String 90 pearls onto thread.

Rnds 1-4: Work same as Rnds 1-4 of Head and Body: 24 sc.

Rnd 5: Slip st in next sc, ch 4, (dc in next sc, ch 1) around; join with slip st to first dc: 24 dc.

Rnd 6: Ch 8, **turn**; skip next dc, (dc in next dc, ch 5, skip next dc) around; join with slip st to first dc: 12 dc.

Rnd 7: Ch 5, sc in third ch of next ch-5, add pearl, ch 2, ★ dc in next dc, ch 2, sc in third ch of next ch-5, add pearl, ch 2; repeat from ★ around; join with slip st to first dc.

Continued on page 106.

Rnd 8: Ch 5, dc in same st, ch 5, dc in next dc, ch 5, ★ (dc, ch 2, dc) in next dc, ch 5, dc in next dc, ch 5; repeat from ★ around; join with slip st to first dc: 18 dc.

Rnd 9: Ch 8, (dc in next dc, ch 2, sc in third ch of next ch-5, add pearl, ch 2) twice, ★ dc in next dc, ch 5, (dc in next dc, ch 2, sc in third ch of next ch-5, add pearl, ch 2) twice; repeat from ★ around; join with slip st to first dc.

Rnd 10: Ch 5, dc in same st, ch 2, sc in third ch of next ch-5, add pearl, ch 2, (dc, ch 2, dc) in next dc, ch 5, dc in next dc, ch 5, ★ (dc, ch 2, dc) in next dc, ch 2, sc in third ch of next ch-5, add pearl, ch 2, (dc, ch 2, dc) in next dc, ch 5, dc in next dc, ch 5; repeat from ★ around; join with slip st to first dc: 30 dc.

Rnd 11: Ch 8, dc in next dc, (ch 5, dc in next dc) twice, ★ (ch 2, sc in third ch of next ch-5, add pearl, ch 2, dc in next dc) twice, (ch 5, dc in next dc) 3 times; repeat from ★ around to last 2 ch-5 sps, ch 2, sc in third ch of next ch-5, add pearl, ch 2, dc in next dc, ch 2, sc in third ch of last ch-5, add pearl, ch 2; join with slip st to first dc.

Rnd 12: Ch 5, sc in third ch of next ch-5, add pearl, ch 2, (dc in next dc, ch 2, sc in third ch of next ch-5, add pearl, ch 2) twice, (dc in next dc, ch 5) twice, ★ (dc in next dc, ch 2, sc in third ch of next ch-5, add pearl, ch 2) 3 times, (dc in next dc, ch 5) twice; repeat from ★ around; join with slip st to first dc.

Rnd 13: Slip st in next ch-2 sp, ch 1, sc in same sp, [(4 dc, add pearl, 3 dc) in next ch-2 sp, sc in next ch-2 sp] twice, (4 dc, add pearl, 3 dc) in next ch-2 sp, (sc, 4 dc, add pearl, 3 dc) in each of next 2 ch-5 sps, ★ [sc in next ch-2 sp, (4 dc, add pearl, 3 dc) in next ch-2 sp] 3 times, (sc, 4 dc, add pearl, 3 dc) in each of next 2 ch-5 sps; repeat from ★ around; join with slip st to first sc; finish off.

FINISHING

See Starching and Blocking, page 124.

Using photo as a guide, glue Halo to Head.

FESTIVE WREATH

*D*isplay this lovely wreath in a window or on the front door to spread your warmest holiday wishes! The vibrant decoration is worked around a metal ring using cheery Christmas colors and is finished with a satin bow.

Finished Size: 8½" in diameter

MATERIALS
Bedspread Weight Cotton Thread (size 10):
    White - 145 yards
    Green - 60 yards
    Red - 30 yards
Steel crochet hook, size 5 (1.90 mm) **or** size needed for gauge
5" Metal ring
Ribbon
Tapestry needle
Optional - spray starch

GAUGE: 16 dc = 2"

STITCH GUIDE

PICOT
Ch 3, (dc, ch 2, slip st) in third ch from hook, (ch 2, dc, ch 2, slip st) twice in same ch.

BAND
Rnd 1 (Right side)**:** With White, (ch 3, dc in third ch from hook) 120 times; being careful not to twist chs, join with slip st to first ch to form a ring.

Note: Loop a short piece of thread around any stitch to mark Rnd 1 as **right** side.

Rnd 2: Slip st in first ch-2 sp, ch 1, sc in same sp, (ch 3, sc in next ch-2 sp) around, ch 1, hdc in first sc to form last sp: 120 sps.

Rnds 3 and 4: Ch 1, sc in same sp, (ch 3, sc in next ch-3 sp) around, ch 1, hdc in first sc to form last sp.

Rnd 5: Ch 1, sc in same sp, ch 3, (sc in next ch-3 sp, ch 3) around; join with slip st to first sc, finish off.

Rnd 6: With **right** side facing, join Green with sc in last ch-3 sp made *(see Joining With Sc, page 122)*; work Picot, sc in same ch-3 sp, ★ (ch 3, sc in next ch-3 sp) 3 times, work Picot, sc in same ch-3 sp; repeat from ★ around to last 2 ch-3 sps, ch 3, (sc in next ch-3 sp, ch 3) twice; join with slip st to first sc, finish off: 40 Picots.

Rnd 7: With **right** side facing, join White with sc in last ch-3 sp made (to right of first Picot); working **behind** Picots, (ch 3, sc in next ch-3 sp) around, ch 1, hdc in first sc to form last sp: 120 sps.

Rnd 8: Ch 1, sc in same sp, ch 3, (sc in next ch-3 sp, ch 3) around; join with slip st to first sc, finish off.

Rnd 9: With Red, repeat Rnd 6.

Rnds 10 and 11: Repeat Rnds 7 and 8.

Rnds 12 and 13: Repeat Rnds 6 and 7.

Rnd 14: Repeat Rnd 3.

Rnd 15: Ch 1, sc in same sp, work Picot, sc in same ch-3 sp, ★ (ch 3, sc in next ch-3 sp) 3 times, work Picot, sc in same ch-3 sp; repeat from ★ around to last 2 ch-3 sps, ch 3, (sc in next ch-3 sp, ch 3) twice; join with slip st to first sc, finish off: 40 Picots.

FINISHING

Sew Rnd 4 of Band to ring. Spray back of Wreath with starch if desired. Attach ribbon bow.

POINSETTIA DOILY

The beauty of the traditional Christmas flower is gracefully recreated in our stunning Yuletide doily. This pretty poinsettia will bring holiday spirit to any room!

Finished Size: 16" in diameter

MATERIALS
Bedspread Weight Cotton Thread (size 10):
Red - 90 yards
Ecru- 80 yards
Green - 35 yards
Tan - 10 yards
Steel crochet hook, size 3 (2.10 mm) **or** size needed for gauge

GAUGE: Rnds 1-3 of Center = 3½"

STITCH GUIDE

PICOT
Slip st in third ch from hook.

CENTER
With Tan, ch 6; join with slip st to form a ring.

Rnd 1 (Right side)**:** Ch 1, (sc in ring, ch 4, work Picot, ch 1) 5 times; join with slip st to first sc: 10 ch-1 sps.

Note: Loop a short piece of thread around any stitch to mark Rnd 1 as **right** side.

Rnd 2: Slip st in first ch-1 sp, ch 1, sc in same sp, (ch 6, sc in next ch-1 sp) around, ch 3, dc in first sc to form last ch-6 sp: 10 ch-6 sps.

Rnd 3: Ch 1, sc in same sp, ch 6, work Picot, ch 3, ★ sc in next ch-6 sp, ch 6, work Picot, ch 3; repeat from ★ around; join with slip st to first sc, finish off: 20 ch-3 sps.

Rnd 4: With **right** side facing, join Red with slip st in ch-3 sp **before** first Picot; ch 3 **(counts as first dc, now and throughout)**, dc in same sp, ch 2, (2 dc in next ch-3 sp, ch 2) around; join with slip st to first dc: 20 ch-2 sps.

Rnd 5: Ch 3, dc in next dc, ch 3, (dc, ch 3) twice in next ch-2 sp, ★ dc in next 4 dc, ch 3, (dc, ch 3) twice in next ch-2 sp; repeat from ★ around to last 2 dc, dc in last 2 dc; join with slip st to first dc: 30 ch-3 sps.

Rnd 6: Ch 3, dc in next dc, ch 3, skip next ch-3 sp, 5 dc in next ch-3 sp, ch 3, skip next ch-3 sp, dc in next 2 dc, ch 1, ★ dc in next 2 dc, ch 3, skip next ch-3 sp, 5 dc in next ch-3 sp, ch 3, skip next ch-3 sp, dc in next 2 dc, ch 1; repeat from ★ around; join with slip st to first dc.

Rnds 7 and 8: Ch 3, dc in next dc, ch 3, dc in next 5 dc, ch 3, dc in next 2 dc, ch 1, ★ dc in next 2 dc, ch 3, dc in next 5 dc, ch 3, dc in next 2 dc, ch 1; repeat from ★ around; join with slip st to first dc, do **not** finish off.

FIRST PETAL
Row 1: Ch 3, do **not** turn; dc in next dc, ch 3, dc in next dc, (ch 1, dc in next dc) 4 times, ch 3, dc in next 2 dc, leave remaining sts unworked: 9 dc.

Row 2: Ch 3, **turn**; dc in next dc, ch 3, (sc in next ch-1 sp, ch 3) 4 times, skip next ch-3 sp, dc in last 2 dc.

Row 3: Ch 3, turn; dc in next dc, ch 3, skip next ch-3 sp, (sc in next ch-3 sp, ch 3) 3 times, dc in last 2 dc.

Row 4: Ch 3, turn; dc in next dc, ch 3, skip next ch-3 sp, (sc in next ch-3 sp, ch 3) twice, dc in last 2 dc.

Row 5: Ch 3, turn; dc in next dc, ch 3, skip next ch-3 sp, sc in next ch-3 sp, ch 3, dc in last 2 dc.

Row 6: Ch 2, turn; ★ YO, insert hook in **next** dc, YO and pull up a loop, YO and draw through 2 loops on hook; repeat from ★ 2 times **more**, YO and draw through all 4 loops on hook (point made); finish off.

REMAINING 9 PETALS
Row 1: With **right** side of Center facing, join Red with slip st in next dc on Rnd 8; (ch 3, dc in next dc) twice, (ch 1, dc in next dc) 4 times, ch 3, dc in next 2 dc, leave remaining sts unworked: 9 dc.

Rows 2-6: Work same as First Petal.

FIRST LEAF
Row 1: With **right** side of Center facing, join Green with slip st in any unworked ch-1 sp on Rnd 8 **between** Petals; ch 3, (dc, ch 3, 2 dc) in same sp.

Row 2: Ch 3, turn; dc in next dc, ch 3, dc in next ch-3 sp, (ch 1, dc in same sp) 4 times, ch 3, dc in last 2 dc: 4 ch-1 sps.

Rows 3-7: Work same as Rows 2-6 of First Petal.

Repeat in each unworked ch-1 sp between Petals for remaining 9 Leaves.

BODY

Rnd 1: With **right** side facing and working around Leaves and Petals, join Ecru with slip st in last dc on Row 3 of any Leaf (left side); ch 1, sc in same st, ★ † sc in top of next dc on Row 3 of next Petal, ch 5, (sc in top of next dc, ch 5) twice, sc around point of Petal, (ch 5, sc in top of next dc) 3 times, sc in top of next dc on Row 3 of next Leaf, ch 5, (sc in top of next dc, ch 5) 3 times, sc around point of Leaf †, (ch 5, sc in top of next dc) 4 times; repeat from ★ 8 times **more**, then repeat from † to † once, (ch 5, sc in top of next dc) 3 times, ch 2, dc in first sc to form last ch-5 sp: 140 ch-5 sps.

Rnd 2: Ch 1, sc in same sp, ch 3, sc in next ch-5 sp, (ch 5, sc in next ch-5 sp) 5 times, ch 3, sc in next ch-5 sp, ★ (ch 5, sc in next ch-5 sp) 7 times, ch 3, sc in next ch-5 sp, (ch 5, sc in next ch-5 sp) 5 times, ch 3, sc in next ch-5 sp; repeat from ★ around to last 6 ch-5 sps, (ch 5, sc in next ch-5 sp) 6 times, ch 2, dc in first sc to form last ch-5 sp: 120 ch-5 sps and 20 ch-3 sps.

Rnd 3: Ch 1, sc in same sp, ch 3, skip next ch-3 sp, sc in next ch-5 sp, (ch 5, sc in next ch-5 sp) 4 times, ch 3, skip next ch-3 sp, sc in next ch-5 sp, ★ (ch 5, sc in next ch-5 sp) 6 times, ch 3, skip next ch-3 sp, sc in next ch-5 sp, (ch 5, sc in next ch-5 sp) 4 times, ch 3, skip next ch-3 sp, sc in next ch-5 sp; repeat from ★ around to last 5 ch-5 sps, (ch 5, sc in next ch-5 sp) 5 times, ch 2, dc in first sc to form last ch-5 sp: 100 ch-5 sps and 20 ch-3 sps.

Rnd 4: Ch 1, sc in same sp, ch 3, skip next ch-3 sp, sc in next ch-5 sp, (ch 5, sc in next ch-5 sp) 3 times, ch 3, skip next ch-3 sp, sc in next ch-5 sp, ★ (ch 5, sc in next ch-5 sp) 5 times, ch 3, skip next ch-3 sp, sc in next ch-5 sp, (ch 5, sc in next ch-5 sp) 3 times, ch 3, skip next ch-3 sp, sc in next ch-5 sp; repeat from ★ around to last 4 ch-5 sps, (ch 5, sc in next ch-5 sp) 4 times, ch 2, dc in first sc to form last ch-5 sp: 80 ch-5 sps and 20 ch-3 sps.

Continued on page 110.

Rnd 5: Ch 9 (counts as first tr plus ch 5), skip next ch-3 sp, (tr in next ch-5 sp, ch 5) 3 times, skip next ch-3 sp, tr in next ch-5 sp, (ch 5, sc in next ch-5 sp) 3 times, ★ ch 5, tr in next ch-5 sp, ch 5, skip next ch-3 sp, (tr in next ch-5 sp, ch 5) 3 times, skip next ch-3 sp, tr in next ch-5 sp, (ch 5, sc in next ch-5 sp) 3 times; repeat from ★ around, ch 2, dc in first tr to form last ch-5 sp: 80 ch-5 sps.

Rnd 6: Ch 1, sc in same sp, ch 5, (sc in next ch-5 sp, ch 5) around; join with slip st to first sc, finish off.

Rnd 7: With **right** side facing, join Red with slip st in any ch-5 sp; ch 1, sc in same sp, ch 3, (2 dc, ch 4, work Picot, ch 1, 2 dc) in next ch-5 sp, ch 3, ★ sc in next ch-5 sp, ch 3, (2 dc, ch 4, work Picot, ch 1, 2 dc) in next ch-5 sp, ch 3; repeat from ★ around; join with slip st to first sc, finish off.

See Washing and Blocking, page 124.

DIVINE LITTLE ANGEL

*T*his quick-to-crochet clothespin angel is sure to become a holiday favorite! You'll want to create a multitude of the divine little dolls to trim your tree, share with friends, or decorate gifts.

MATERIALS
Bedspread Weight Cotton Thread (size 10):
  Red - 35 yards
  Cream - 20 yards
Steel crochet hook, size 6 (1.80 mm) **or** size needed for gauge
3³⁄₄" round, slotted clothespin
Craft glue
10" length of ¹⁄₈"w ribbon

GAUGE: 16 dc and 8 rows = 2"

STITCH GUIDE

CLUSTER
★ YO, insert hook in ch indicated, YO and pull up a loop, YO and draw through 2 loops on hook; repeat from ★ once **more**, YO and draw through all 3 loops on hook *(Figs. 12a & b, page 121)*.

DRESS
BODICE
With Red and leaving an 18" length at beginning for Neck Edging, ch 14; being careful not to twist ch, join with slip st to form a ring.

Rnd 1 (Right side)**:** Ch 3 **(counts as first dc, now and throughout)**, dc in same st, 2 dc in next ch, † ch 1, (dc, ch 1) 3 times in next ch, (dc, ch 1) twice in next ch, (dc, ch 1) 3 times in next ch †, 2 dc in each of next 4 chs, repeat from † to † once, 2 dc in each of last 2 chs; join with slip st to first dc: 32 dc.

Note: Loop a short piece of thread around any stitch to mark Rnd 1 as **right** side.

Rnd 2: Ch 3, dc in next 3 dc, ch 1, skip next 9 ch-1 sps (armhole), dc in next 8 dc, ch 1, skip next 9 ch-1 sps (armhole), dc in last 4 dc; join with slip st to first dc, do **not** finish off: 16 dc.

SKIRT
Rnd 1: Ch 6, work Cluster in third ch from hook; working in each dc and in each ch around, dc in next st, ch 3, work Cluster in third ch from hook, † (dc, ch 3, work Cluster in third ch from hook) twice in next st, (dc in next st, ch 3, work Cluster in third ch from hook) 3 times, (dc, ch 3, work Cluster in third ch from hook) twice in next st †, (dc in next st, ch 3, work Cluster in third ch from hook) 4 times, repeat from † to † once, (dc in next st, ch 3, work Cluster in third ch from hook) twice; join with slip st to third ch of beginning ch-6: 22 Clusters.

Rnds 2-6: Ch 6, work Cluster in third ch from hook, ★ dc in next dc, ch 3, work Cluster in third ch from hook; repeat from ★ around; join with slip st to third ch of beginning ch-6.

Rnd 7: With **right** side facing, join Cream with sc in same st as joining *(see Joining With Sc, page 122)*; ch 4, (sc in next dc, ch 4) around; join with slip st to first sc: 22 ch-4 sps.

Rnd 8: Ch 5, slip st in next ch-4 sp, ch 2, ★ dc in next sc, ch 2, slip st in next ch-4 sp, ch 2; repeat from ★ around; join with slip st to third ch of beginning ch-5: 44 ch-2 sps.

Rnd 9: (Slip st in next ch-2 sp, ch 2) around; join with slip st to first slip st, finish off.

WING

Rnd 1: With **right** side facing and working in free loop of ch-1 *(Fig. 20b, page 122)* **and** in skipped ch-1 sps of armhole, join Cream with sc in free loop of ch-1 at underarm; ch 3, sc around post of next dc *(Fig. 15, page 121)*, ch 3, (sc in next ch-1 sp, ch 3) 9 times, sc around post of next dc, ch 1, hdc in first sc to form last ch-3 sp: 12 ch-3 sps.

Rnds 2 and 3: Sc in same sp, (ch 3, sc in next ch-3 sp) around, ch 1, hdc in first sc to form last ch-3 sp.

Rnd 4: Sc in same sp, ch 3, work Cluster in third ch from hook, ★ sc in next ch-3 sp, ch 3, work Cluster in third ch from hook; repeat from ★ around; join with slip st to first sc, finish off.

Repeat for second Wing.

HALO

Rnd 1 (Right side): With Red, ch 2, 8 sc in second ch from hook; join with slip st to first sc.

Rnd 2: Ch 6, work Cluster in third ch from hook, ★ dc in next sc, ch 3, work Cluster in third ch from hook; repeat from ★ around; join with slip st to third ch of beginning ch-6, finish off.

FINISHING
NECK EDGING

With **right** side facing and working in free loops of beginning ch, insert hook in same ch as joining, using beginning length, YO and pull up a loop; ch 1, (slip st in next ch, ch 1) around; join with slip st to first slip st, finish off.

Weave ribbon through sts on Rnd 2 of Bodice.

Using photo as a guide, place Dress on clothespin and glue Halo in place.

HEAVENLY PILLOWS

Bring a little piece of heaven into your home by embellishing bright pillows with crocheted angels. By using different thread weights, our motif works up in three sizes that are perfect for decorating a variety of cushions. The pillows also make glorious gifts!

Finished Size: Size 10 thread - 6½" x 7"
Size 20 thread - 5½" x 6"
Size 30 thread - 4½" x 5"

MATERIALS
Cotton Crochet Thread (size 10, 20, 30):
1 ball
Steel crochet hook,
Size 10 thread - size 6 (1.80 mm)
Size 20 thread - size 8 (1.50 mm)
Size 30 thread - size 10 (1.30 mm)
or size needed for gauge
Sewing needle and thread
Purchased pillow

GAUGE: Size 10 thread, 16 dc = 2"
Size 20 thread, 20 dc = 2"
Size 30 thread, 24 dc = 2"

STITCH GUIDE

DC DECREASE (uses next 2 dc)
★ YO, insert hook in **next** dc, YO and pull up a loop, YO and draw through 2 loops on hook; repeat from ★ once **more**, YO and draw through all three loops on hook **(counts as one dc)**.
SC DECREASE (uses next 2 dc)
Pull up a loop in each of next 2 sts, YO and draw through all 3 loops on hook **(counts as one sc)**.

HEAD AND BODICE
Ch 8.

Row 1: 2 Dc in fourth ch from hook, dc in next 3 chs, 3 dc in last ch: 9 sts.

Row 2 (Right side)**:** Ch 3 **(counts as first dc, now and throughout)**, turn; 2 dc in first dc, dc in next 7 dc, 3 dc in last st: 13 dc.

Note: Loop a short piece of thread around any stitch to mark Row 2 as **right** side.

Rows 3 and 4: Ch 3, turn; dc in next dc and in each dc across.

Row 5: Ch 2, turn; dc in next 10 dc, dc decrease: 11 dc.

Row 6: Ch 1, turn; sc decrease twice, sc in next 3 dc, sc decrease twice: 7 sc.

Rows 7 and 8: Ch 1, turn; sc in each sc across.

Row 9: Ch 3, turn; 2 dc in first sc, 3 dc in each sc across: 21 dc.

Row 10: Ch 3, turn; dc in same st, dc in next dc and in each dc across to last dc, 2 dc in last dc: 23 dc.

Row 11: Ch 3, turn; dc in next 13 dc, place marker around last dc made for Skirt placement, dc in last 9 dc.

Row 12: Ch 1, turn; sc in first dc, (ch 3, skip next dc, sc in next dc) across to last 2 dc, ch 1, skip next dc, hdc in last dc to form last ch-3 sp: 11 ch-3 sps.

Row 13: Ch 1, turn; sc in same sp, ★ ch 3, (dc, ch 1, tr, ch 1, dc) in next ch-3 sp, ch 3, sc in next ch-3 sp; repeat from ★ across.

Row 14: Ch 1, turn; sc in first sc, ★ ch 5, skip next dc, (sc, ch 5, sc) in next tr, ch 5, skip next dc, sc in next sc; repeat from ★ across: finish off.

SKIRT
Row 1: With **right** side facing, fold last 3 rows to **front**, join thread with slip st in marked dc; ch 3, 4 dc in same st, 5 dc in each of next 2 unworked dc, leave remaining dc unworked: 15 dc.

Rows 2 and 3: Ch 4 **(counts as first dc plus ch 1, now and throughout)**, turn; dc in next dc, (ch 1, dc in next dc) across: 14 ch-1 sps.

Row 4: Ch 4, turn; dc in next ch-1 sp, ch 1, dc in next dc, ch 1, dc in next ch-1 sp, (ch 1, dc in next dc) 11 times, (ch 1, dc in next ch-1 sp, ch 1, dc in next dc) twice: 19 dc.

Row 5: Ch 4, turn; dc in next dc, (ch 1, dc in next dc) across: 18 ch-1 sps.

Rows 6-9: Ch 5 **(counts as first dc plus ch 2)**, turn; dc in next dc, (ch 2, dc in next dc) across.

Row 10: Turn; slip st in first ch-2 sp, ch 1, sc in same sp, (ch 5, sc in next ch-2 sp) across to last ch-2 sp, ch 2, dc in last ch-2 sp to form last ch-5 sp: 17 ch-5 sps.

Row 11: Ch 1, turn; sc in same sp, ★ ch 3, (dc, ch 3, tr, ch 3, dc) in next ch-5 sp, ch 3, sc in next ch-5 sp; repeat from ★ across.

Row 12: Ch 1, turn; sc in first sc, ★ ch 3, skip next ch-3 sp, sc in next ch-3 sp, ch 3, dc in next tr, ch 3, sc in next ch-3 sp, ch 3, skip next ch-3 sp, sc in next sc; repeat from ★ across.

Row 13: Ch 1, turn; sc in first sc, ★ ch 5, skip next 2 ch-3 sps, (sc, ch 5, sc) in next dc, ch 5, skip next 2 ch-3 sps, sc in next sc; repeat from ★ across; finish off.

Continued on page 114.

WINGS

Ch 16; join with slip st to form a ring.

Row 1: Ch 4 **(counts as first tr)**, 24 tr in ring; do **not** join: 25 tr.

Row 2 (Right side)**:** Ch 5 **(counts as first tr plus ch 1, now and throughout)**, turn; (tr in next tr, ch 1) 10 times, (tr, ch 4, sc) in next tr, ch 4, sc in next tr, ch 4, (sc, ch 4, tr) in next tr, (ch 1, tr in next tr) across.

Note: Mark Row 2 as **right** side.

Row 3: Ch 6 **(counts as first tr plus ch 2, now and throughout)**, turn; (tr in next tr, ch 2) 10 times, (tr, ch 4, sc) in next tr, ch 4, sc in next sc, ch 9, skip next sc, sc in next sc, ch 4, (sc, ch 4, tr) in next tr, (ch 2, tr in next tr) across.

Row 4: Ch 6, turn; (tr in next tr, ch 2) 10 times, (tr, ch 4, sc) in next tr, ch 4, (sc in next sc, ch 4) twice, working around ch-9 sp, sc in next sc one row **below**, ch 4, (sc in next sc, ch 4) twice, (sc, ch 4, tr) in next tr, (ch 2, tr in next tr) across; do **not** finish off.

FIRST EDGING

Row 1: Ch 1, turn; sc in first tr, (ch 5, sc in next tr) 10 times, ch 2, dc in next tr to form last ch-5 sp, skip next 8 sps, place marker around next tr for Second Edging placement, leave remaining sts unworked: 11 ch-5 sps.

Rows 2-4: Work same as Skirt Rows 11-13.

SECOND EDGING

Row 1: With **wrong** side facing, join thread with slip st in marked tr; ch 1, sc in same st, (ch 5, sc in next tr) 10 times, ch 2, dc in last tr to form last ch-5 sp: 11 ch-5 sps.

Rows 2-4: Work same as Skirt Rows 11-13.

Sew Wings to back of Angel.
Sew to pillow.

TIMELESS TABLECLOTH

*D*rape *your holiday table in beauty and elegance with this timeless tablecloth. Fashioned from hexagonal motifs that are joined as you go, the lacy covering can be made from either size 10 or 20 cotton thread. A delicate border of cluster stitches completes this luxurious piece.*

Finished Size: With size 10 thread, 52" x 69"
With size 20 thread, 55" x 72"

Note: Instructions are written for size 10 and size 20 weight thread. Size 10 is given with size 20 in parentheses. Instructions will be easier to read if you circle all the numbers pertaining to your chosen size. If only one number is given, then it applies to both sizes.

MATERIALS

Cotton Crochet Thread (size 10 or 20):
    19 balls (225 yards per ball)
Steel crochet hook, size 6 (1.80 mm) for size
    10 thread **or** size 8 (1.50 mm) for size 20 thread
    or size needed for gauge

GAUGE: Each Motif = 5(4)" (from point to point)

STITCH GUIDE

BEGINNING CLUSTER
Ch 4, ★ YO twice, insert hook in same sp, YO and pull up a loop, (YO and draw through 2 loops on hook) twice; repeat from ★ 3 times **more**, YO and draw through all 5 loops on hook *(Figs. 12a & b, page 121)*.

CLUSTER
★ YO twice, insert hook in st or sp indicated, YO and pull up a loop, (YO and draw through 2 loops on hook) twice; repeat from ★ 4 times **more**, YO and draw through all 6 loops on hook.

PICOT
Slip st in fourth ch from hook.

BEGINNING 3-TR CLUSTER
Ch 4, ★ YO twice, insert hook in same sp, YO and pull up a loop, (YO and draw through 2 loops on hook) twice; repeat from ★ once **more**, YO and draw through all 3 loops on hook.

3-TR CLUSTER
★ YO twice, insert hook in st or sp indicated, YO and pull up a loop, (YO and draw through 2 loops on hook) twice; repeat from ★ 2 times **more**, YO and draw through all 4 loops on hook.

Continued on page 116.

FIRST MOTIF

Rnd 1 (Right side): Ch 7, dc in seventh ch from hook, ch 3, (dc, ch 3) 4 times in same ch; join with slip st to fourth ch of beginning ch-7: 6 ch-3 sps.

Note: Loop a short piece of thread around any stitch to mark Rnd 1 as **right** side.

Rnd 2: Slip st in first ch-3 sp, ch 1, (sc, ch 4, 5 tr, ch 4, sc) in same sp and in each ch-3 sp around; join with slip st to first sc.

Rnd 3: Slip st in first 4 chs, sc in same ch and in next 2 tr, (sc, ch 4, sc) in next tr, sc in next 2 tr and in top of next ch-4, ★ ch 3, sc in top of next ch-4 and in next 2 tr, (sc, ch 4, sc) in next tr, sc in next 2 tr and in top of next ch-4; repeat from ★ around, ch 1, hdc in first sc to form last ch-3 sp: 48 sc and 6 ch-3 sps.

Rnd 4: Ch 5 **(counts as first dc plus ch 2)**, (dc, ch 2, dc) in top of same hdc, ch 3, (dc, ch 3, dc) in next ch-4 sp, ch 3, ★ [dc, (ch 2, dc) twice] in center ch of next ch-3, ch 3, (dc, ch 3, dc) in next ch-4 sp, ch 3; repeat from ★ around; join with slip st to first dc: 30 dc and 30 sps.

Rnd 5: Slip st in first sp, work beginning Cluster, ★ † ch 3, work Cluster in next dc, ch 3, work Cluster in next ch-2 sp, ch 5, skip next ch-3 sp, (tr, ch 3, tr) in center ch of next ch-3, ch 5, skip next ch-3 sp †, work Cluster in next ch-2 sp; repeat from ★ 4 times **more**, then repeat † to † once; join with slip st to top of beginning Cluster: 18 Clusters.

Rnd 6: Slip st in first sp, work beginning Cluster, ★ † ch 7, work Picot, ch 3, work Cluster in next ch-3 sp, ch 7, (sc, ch 4, work Picot, sc) in next ch-3 sp, ch 7 †, work Cluster in next ch-3 sp; repeat from ★ 4 times **more**, then repeat from † to † once; join with slip st to top of beginning Cluster, finish off.

REMAINING MOTIFS

Tablecloth is assembled by joining 16(20) Motifs into a center strip *(Fig. 1)*, then by joining additional Motifs to each side of center strip until outside strips have 10(12) Motifs.

Fig. 1

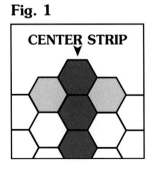

Rnds 1-5: Work same as First Motif.

Rnd 6: Work One, Two, or Three Side Joining.

ONE SIDE JOINING

Slip st in first sp, work beginning Cluster, ★ ch 7, work Picot, ch 3, work Cluster in next ch-3 sp, ch 7, (sc, ch 4, work Picot, sc) in next ch-3 sp, ch 7, work Cluster in next ch-3 sp; repeat from ★ 3 times **more**, ch 3, holding Motifs with **wrong** sides together, slip st in corresponding Picot of **previous** Motif *(Fig. 22, page 120)*, ch 3, work Cluster in next ch-3 sp of **new Motif**, ch 7, sc in next ch-3 sp, ch 2, slip st in next Picot on **previous Motif**, ch 2, sc in same ch-3 sp on **new Motif**, ch 7, work Cluster in next ch-3 sp, ch 3, slip st in next Picot on **previous Motif**, ch 3, work Cluster in next ch-3 sp on **new Motif**, ch 7, (sc, ch 4, work Picot, sc) in next ch-3 sp, ch 7; join with slip st to top of beginning Cluster, finish off.

TWO SIDE JOINING

Slip st in first sp, work beginning Cluster, ★ ch 7, work Picot, ch 3, work Cluster in next ch-3 sp, ch 7, (sc, ch 4, work Picot, sc) in next ch-3 sp, ch 7, work Cluster in next ch-3 sp; repeat from ★ 2 times **more**, ch 3, holding Motifs with **wrong** sides together, slip st in corresponding Picot of **previous Motif**, ch 3, work Cluster in next ch-3 sp of **new Motif**, † ch 7, sc in next ch-3 sp, ch 2, slip st in next Picot on **previous Motif**, ch 2, sc in same ch-3 sp on **new Motif**, ch 7, work Cluster in next ch-3 sp, ch 3, slip st in next Picot on **previous Motif**, ch 3, work Cluster in next ch-3 sp on **new Motif** †, repeat from † to † once **more**, ch 7, (sc, ch 4, work Picot, sc) in next ch-3 sp, ch 7; join with slip st to top of beginning Cluster, finish off.

THREE SIDE JOINING

Slip st in first sp, work beginning Cluster, ★ ch 7, work Picot, ch 3, work Cluster in next ch-3 sp, ch 7, (sc, ch 4, work Picot, sc) in next ch-3 sp, ch 7, work Cluster in next ch-3 sp; repeat from ★ once **more**, ch 3, holding Motifs with **wrong** sides together, slip st in corresponding Picot of **previous Motif**, ch 3, work Cluster in next ch-3 sp of **new Motif**, † ch 7, sc in next ch-3 sp, ch 2, slip st in next Picot on **previous Motif**, ch 2, sc in same ch-3 sp on **new Motif**, ch 7, work Cluster in next ch-3 sp, ch 3, slip st in next Picot on **previous Motif**, ch 3, work Cluster in next ch-3 sp on **new Motif** †, repeat from † to † 2 times **more**, ch 7, (sc, ch 4, work Picot, sc) in next ch-3 sp, ch 7; join with slip st to top of beginning Cluster, finish off.

EDGING

Rnd 1: With **right** side facing, join thread with slip st in ch-7 sp at point A on last strip *(Fig. 2)*; ch 6, tr in same sp, (ch 2, tr in same sp) 7 times, ch 3, ★ † tr in next ch-7 sp, (ch 2, tr in same sp) 8 times, ch 3, sc in next Picot, ch 3, tr in next ch-7 sp, (ch 2, tr in same sp) 8 times, ch 3, [tr in next ch-7 sp, (ch 2, tr in same sp) 4 times, ch 3] twice †, repeat from † to † across to next corner Motif, tr in next ch-7 sp, (ch 2, tr in same sp) 8 times, ch 3, sc in next Picot, ch 3, tr in next ch-7 sp, (ch 2, tr in same sp) 8 times, ch 3; repeat from ★ 4 times **more**, then repeat from † to † across to last ch-7 sp on first corner Motif, tr in last ch-7 sp, (ch 2, tr in same sp) 8 times, ch 3, sc in last Picot, ch 3; join with slip st to fourth ch of beginning ch-6.

Rnd 2: Slip st in first ch-2 sp, work beginning 3-tr Cluster, (ch 3, work 3-tr Cluster in next ch-2 sp) 7 times, ★ † skip next ch-3 sp, [work 3-tr Cluster in next ch-2 sp, (ch 3, work 3-tr Cluster in next ch-2 sp) 7 times] twice, [skip next ch-3 sp, work 3-tr Cluster in next ch-2 sp, (ch 3, work 3-tr Cluster in next ch-2 sp) 3 times] twice †, repeat from † to † across to next corner Motif, skip next ch-3 sp, [work 3-tr Cluster in next ch-2 sp, (ch 3, work 3-tr Cluster in next ch-2 sp) 7 times] twice; repeat from ★ 4 times **more**, then repeat from † to † across to first corner Motif, skip next ch-3 sp, work 3-tr Cluster in next ch-2 sp, (ch 3, work 3-tr Cluster in next ch-2 sp) 7 times; join with slip st to top of beginning 3-tr Cluster.

Rnd 3: Slip st in first ch-3 sp, ch 1, sc in same sp, [ch 8, skip next ch-3 sp, work 3-tr Cluster in next ch-3 sp, (ch 3, work 3-tr Cluster in next ch-3 sp) twice, ch 8, skip next ch-3 sp, sc in next ch-3 sp, ch 5, sc in next ch-3 sp] 3 times, ch 5, skip next 3 Clusters, tr in sp **before** next Cluster, ch 5, skip next 2 ch-3 sps, sc in next ch-3 sp, ch 5, sc in next ch-3 sp, ★ † [ch 8, skip next ch-3 sp, work 3-tr Cluster in next ch-3 sp, (ch 3, work 3-tr Cluster in next ch-3 sp) twice, ch 8, skip next ch-3 sp, sc in next ch-3 sp, ch 5, sc in next ch-3 sp] twice, ch 5, skip next 3 Clusters, tr in sp **before** next Cluster, ch 5, skip next 2 ch-3 sps, sc in next ch-3 sp, ch 5, sc in next ch-3 sp †, repeat from † to † across to next corner Motif, [ch 8, skip next ch-3 sp, work 3-tr Cluster in next ch-3 sp, (ch 3, work 3-tr Cluster in next ch-3 sp) twice, ch 8, skip next ch-3 sp, sc in next ch-3 sp, ch 5, sc in next ch-3 sp] 4 times, ch 5, skip next 3 Clusters, tr in sp **before** next Cluster, ch 5, skip next 2 ch-3 sps, sc in next ch-3 sp, ch 5, sc in next ch-3 sp; repeat from ★ 4 times **more**, then repeat from † to † across to first corner Motif, ch 8, skip next ch-3 sp, work 3-tr Cluster in next ch-3 sp, (ch 3, work 3-tr Cluster in next ch-3 sp) twice, ch 8, skip next ch-3 sp, sc in next ch-3 sp, ch 2, dc in first sc to form last ch-5 sp.

Rnd 4: Work beginning 3-tr Cluster, ch 8, work 3-tr Cluster in next ch-3 sp, ch 7, slip st in fifth ch from hook, ch 2, work 3-tr Cluster in next ch-3 sp, ch 8, [in next ch-5 sp work (3-tr Cluster, ch 7, slip st in fifth ch from hook, ch 2, 3-tr Cluster), ch 8, work 3-tr Cluster in next ch-3 sp, ch 7, slip st in fifth ch from hook, ch 2, work 3-tr Cluster in next ch-3 sp, ch 8] twice, (3 tr, ch 5, slip st in fifth ch from hook, 3 tr) in next ch-5 sp, ch 5, sc in next tr, ch 5, skip next ch-5 sp, (3 tr, ch 5, slip st in fifth ch from hook, 3 tr) in next ch-5 sp, ch 8, ★ † work 3-tr Cluster in next ch-3 sp, ch 7, slip st in fifth ch from hook, ch 2, work 3-tr Cluster in next ch-3 sp, ch 8, work (3-tr Cluster, ch 7, slip st in fifth ch from hook, ch 2, 3-tr Cluster) in next ch-5 sp, ch 8, work 3-tr Cluster in next ch-3 sp, ch 7, slip st in fifth ch from hook, ch 2, work 3-tr Cluster in next ch-3 sp, ch 8, (3 tr, ch 5, slip st in fifth ch from hook, 3 tr) in next ch-5 sp, ch 5, sc in next tr, ch 5, skip next ch-5 sp, (3 tr, ch 5, slip st in fifth ch from hook, 3 tr) in next ch-5 sp, ch 8 †, repeat from † to † across to next corner Motif, work 3-tr Cluster in next ch-3 sp, ch 7, slip st in fifth ch from hook, ch 2, work 3-tr Cluster in next ch-3 sp, ch 8, [work (3-tr Cluster, ch 7, slip st in fifth ch from hook, ch 2, 3-tr Cluster) in next ch-5 sp, ch 8, work 3-tr Cluster in next ch-3 sp, ch 7, slip st in fifth ch from hook, ch 2, work 3-tr Cluster in next ch-3 sp, ch 8] 3 times, (3 tr, ch 5, slip st in fifth ch from hook, 3 tr) in next ch-5 sp, ch 5, sc in next tr, ch 5, skip next ch-5 sp, (3 tr, ch 5, slip st in fifth ch from hook, 3 tr) in next ch-5 sp, ch 8; repeat from ★ 4 times **more**, then repeat from † to † across to first corner Motif, work 3-tr Cluster in next ch-3 sp, ch 7, slip st in fifth ch from hook, ch 2, work 3-tr Cluster in next ch-3 sp, ch 8, work 3-tr Cluster in same sp as beginning Cluster, ch 7, slip st in fifth ch from hook, ch 2; join with slip st to top of beginning Cluster, finish off.

Fig. 2

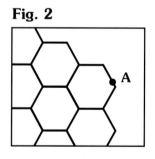

117

GENERAL INSTRUCTIONS

ABBREVIATIONS

BLO	Back Loop(s) Only
BPdc	Back Post double crochet(s)
ch(s)	chain(s)
dc	double crochet(s)
dtr	double treble crochet(s)
FLO	Front Loop(s) Only
FPdc	Front Post double crochet(s)
hdc	half double crochet(s)
htr	half treble crochet(s)
mm	millimeters
Rnd(s)	Round(s)
sc	single crochet(s)
sp(s)	space(s)
st(s)	stitch(es)
tr	treble crochet(s)
tr tr	triple treble crochet(s)
YO	yarn over

★ — work instructions following ★ as many **more** times as indicated in addition to the first time.

† to † — work all instructions from first † to second † **as many** times as specified.

( ) or [ ] — work enclosed instructions **as many** times as specified by the number immediately following **or** work all enclosed instructions in the stitch or space indicated **or** contains explanatory remarks.

GAUGE

Correct gauge is essential for proper size. Hook size given in instructions is merely a guide and should never be used without first making a sample swatch approximately 2" square in the stitch, thread, and hook specified. Or, if piece is worked in rounds, make a sample swatch of the rounds indicated in the thread and hook specified. Then measure the swatch, counting your stitches and rows or rounds carefully. If your swatch is smaller than specified, try again with a larger size hook; if larger, try again with a smaller size. Keep trying until you find the size that will give you the specified gauge. DO NOT HESITATE TO CHANGE HOOK SIZE TO OBTAIN CORRECT GAUGE.

THREAD

There are many types, weights (or sizes), and colors of crochet thread available. The type usually indicates the size, but it can also refer to texture, ranging from smooth to coarse or from plain to metallic, or refer to the composition — crochet thread can contain as many as six cords that may be twisted loosely or tightly. The type of thread you choose to use will depend primarily on the weight (or size) recommended in the instructions and on the finished look you desire.

Thread weights (or sizes) range from a thick size 3 to a thin, very delicate size 150. **The higher the number, the finer the thickness of the thread.** The most commonly used thread is bedspread weight cotton thread, size 10. This size is featured in many of the designs throughout this book. The Heavenly Pillows, page 112, feature sizes 20 and 30, which are more delicate threads; Always remember to check the label for the dye lot number and to purchase enough of one color from the same dye lot to complete your project. The following list includes some of brands of bedspread weight cotton that may be used for the designs in this book:

Anchor "Mercer Crochet"
DMC "Baroque"
DMC "Cebelia"
DMC "Cordonnet"
Grandma's Best
J. & P. Coats "Knit-Cro-Sheen"
J. & P. Coats "South Maid"
Lily "Daisy"
Opera

HOLDING THE THREAD

If you are a beginning crocheter or if you usually crochet with yarn, it may require some practice for you to adjust to holding thread. Try wrapping the thread around your little finger once or twice to help you obtain or maintain the correct gauge. Don't hesitate to experiment with holding the thread in different ways to find the method that allows you to control the thread and still produce firm, uniform stitches.

HOOK SIZES

Crochet hooks used for thread work are made of steel, bone, or wood, the most popular of which is the steel hook. Sizes range from size 00 (3.50 mm) to a very small size 14 (.75 mm) and, as in thread sizes, **the higher the size number, the smaller the hook**.

BASIC STITCH GUIDE

CHAIN
(abbreviated ch)
To work a chain stitch, begin with a slip knot on the hook. Bring the yarn **over** hook from back to front, catching the yarn with the hook and turning the hook slightly toward you to keep the yarn from slipping off. Draw the yarn through the slip knot *(Fig. 1)* **(first chain st made)**.

Fig. 1

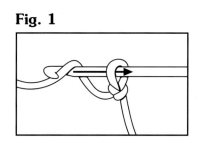

WORKING INTO THE CHAIN
When beginning a first row of crochet in a chain, always skip the first ch from the hook and work into the second ch from the hook (for single crochet), third chain from the hook (for half double crochet), fourth chain from the hook (for double crochet), etc. *(Fig. 2a)*.

Fig. 2a

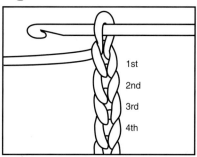

Method 1: Insert hook into back ridge of each chain *(Fig. 2b)*.
Method 2: Insert hook under top two strands of each chain *(Fig. 2c)*.

Fig. 2b   **Fig. 2c**

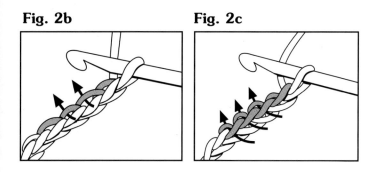

SLIP STITCH
(abbreviated slip st)
This stitch is used to attach new yarn, to join work, or to move the yarn across a group of stitches without adding height. Insert hook in stitch or space indicated, YO and draw through stitch **and** through loop on hook *(Fig. 3)*.

Fig. 3

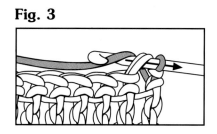

MAKING A BEGINNING RING
Chain amount indicated in instructions. Being careful not to twist chain, slip stitch in first chain to form a ring *(Fig. 4)*.

Fig. 4

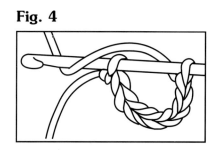

SINGLE CROCHET
(abbreviated sc)
Insert hook in stitch or space indicated, YO and pull up a loop, YO and draw through both loops on hook *(Fig. 5)*.

Fig. 5

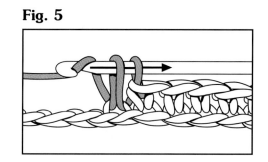

HALF DOUBLE CROCHET
(abbreviated hdc)

YO, insert hook in stitch or space indicated, YO and pull up a loop (3 loops on hook), YO and draw through all 3 loops on hook *(Fig. 6)*.

Fig. 6

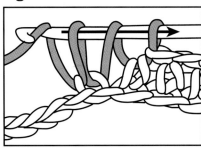

DOUBLE CROCHET
(abbreviated dc)

YO, insert hook in stitch or space indicated, YO and pull up a loop (3 loops on hook), YO and draw through 2 loops on hook *(Fig. 7a)*, YO and draw through remaining 2 loops on hook *(Fig. 7b)*.

Fig. 7a   **Fig. 7b**

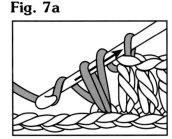

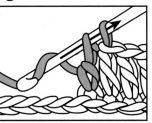

HALF TREBLE CROCHET
(abbreviated htr)

YO twice, insert hook in stitch or space indicated, YO and pull up a loop (4 loops on hook), YO and draw through 2 loops on hook *(Fig. 8a)*, YO and draw through all 3 loops on hook *(Fig. 8b)*.

Fig. 8a   **Fig. 8b**

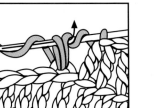
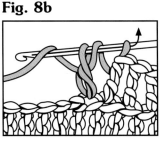

TREBLE CROCHET
(abbreviated tr)

YO twice, insert hook in stitch or space indicated, YO and pull up a loop (4 loops on hook) *(Fig. 9a)*, (YO and draw through 2 loops on hook) 3 times *(Fig. 9b)*.

Fig. 9a   **Fig. 9b**

DOUBLE TREBLE CROCHET
(abbreviated dtr)

YO 3 times, insert hook in stitch or space indicated, YO and pull up a loop (5 loops on hook) *(Fig. 10a)*, (YO and draw through 2 loops on hook) 4 times *(Fig. 10b)*.

Fig. 10a   **Fig. 10b**

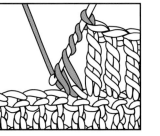

TRIPLE TREBLE CROCHET
(abbreviated tr tr)

YO 4 times, insert hook in stitch or space indicated, YO and pull up a loop (6 loops on hook) *(Fig. 11a)*, (YO and draw through 2 loops on hook) 5 times *(Fig. 11b)*.

Fig. 11a   **Fig. 11b**

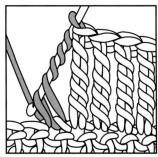

PATTERN STITCHES

CLUSTER

A Cluster can be worked all in the same stitch or space *(Figs. 12a & b)* or across several stitches *(Figs. 12c & d)*.

Fig. 12a

Fig. 12b

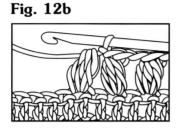

Fig. 12c

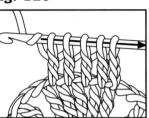

Fig. 12d

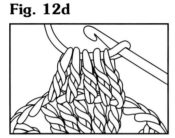

POPCORN

5 Dc in next dc, drop loop from hook, insert hook in first dc of 5-dc group, hook dropped loop and draw through *(Fig. 13)*.

Fig. 13

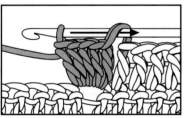

PUFF STITCH

★ YO, insert hook in stitch indicated, YO and pull up a loop even with loop on hook; repeat from ★ as many as instructed, YO and draw through all loops on hook *(Fig. 14)*.

Fig. 14

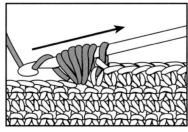

POST STITCH

Work around post of stitch indicated, inserting hook in direction of arrow *(Fig. 15)*.

Fig. 15

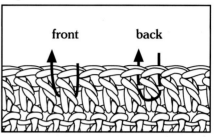

front   back

FRONT POST DOUBLE CROCHET
(abbreviated FPdc)

YO, insert hook from **front** to **back** around post of stitch indicated *(Fig. 15)*, YO and pull up a loop (3 loops on hook) *(Fig. 16)*, (YO and draw through 2 loops on hook) twice.

Fig. 16

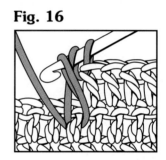

BACK POST DOUBLE CROCHET
(abbreviated BPdc)

YO, insert hook from **back** to **front** around post of stitch indicated *(Fig. 15)*, YO and pull up a loop (3 loops on hook) *(Fig. 17)*, (YO and draw through 2 loops on hook) twice.

Fig. 17

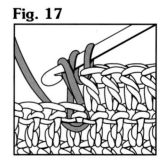

STITCHING TIPS

HOW TO DETERMINE THE RIGHT SIDE

Most designs are made with the **front** of the stitch as the **right** side. Notice that the **front** of the stitches is smooth *(Fig. 18a)* and the **back** of the stitches is bumpy *(Fig. 18b)*. For easy identification, it may be helpful to loop a short piece of thread around any stitch to mark **right** side.

Fig. 18a

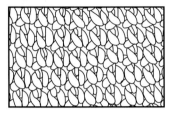

Fig. 18b

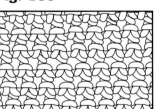

MULTIPLES

The multiple of chains plus the number of extra chains needed for the foundation row is given in some patterns. This enables you to make the piece any size you want by determining the exact number of stitches evenly divisible by the multiple.

For example, a multiple of 6 chains would require 6, 12, 18, 24, etc., chains for the first row. A multiple of 6 chains plus 2 would require 8, 14, 20, 26, etc., chains for the first row.

FILET CROCHET

Filet Crochet, which is also called the Square or Net Stitch, is a combination of blocks of double crochets and spaces of chain stitches. On most charts, the blocks are represented by solid squares or by an X, and the spaces are represented by open squares. Charts are usually worked from right to left on right side rows and from left to right on wrong side rows. Gauge is extremely important to achieve the desired design in Filet crochet. If your rows are too tall or if you have too few stitches per inch, your design will be out of proportion. It will be well worth your time to check your gauge by making several swatches *(see Gauge, page 118)*. For best results, work Filet Crochet firmly and evenly *(see Holding the Thread, page 118)*.

MARKERS

Markers are used to help distinguish the beginning of each round being worked. Place a 2" scrap piece of thread around the first stitch of each round, moving marker after each round is complete. Remove when no longer needed.

JOINING WITH SC

When instructed to join with sc, begin with a slip knot on hook. Insert hook in stitch or space indicated, YO and pull up a loop, YO and draw through both loops on hook.

BACK OR FRONT LOOP ONLY

Work only in loop(s) indicated by arrow *(Fig. 19)*.

Fig. 19

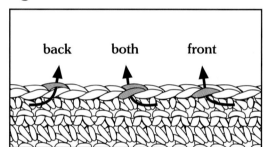

FREE LOOPS

After working in Back or Front Loops Only on a row or round there will be a ridge of unused loops. These are called the free loops. Later, when instructed to work in the free loops of the same row or round, work in these loops *(Fig. 20a)*.

When instructed to work in free loops of a beginning chain, work in loop indicated by arrow *(Fig. 20b)*.

Fig. 20a

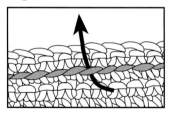

Fig. 20b

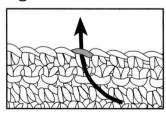

ADDING ON DC

When instructed to add on dc at the end of a row, YO, insert hook into base of last dc made *(Fig. 21)*, YO and pull up a loop, YO and draw through one loop on hook, (YO and draw through 2 loops on hook) twice. Repeat as many times as instructed.

Fig. 21

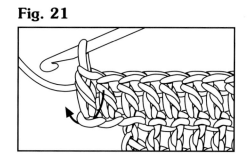

NO-SEW JOINING

Hold Motifs with wrong sides together. Work slip st into stitch or space as indicated *(Fig. 22)*.

Fig. 22

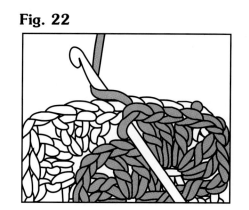

FINISHING

WHIPSTITCH

With **wrong** sides together, sew through both pieces once to secure the beginning of the seam, leaving an ample yarn end to weave in later. Insert the needle from **front** to **back** through **both** loops of **each** piece *(Fig. 23)*. Bring the needle around and insert it from **front** to **back** through the next loops of **both** pieces.

Repeat along the edge, being careful to match stitches and rows. Continue in this manner across, keeping sewing yarn fairly loose and being careful to match stitches.

Fig. 23

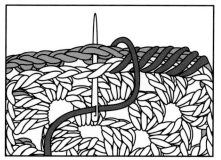

TASSEL

Cut a piece of cardboard 3" wide and as long as you want your finished tassel to be. Wind a double strand of thread around the cardboard approximately 12 times. Cut an 18" length of thread and insert it under all of the strands at the top of the cardboard; pull up **tightly** and tie securely. Leave the thread ends long enough to attach the tassel. Cut the thread at the opposite end of the cardboard; remove cardboard *(Fig. 24a)*. Cut a 6" length of thread and wrap it **tightly** around the tassel twice, $1/2$" below the top *(Fig. 24b)*; tie securely. Trim the ends.

Fig. 24a

Fig. 24b

WASHING

For a more professional look, thread projects should be washed and blocked. Using a mild detergent and warm water and being careful not to rub, twist, or wring, gently squeeze suds through the piece. Rinse several times in cool, clear water. Roll piece in a clean terry towel and gently press out the excess moisture.

BLOCKING

Lay piece on a flat surface and shape to proper size; where needed, pin in place using stainless steel pins. Allow to dry **completely**. Doilies can be spray starched for extra crispness.

STARCHING AND BLOCKING TIPS

1. If using the same fabric stiffener for both white and colored items, starch the white items first in case thread dye bleeds into the solution.

2. A good blocking board can make pinning easier. You can use heavy cardboard, an ironing board, ceiling board, etc.

3. Stainless steel pins with balls on the end are easier on the fingertips. Fabric stiffener will permanently damage pins used for sewing. These can be set aside for all starching projects.

4. Fabric stiffener can be returned to the bottle after starching if it has not been contaminated with particles and dye. Clip one corner of the bag, then squeeze the bag, forcing the solution to flow into the bottle.

5. An acrylic spray can be used after starching to protect the piece from heat and humidity.

Note: Refer to the following instructions for each specific project.

BUGGY
(Shown on page 91)

1. Wash piece(s) (*see Washing, first column*).

2. Lay piece(s) flat and allow to dry completely.

3. Pour fabric stiffener into resealable plastic bag. Do **not** dilute stiffener. *Note:* This method is permanent and will not wash out.

4. Immerse Buggy pieces in fabric stiffener; remove air and seal the bag. Work solution thoroughly into pieces. Let soak several hours or overnight.

5. Trace two Side patterns and 4 Wheel patterns.

6. Place patterns on blocking board (making sure one Side pattern is reversed) and cover with plastic wrap.

7. Cover cardboard square and cylinder with plastic wrap.

8. Remove pieces from stiffener and squeeze to remove excess; blot with a paper towel several times to remove excess from holes.

9. With **right** side facing, pin Sides and Wheels over patterns.

10. With **right** side facing, pin Middle over cylinder.

11. With **right** side facing, center and pin handle to edge of cardboard square.

12. Allow items to dry **completely**; remove pins.

13. Using photo as a guide, glue Sides to Middle, Wheels to Sides, and Handle to Sides.

BOOTIE
(Shown on page 91)

1. Follow Steps 1 and 2 of Buggy instructions, above.

2. Pour fabric stiffener into resealable plastic bag. Do **not** dilute stiffener. *Note:* This method is permanent and will not wash out.

3. Immerse Bootie in fabric stiffener; remove air and seal the bag. Work solution thoroughly into pieces. Let soak several hours or overnight.

4. Cover blocking board with plastic wrap.

5. Remove Bootie from stiffener and squeeze to remove excess; blot with a paper towel several times to remove excess from holes.

6. Stuff Bootie with plastic wrap and shape as desired.

7. Allow Bootie to dry **completely**.

POTPOURRI BASKETS

(Shown on page 101)

1. Follow Steps 1 and 2 of Buggy instructions, page 124.

2. Pour fabric stiffener into resealable plastic bag. Do **not** dilute stiffener. *Note:* This method is permanent and will not wash out.

3. Immerse Basket in fabric stiffener; remove air and seal the bag. Work solution thoroughly into piece. Let soak several hours or overnight.

4. Draw a line around can 2" from bottom. Place can upside down and cover with plastic wrap.

5. Remove Basket from stiffener and squeeze to remove excess; blot with a paper towel several times to remove excess from holes.

6. With **right** side facing, place Basket over can, matching top Basket to line around can.

7. Allow Basket to dry **completely**.

HEIRLOOM ANGEL

(Shown on page 105)

1. Follow Steps 1 and 2 of Buggy instructions, page 124.

2. Pour fabric stiffener into resealable plastic bag. Do **not** dilute stiffener. *Note:* This method is permanent and will not wash out.

3. Immerse pieces in fabric stiffener; remove air and seal the bag. Work solution thoroughly into pieces. Let soak several hours or overnight.

4. Cover cone and blocking board with plastic wrap.

5. Remove pieces from stiffener and squeeze to remove excess; blot with a paper towel several times to remove excess from holes.

6. With **right** side facing, place Angel over cone, pinning at regular intervals.

7. Stuff Wings with plastic wrap and shape as desired.

8. With **right** side facing, pin Halo to blocking board.

9. Allow pieces to dry **completely**; remove pins.

SO-PRETTY SNOWFLAKES

(Shown on page 103)

1. Follow Steps 1 and 2 of Buggy instructions, page 124.

2. Pour fabric stiffener into resealable plastic bag. Do **not** dilute stiffener. *Note:* This method is permanent and will not wash out.

3. Immerse pieces in fabric stiffener; remove air and seal the bag. Work solution thoroughly into pieces. Let soak several hours or overnight.

4. Trace 3 patterns for each Snowflake by laying tracing paper over the diagram, page 127, and drawing **all** lines.

5. Fold 2 of the patterns in half along dotted line.

6. Cut three 4" x 8" pieces of heavy cardboard. Tape cardboard together along 8" sides to form a triangular tube.

7. Lay the flat blocking pattern on a blocking board. Lay the two folded blocking patterns over the triangular tube; cover all patterns with plastic wrap.

8. Remove Snowflakes from stiffener and squeeze to remove excess; blot with a paper towel several times to remove excess from holes.

9. With **right** side facing, place 2 Snowflakes over triangular tube and pin in place, making sure curved parts are smooth, straight parts are straight, and symmetrical components within the Snowflakes are equal.

10. Remove last Snowflake from stiffener and squeeze to remove excess; blot with a paper towel several times to remove excess from holes.

11. With **right** side facing, pin remaining Snowflake over pattern.

12. Allow to dry **completely**; remove pins.

13. Glue one folded piece to each side of the flat Snowflake *(Fig. 1)*. Allow to dry.

Fig. 1

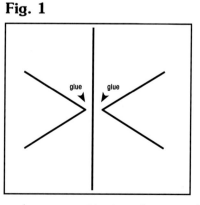

14. Make loop hangers using translucent nylon thread.

SNOWFLAKES
(Shown on pages 96 and 97)

1. Follow Steps 1 and 2 of Buggy instructions, page 124.

2. Pour fabric stiffener into resealable plastic bag. Do **not** dilute stiffener. *Note:* This method is permanent and will not wash out.

3. Immerse Snowflakes in fabric stiffener; remove air and seal the bag. Work solution thoroughly into pieces. Let soak several hours or overnight.

4. Trace pattern for each Snowflake by laying tracing paper over the diagram, page 127, and drawing solid lines.

5. Place pattern on blocking board and cover with plastic wrap.

6. Remove Snowflakes from stiffener and squeeze to remove excess; blot with a paper towel several times to remove excess from holes.

7. With **right** side facing, pin Snowflakes over patterns, making sure curved parts are smooth, straight parts are straight, and symmetrical components within each Snowflake are equal.

8. Allow to dry **completely**; remove pins.

9. Make loop hangers using translucent nylon thread.

RING BEARER'S PILLOW
(Shown on page 48)

1. Follow Steps 1 and 2 of Buggy instructions, page 124.

2. Pour fabric stiffener into resealable plastic bag. Do **not** dilute stiffener. *Note:* This method is permanent and will not wash out.

3. Immerse Bells in fabric stiffener; remove air and seal the bag. Work solution thoroughly into pieces. Let soak several hours or overnight.

4. Cover blocking board with plastic wrap.

5. Remove Bells from stiffener and squeeze to remove excess; blot with a paper towel several times to remove excess from holes.

6. Lightly stuff **wrong** side of each Bell with plastic wrap and shape as desired; pin bottom edge to blocking board.

7. Allow to dry **completely**; remove pins.

PRETTY LITTLE BIRDCAGES
(Shown on page 67)

1. Follow Steps 1 and 2 of Buggy instructions, page 124.

2. Pour fabric stiffener into resealable plastic bag. Do **not** dilute stiffener. *Note:* This method is permanent and will not wash out.

3. Immerse pieces in fabric stiffener; remove air and seal the bag. Work solution thoroughly into pieces. Let soak several hours or overnight.

4. Cover blocking board with plastic wrap.

5. Remove pieces from stiffener and squeeze to remove excess; blot with a paper towel several times to remove excess from holes.

6. With **right** side facing, place each piece over an object covered with plastic wrap that is the same size and shape you want the finished item to be. Pin Bottom at regular intervals.

7. Allow to dry **completely**; remove pins.

BEAUTIFUL BELLS
(Shown on page 63)

1. Follow Steps 1 and 2 of Buggy instructions, page 124.

2. Pour fabric stiffener into resealable plastic bag. Do **not** dilute stiffener. *Note:* This method is permanent and will not wash out.

3. Immerse Bells in fabric stiffener; remove air and seal the bag. Work solution thoroughly into pieces. Let soak several hours or overnight.

4. Cut plastic foam into a 2½" circle. Place plastic bell on top of plastic foam circle and cover both with plastic wrap.

5. Remove Bells from stiffener and squeeze gently to remove excess; blot with a paper towel several times to remove excess from holes.

6. Place crocheted Bell over plastic bell. Place pins into the plastic foam circle at regular intervals, shaping as needed.

7. Place rubber band over the crocheted Bell to help shape.

8. Allow to dry **completely**; remove pins and rubber band.

BEAUTY BOX
(Shown on page 33)

1. Follow Steps 1 and 2 of Buggy instructions, page 124.

2. Pour fabric stiffener into resealable plastic bag. Do **not** dilute stiffener. *Note:* This method is permanent and will not wash out.

3. Immerse pieces in fabric stiffener; remove air and seal the bag. Work solution thoroughly into pieces. Let soak several hours or overnight.

4. Cover blocking board with plastic wrap.

5. Remove pieces from stiffener and squeeze to remove excess; blot with a paper towel several times to remove excess from holes.

6. Lightly stuff **wrong** side of Base with plastic wrap and shape as desired; pin Top to bocking board making sure symmetrical components are equal.

7. Allow to dry **completely**; remove pins.

SNOWFLAKE PATTERN

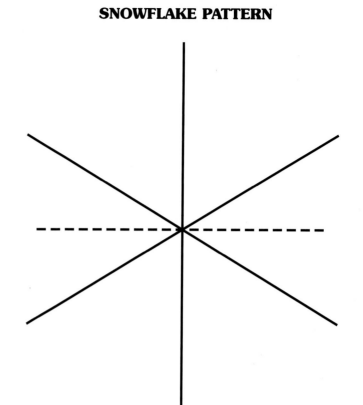

BIB PATTERN

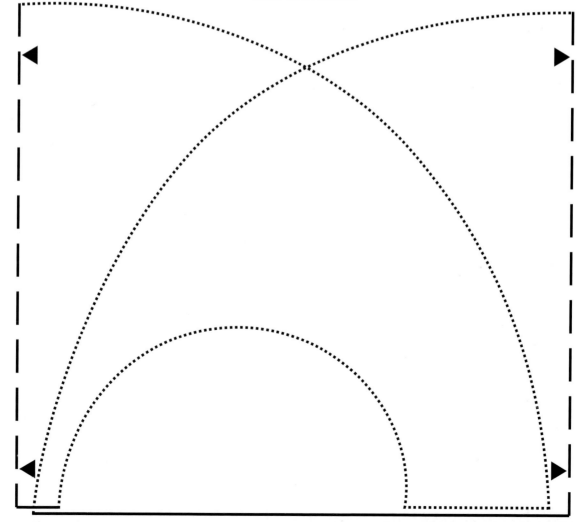

credits

We extend a warm *thank you* to the generous people who allowed us to photograph some of our projects at their homes.

To Magna IV Color Imaging of Little Rock, Arkansas, we say thank you for the superb color reproduction and excellent pre-press preparation. We want to especially thank photographers Larry Pennington, Ken West, Karen Shirey, and Mark Mathews of Peerless Photography, Little Rock, Arkansas, and Jerry R. Davis of Jerry Davis Photography, Little Rock, Arkansas, for their time, patience, and excellent work.

A special word of thanks goes to the talented designers who created the lovely projects in this book:

Dianne Bee: *Dolly's Afghan*, page 52
Jennie Black: *Tea Jacket Bouquet (Tea Jacket and Primrose)*, page 44
Coats & Clark: *Delicate Doily*, page 12
Shobha Govindan: *Floral Table Runner*, page 18
Anne Halliday: *Victorian Sachets*, page 64; *Festive Wreath*, page 106; and *Divine Little Angel*, page 110
Cathy Hardy: *Bride's Sachet Hanger*, page 68
Carol Keppler: *Precious Accents*, page 90
Terry Kimbrough: *Classic Coasters*, page 17; *Fanciful Bookmarks*, page 54; *Strawberry Lace Set*, page 80; *Baby's Bible*, page 84; and *Heavenly Pillows*, page 112
Jennine Korejko: *Tea Jacket Bouquet (Chrysanthemum and Little Dahlia)*, page 44
Lucille LaFlamme: *Timeless Tablecloth*, page 114
Anita Lewis: *Purse Pretties*, page 72
Linda Luder: *Thirsty Bibs*, page 86
Jackie Kelly Mooneyham: *Fantasy Wedding Ensemble*, page 75
Betty Moss: *For Tiny Toes*, page 92
Helen Nissen: *Dainty Candy Dish*, page 70

Cindy Peecher: *Doilies to Love*, page 14
Delsie Rhoades: *Showy Table Topper*, page 8; *Pretty Little Birdcages*, page 66; and *Poinsettia Doily*, page 108
Nanette Seale: *Heirloom Angel*, page 104
Georgia Shaulis: *Sweet Sleeper*, page 88
Faye Shelton: *Beautiful Bells*, page 62, and *Let It Snow!*, page 98
Joan E. Shetler: *Friendly Welcome*, page 36
C. Strohmeyer: *Dreamy Bed Linens*, page 20; *Lacy Towel Sets*, page 29; and *Kitchen Towel Trims*, page 38
Eunice Svinicki: *Lovely Lampshade Cover*, page 10; *Sentimental Bible Set*, page 56; and *Country Kitchen Lace*, page 58
Maggie Weldon: *Beauty Box*, page 32, and *Potpourri Baskets*, page 100
Debra L. Westberry: *Window Charm*, page 34
Lorraine White: *Ornate Edgings*, page 26; *Delightful Dishcloths*, page 40; *Ring Bearer's Pillow*, page 50; and *Baby-Soft Blankets*, page 82